PRINCESS MONONOKE

Original story and screenplay written and directed by
HAYAO MIYAZAKI

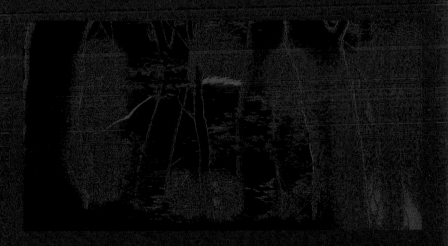

2

STUDIO
GHIBLI
LIBRARY

❰ *Character Introductions* ❱

Ashitaka
■ A young village prince who carries the curse of a rampaging demon god. Heading westward, he's hoping to find a cure for his affliction.

San
■ She is known as Princess Mononoke. Raised by the giant wolf spirit named Moro, she's grown to despise humans and has joined together with a pack of wolves to fight against them.

Kohroku
■ An ox-driver who transports iron manufactured at the mill. Ashitaka rescues him after Moro's attack.

Toki
■ She speaks her mind and is a hard worker. Her coworkers think of her as a straight talker and mother figure. She's married to Kohroku.

Gonza
■ An impulsive man who assists Lady Eboshi. In charge of the accounts, he helps govern Tatara.

Lady Eboshi
(Eboshi Gozen)
■ The leader of the iron town, Tatara. Her rifle shot turned Lord Nago into a curse god. The women laborers at the iron mill respect her.

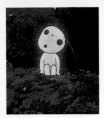

Kodama

■ Spirits of the forest. They spring out of an ancient tree and guide Ashitaka out of the forest.

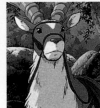

Yakul

■ Part elk and part horse, this faithful "Akashishi" (Red Deer) takes Ashitaka on his journey.

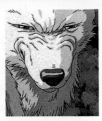

Moro

■ A female wolf god of the forest who understands human speech. She raised the orphan San, but detests humans who tamper with her forest. Her archenemy is Lady Eboshi.

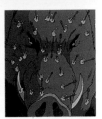

Lord Nago

■ A guardian deity from the forest currently being mined for iron. A rifle shot from Lady Eboshi transformed it into a raging curse god.

The Story So Far

A long time long ago, humans and the spirits of gods lived side by side on Earth. But when mankind began disrupting the harmony of nature, the gods became angry.

In this volatile climate, a guardian deity by the name of Lord Nago suddenly transforms into a raging curse god. Saving his village from attack, Ashitaka kills the monster but acquires the god's curse. Setting off on a journey, the young man hopes to find a cure...

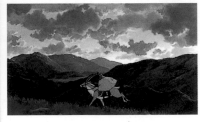

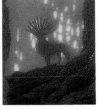

Great Forest Spirit

■ A sacred, untainted forest spirit who controls both life and death. Ashitaka sees it in the deep forest.

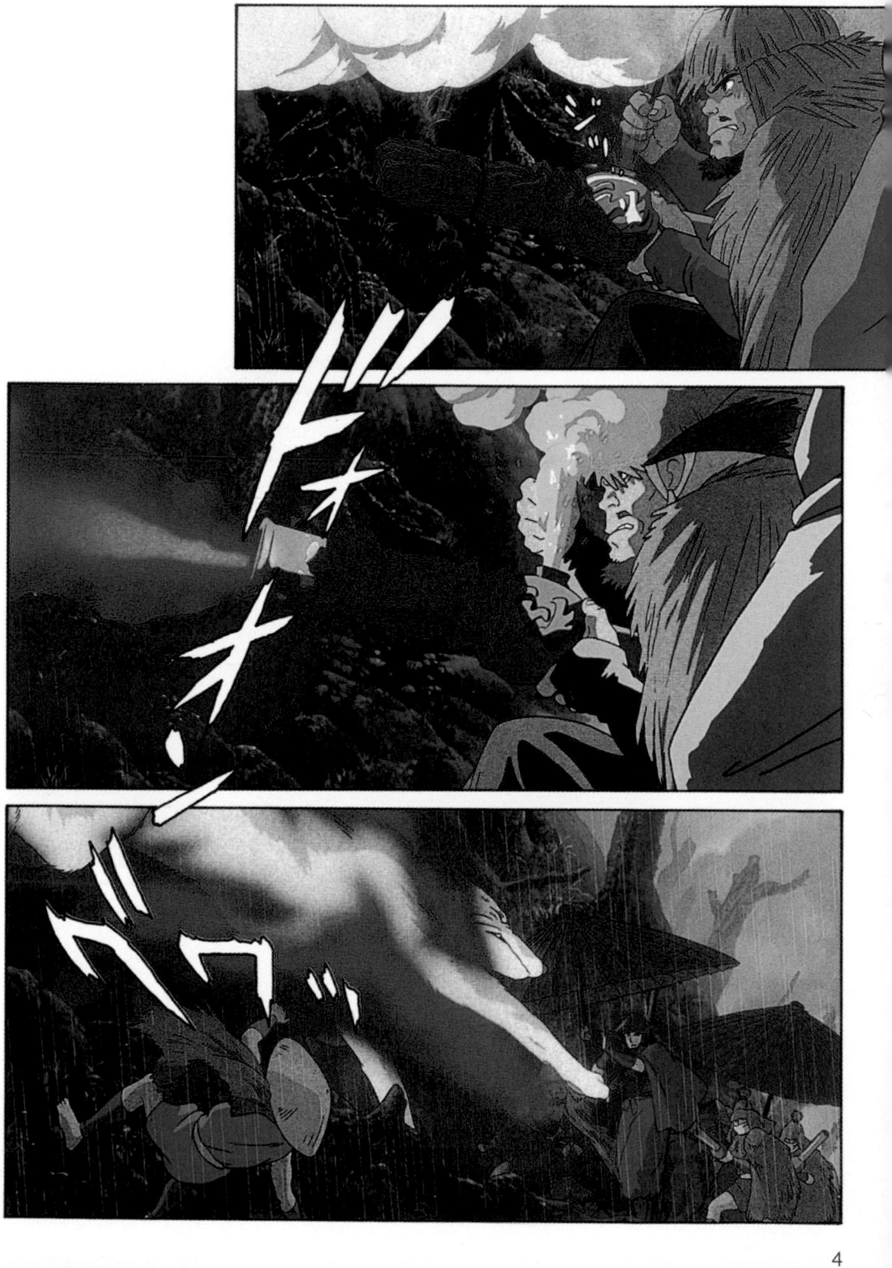
ドォオン
グワッ

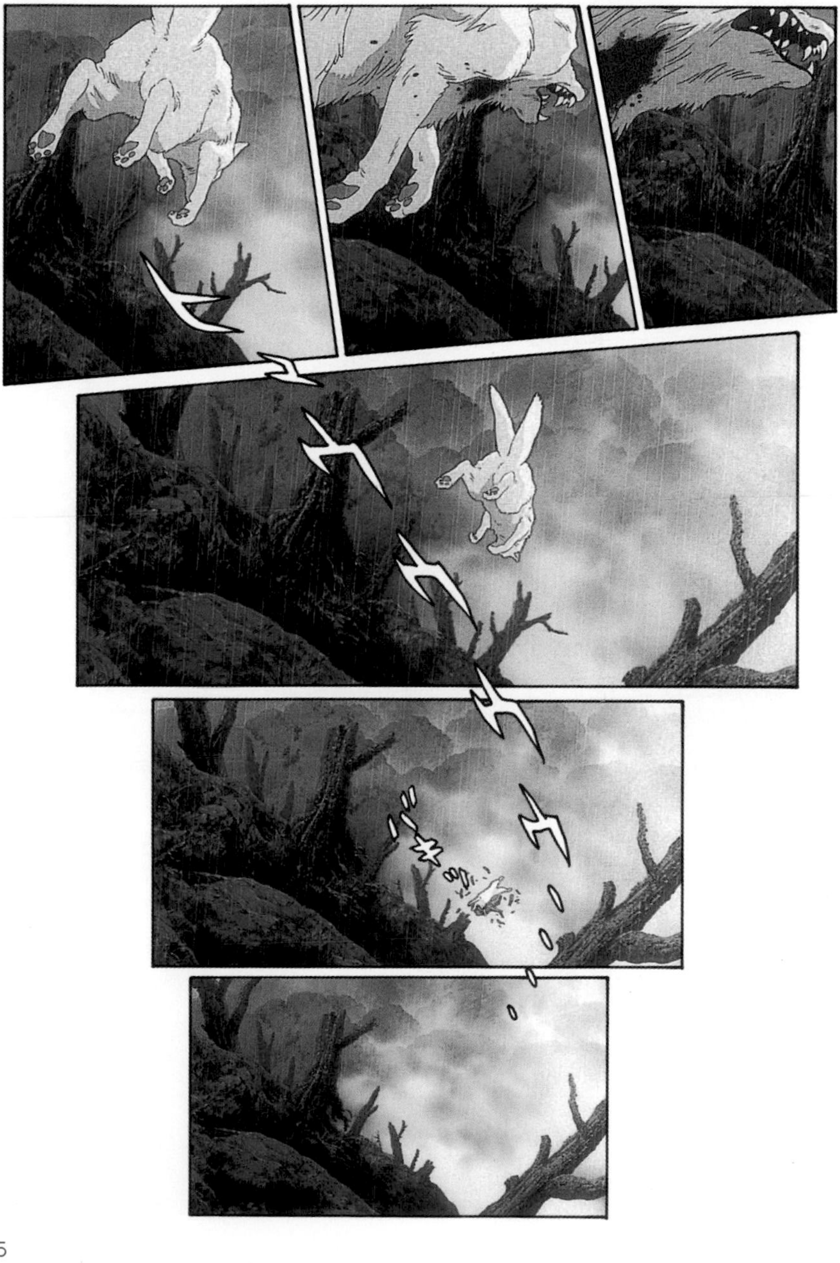

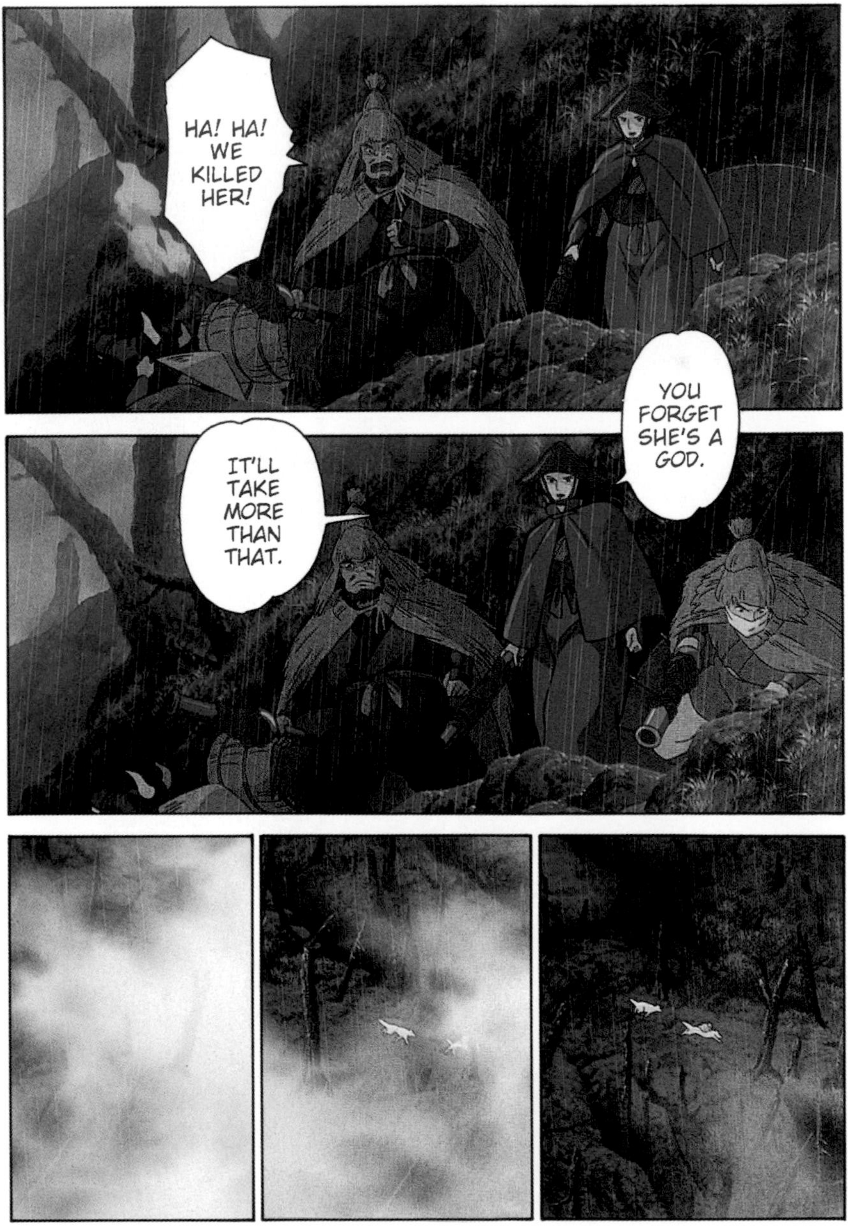
HA! HA! WE KILLED HER!
YOU FORGET SHE'S A GOD.
IT'LL TAKE MORE THAN THAT.

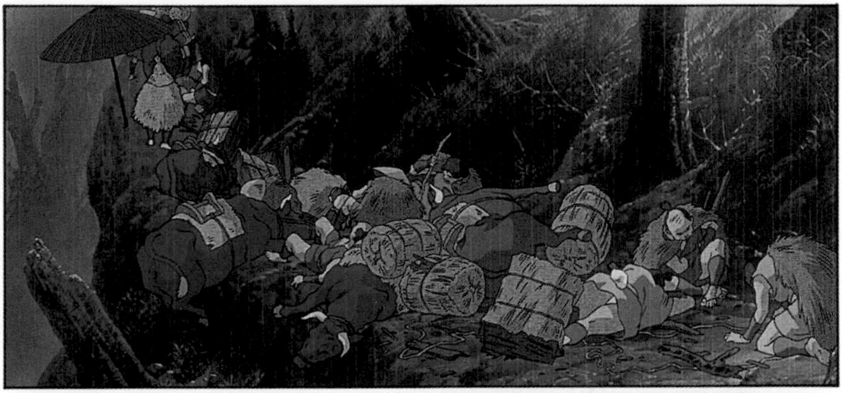

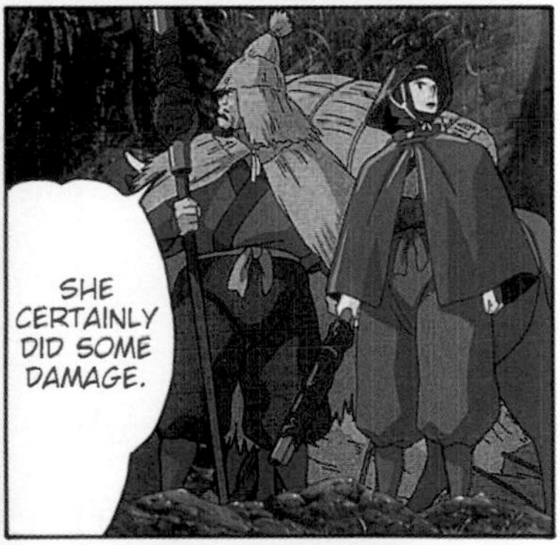
SHE CERTAINLY DID SOME DAMAGE.

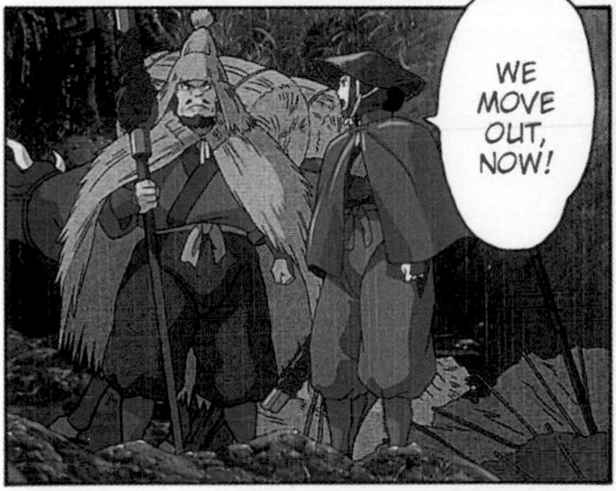
WE MOVE OUT, NOW!

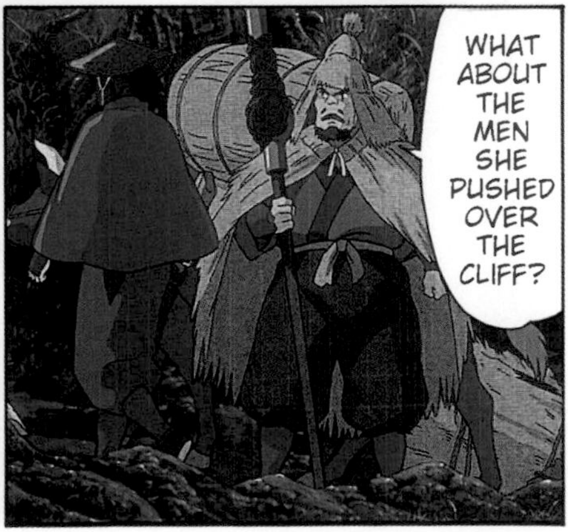
WHAT ABOUT THE MEN SHE PUSHED OVER THE CLIFF?

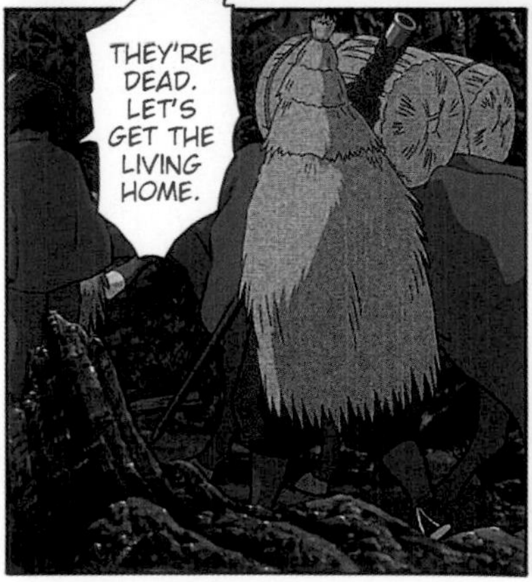
THEY'RE DEAD. LET'S GET THE LIVING HOME.

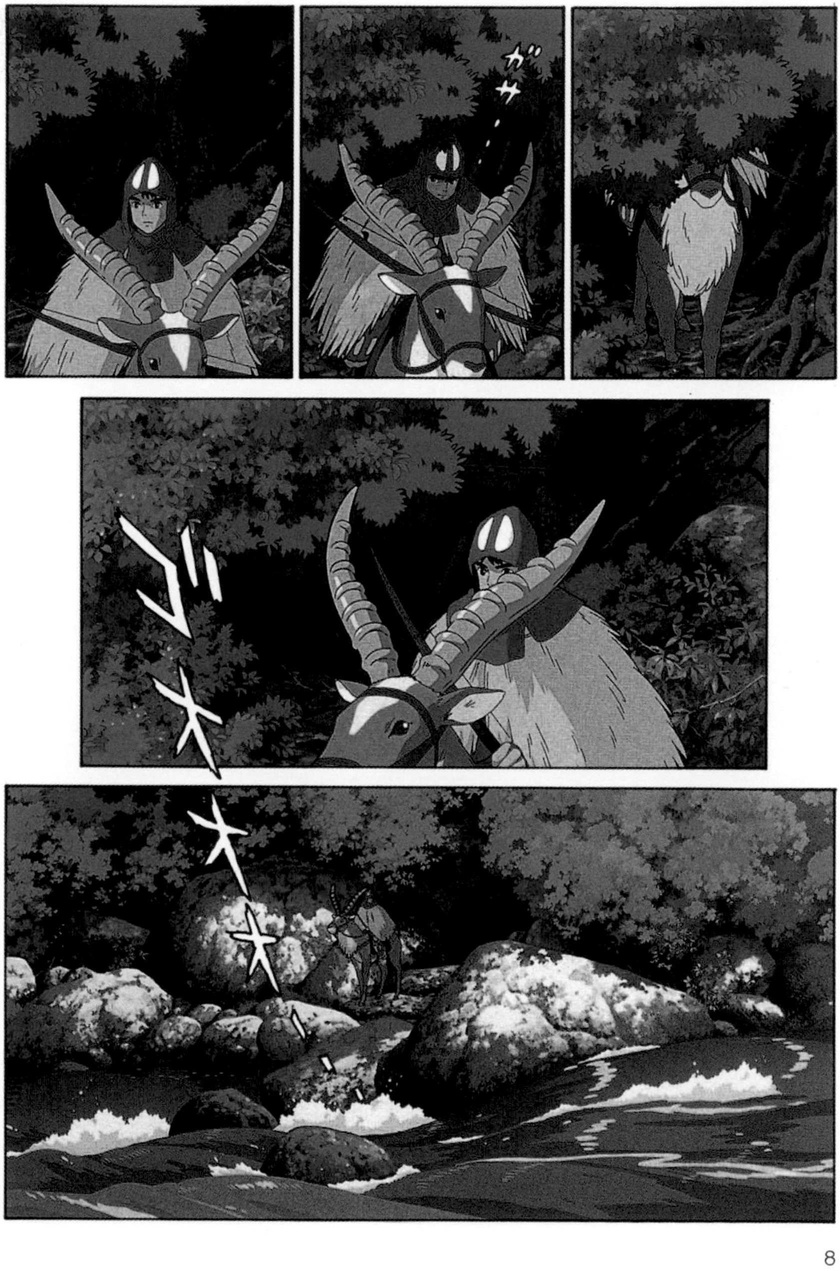
ガサ…
ゾオオオ…

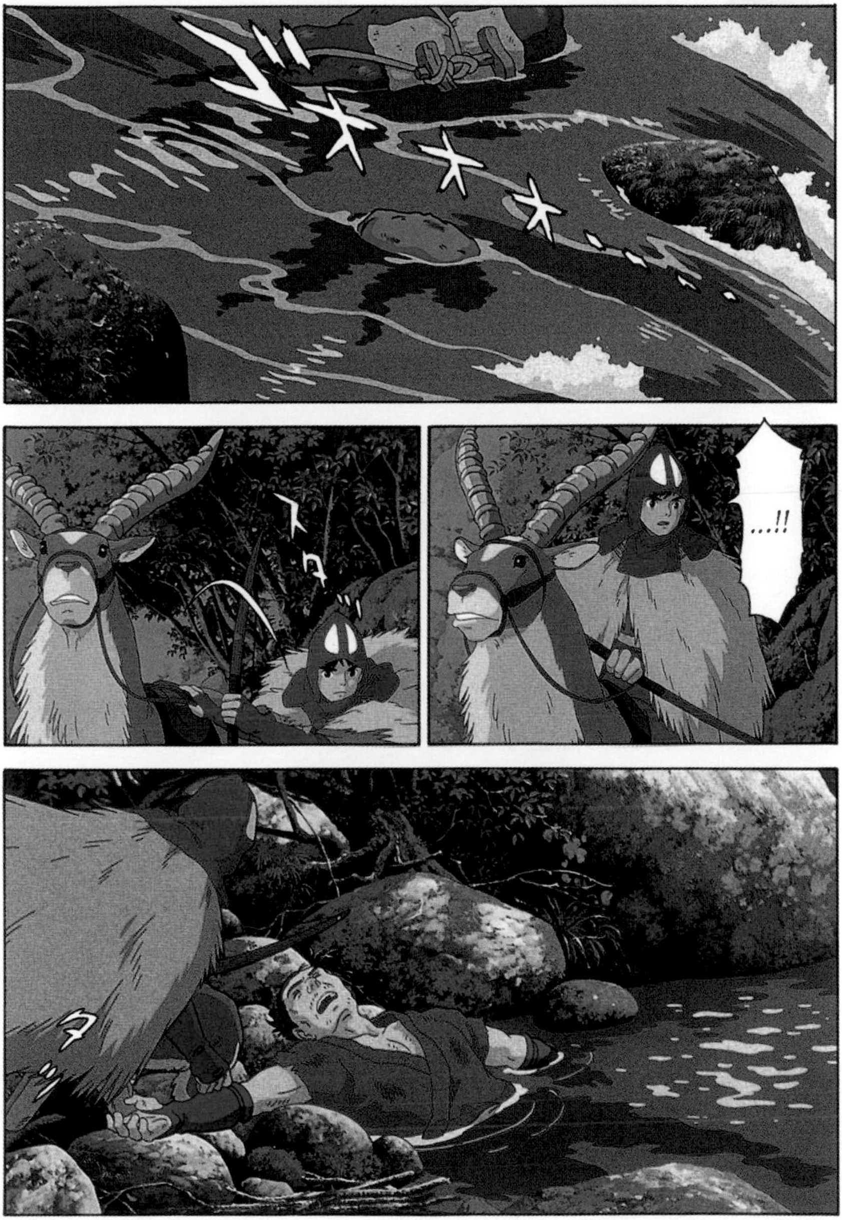
...!!

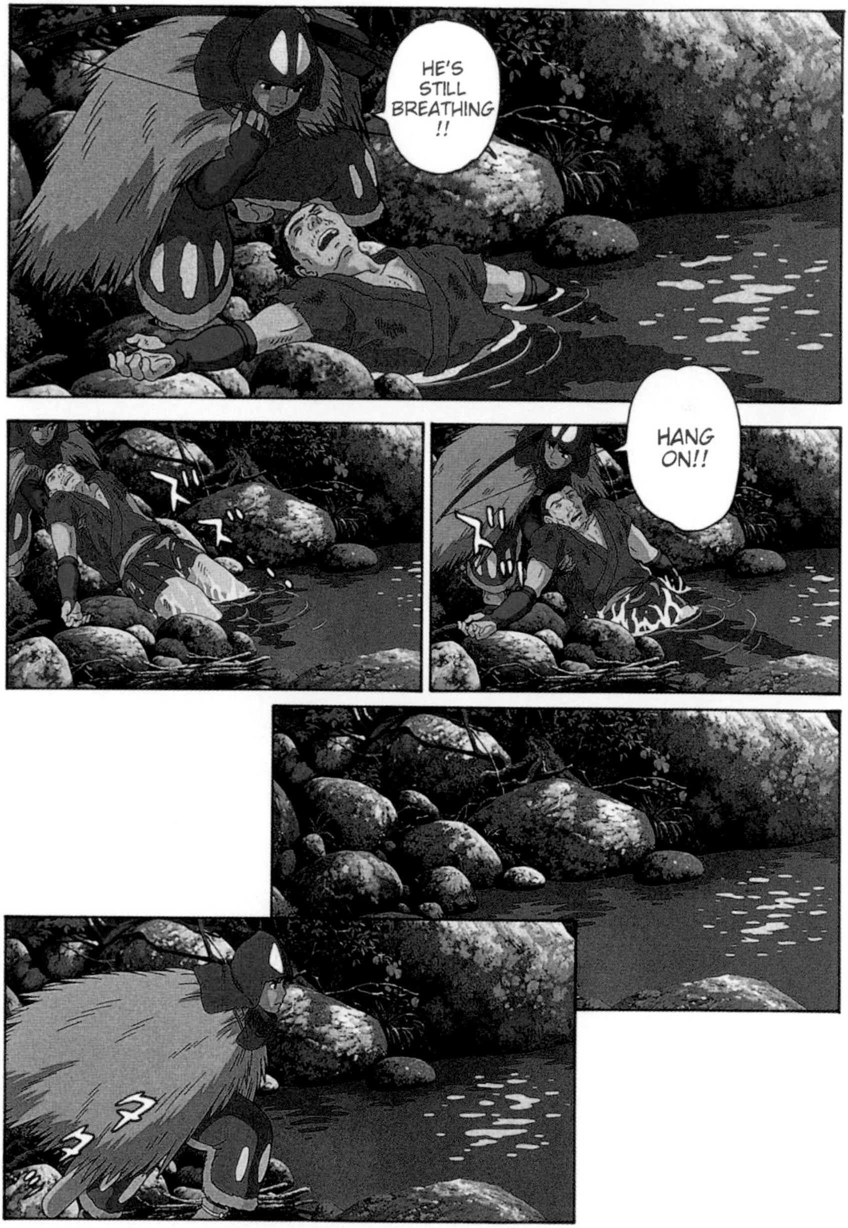
HE'S STILL BREATHING!!
HANG ON!!

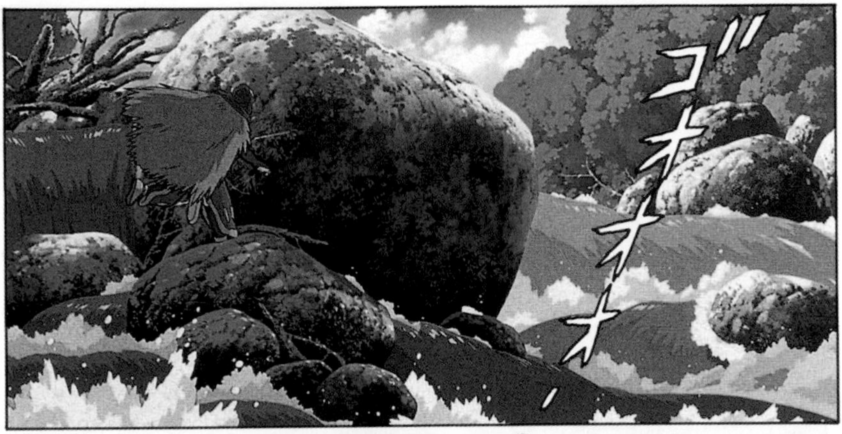
ゴオオオオ
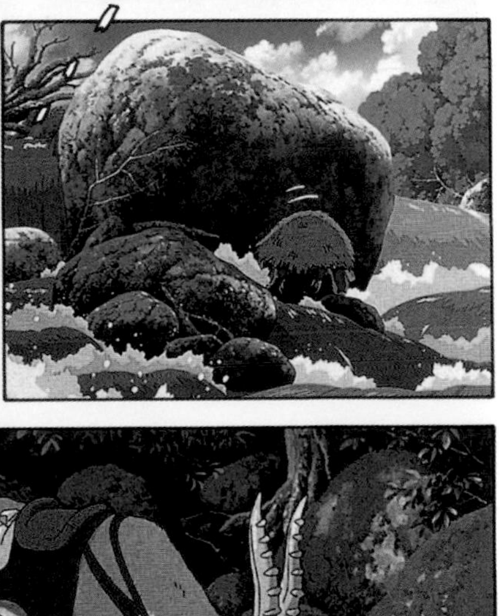
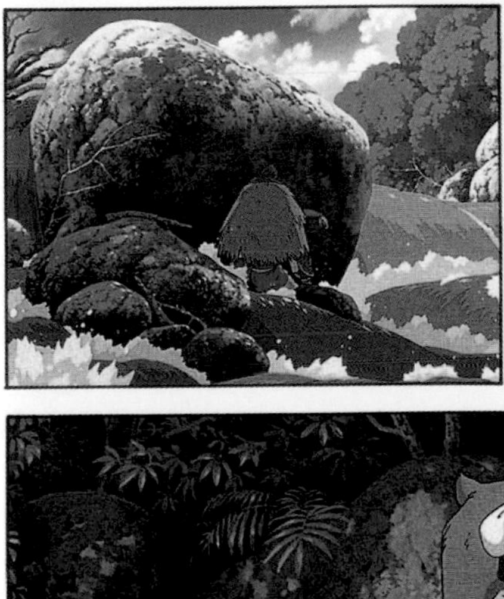
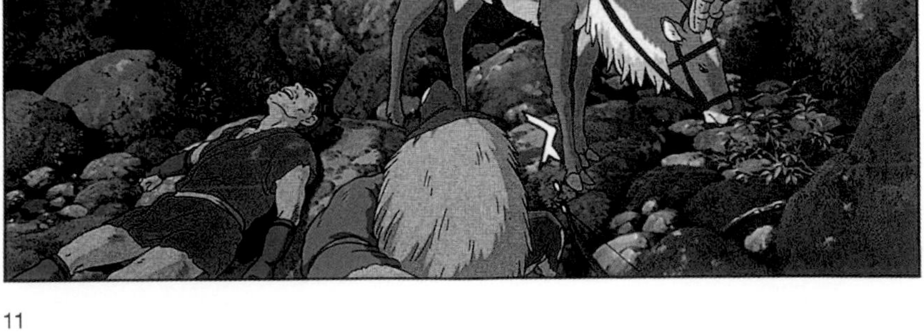
ス

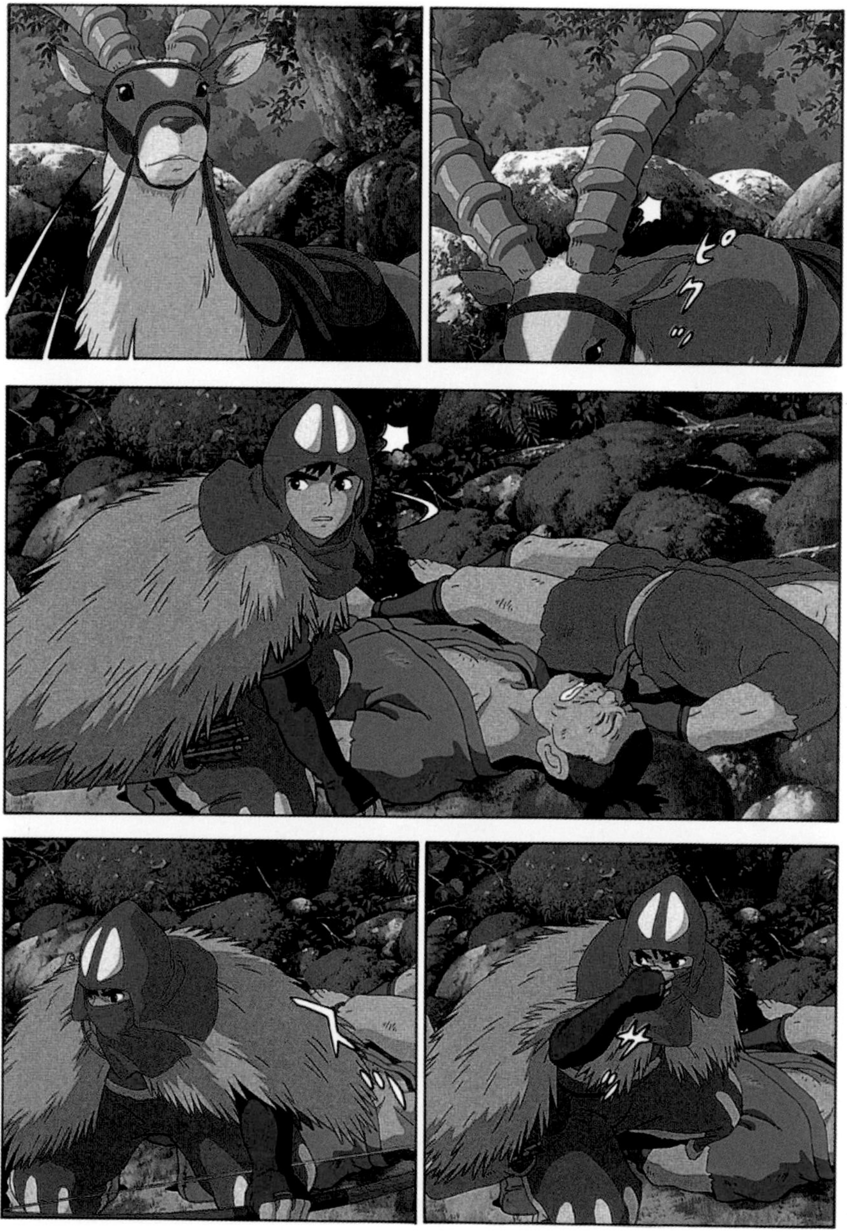
ピクッ

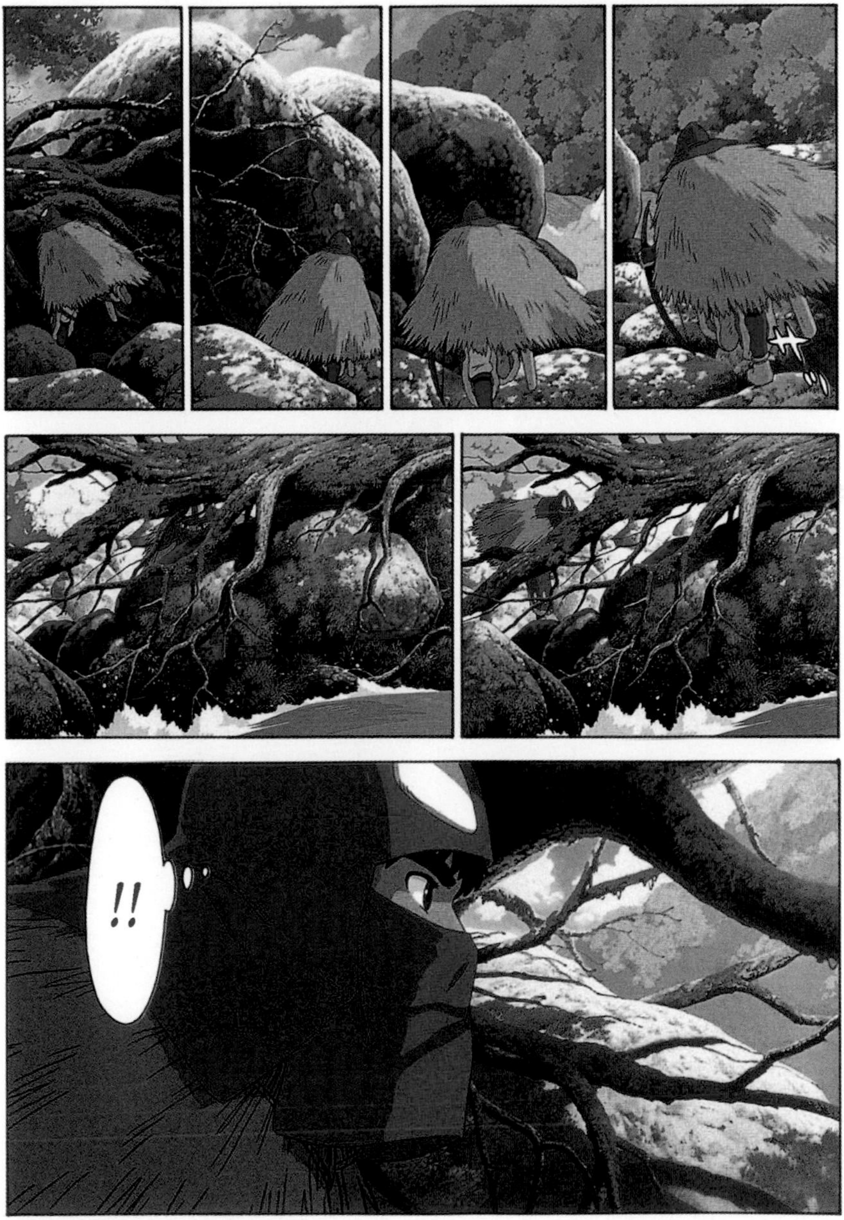
!!

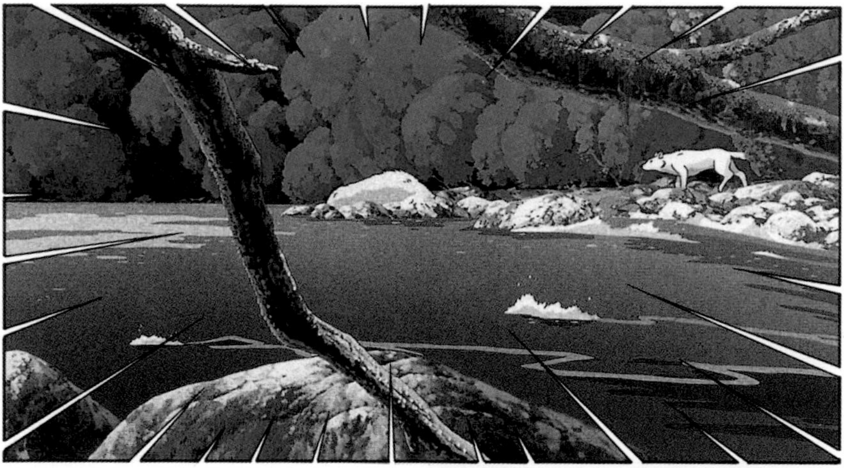

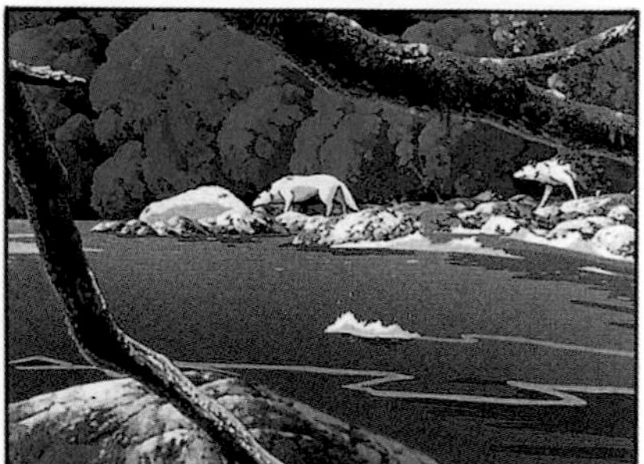

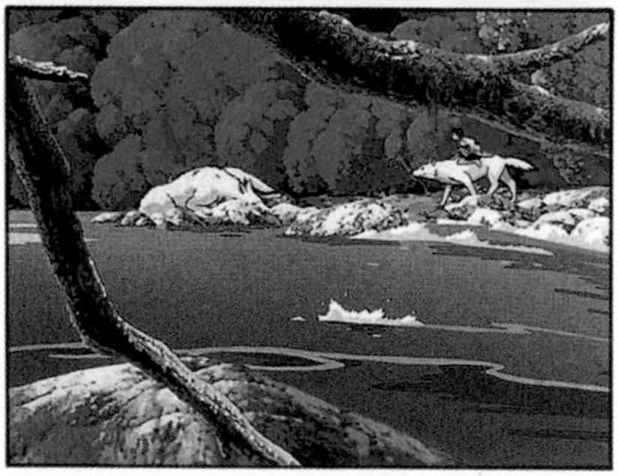

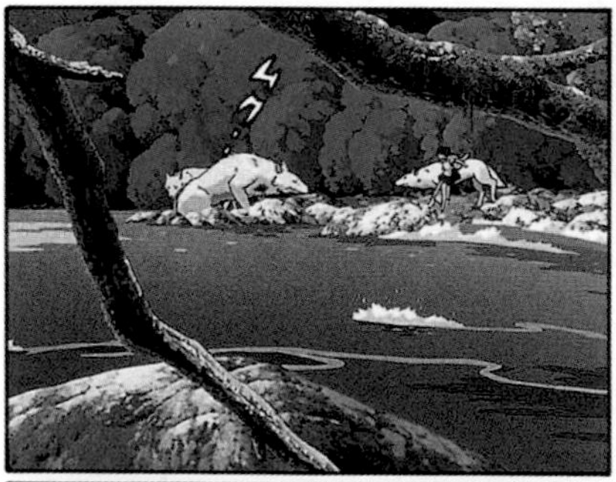
ムク

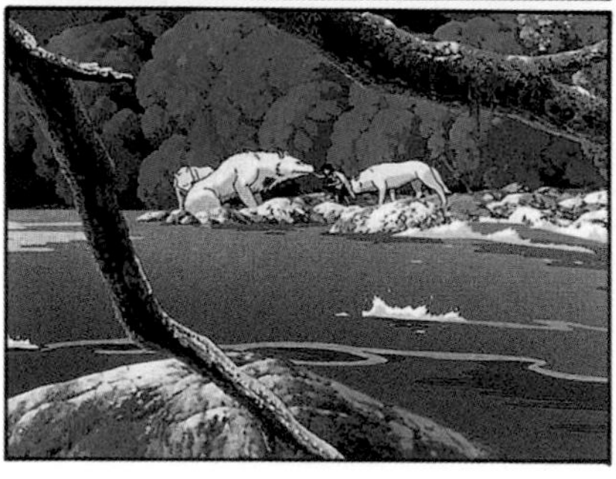

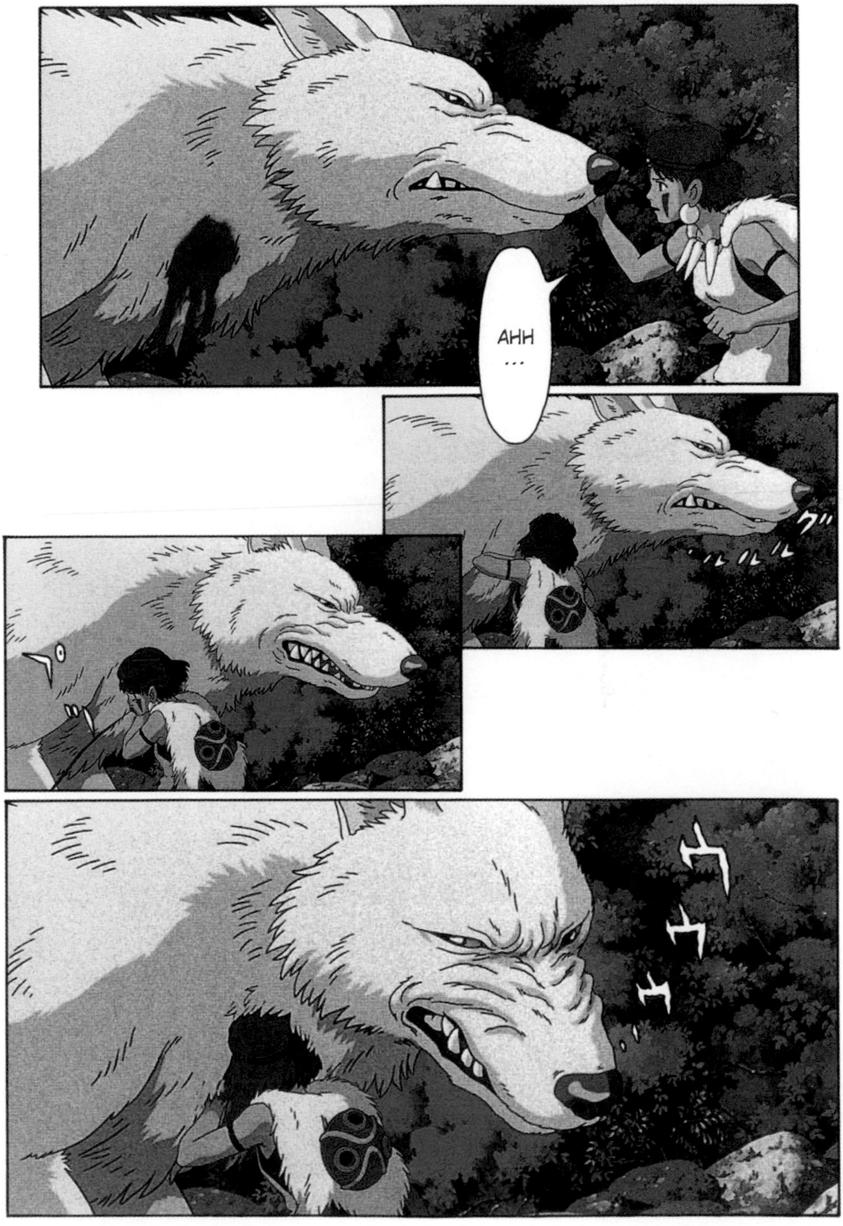
AHH ...

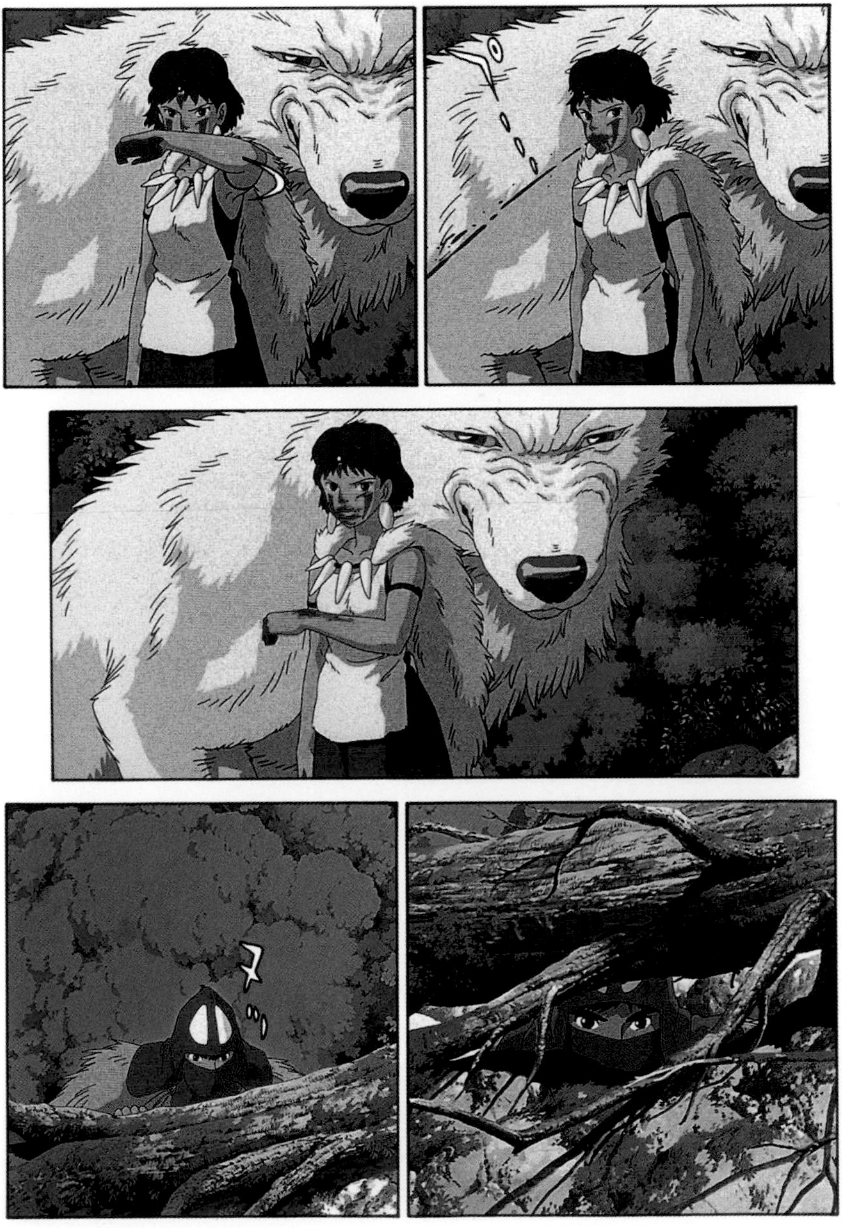

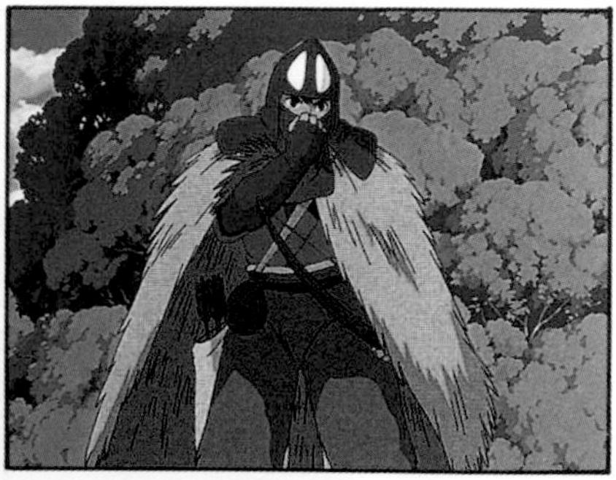
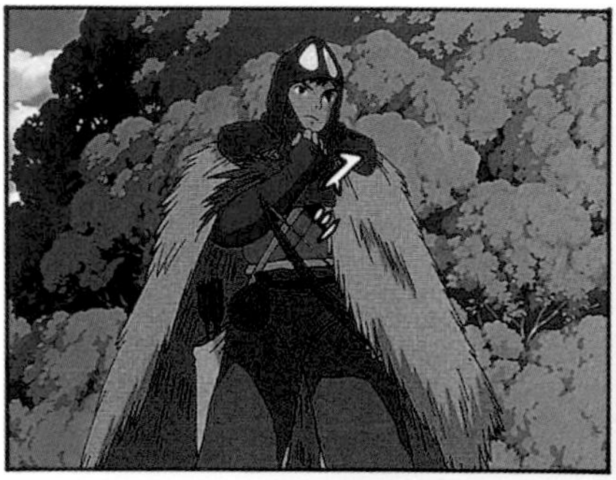
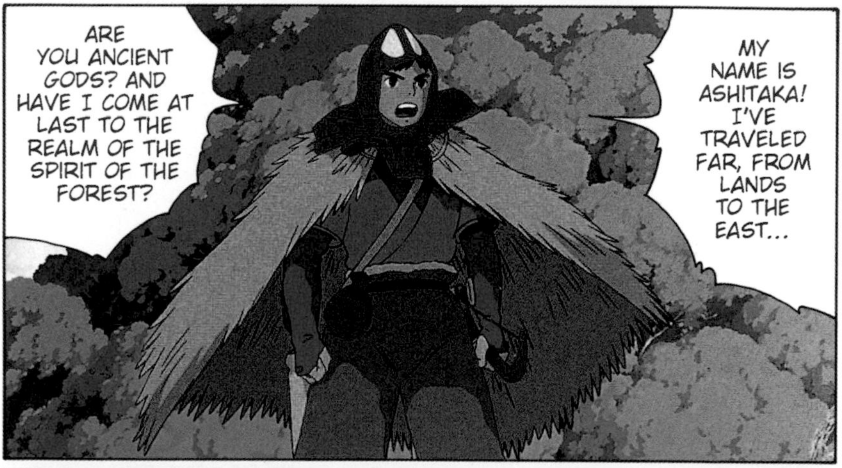
MY NAME IS ASHITAKA! I'VE TRAVELED FAR, FROM LANDS TO THE EAST...
ARE YOU ANCIENT GODS? AND HAVE I COME AT LAST TO THE REALM OF THE SPIRIT OF THE FOREST?
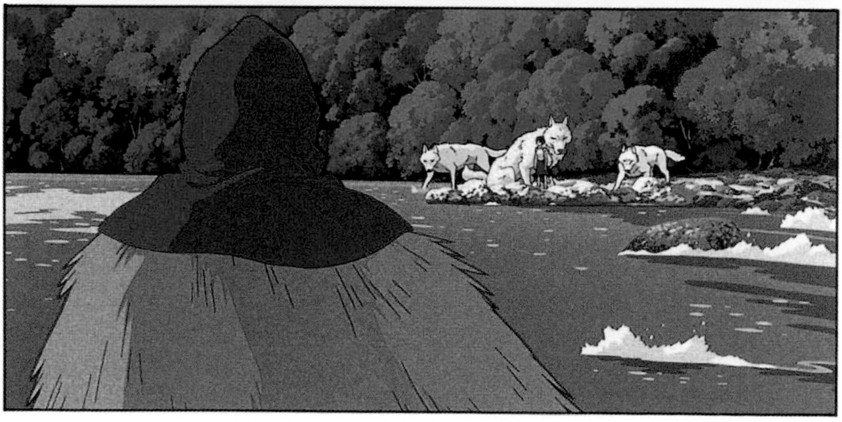

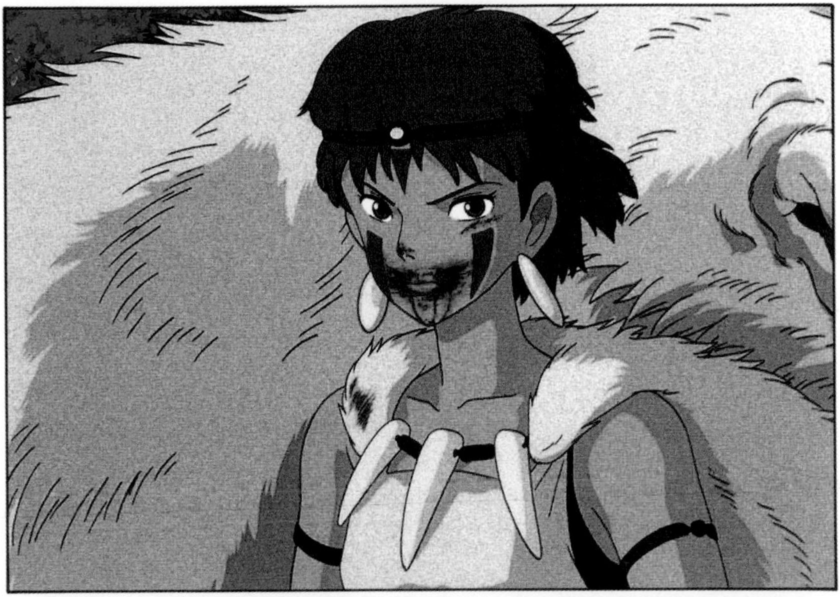

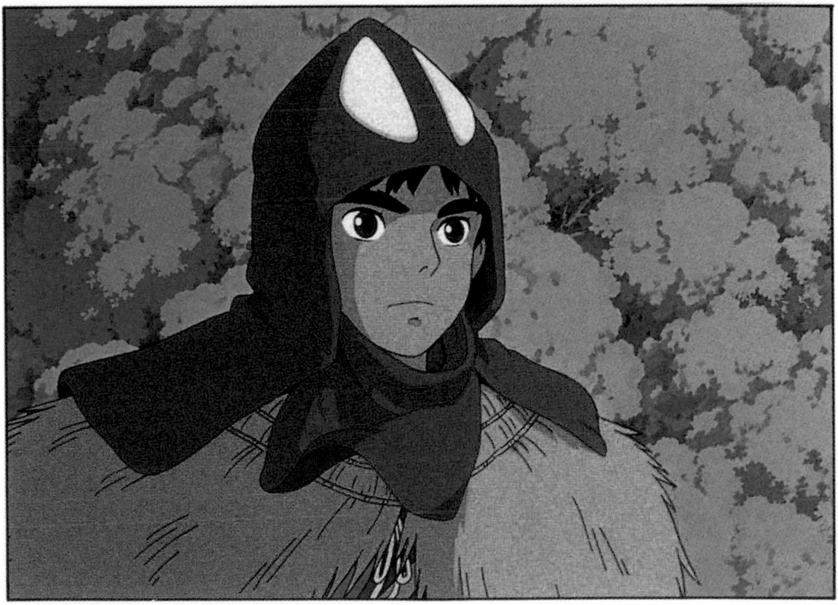

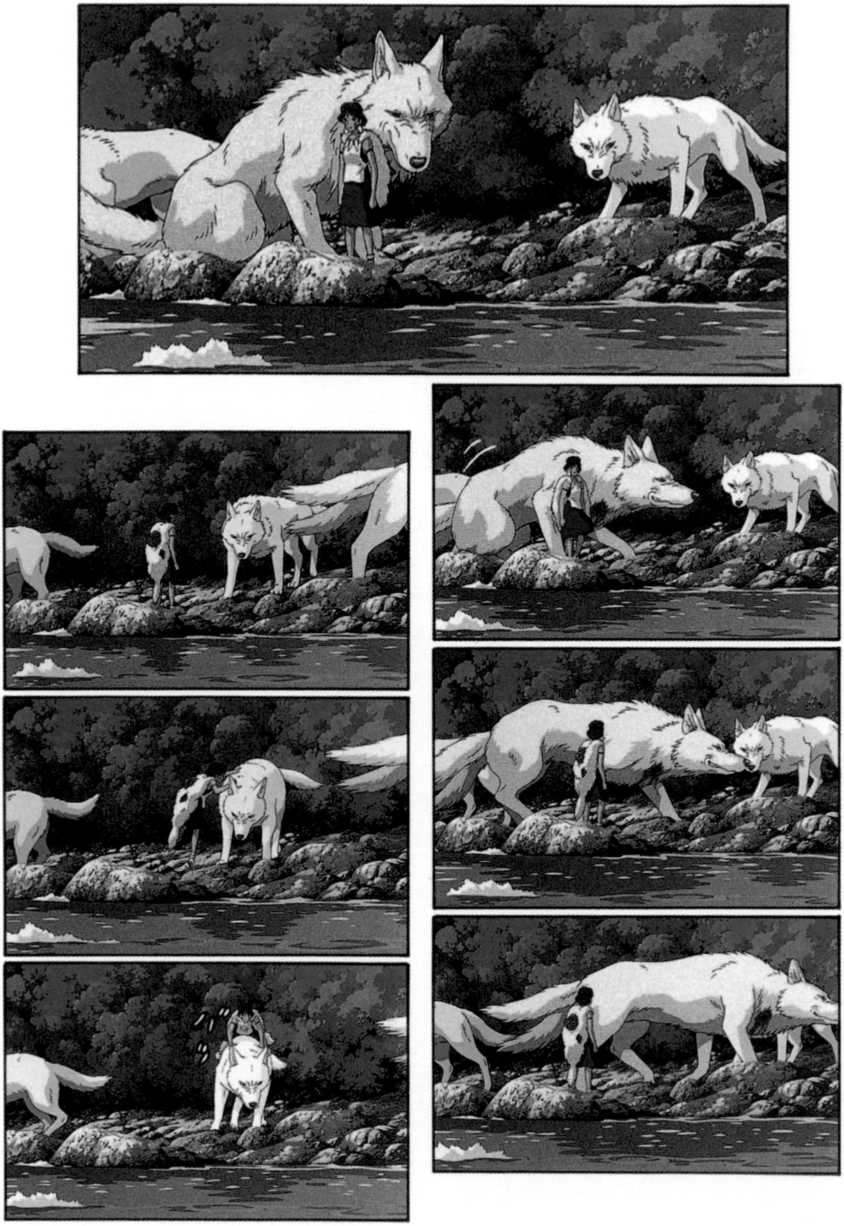

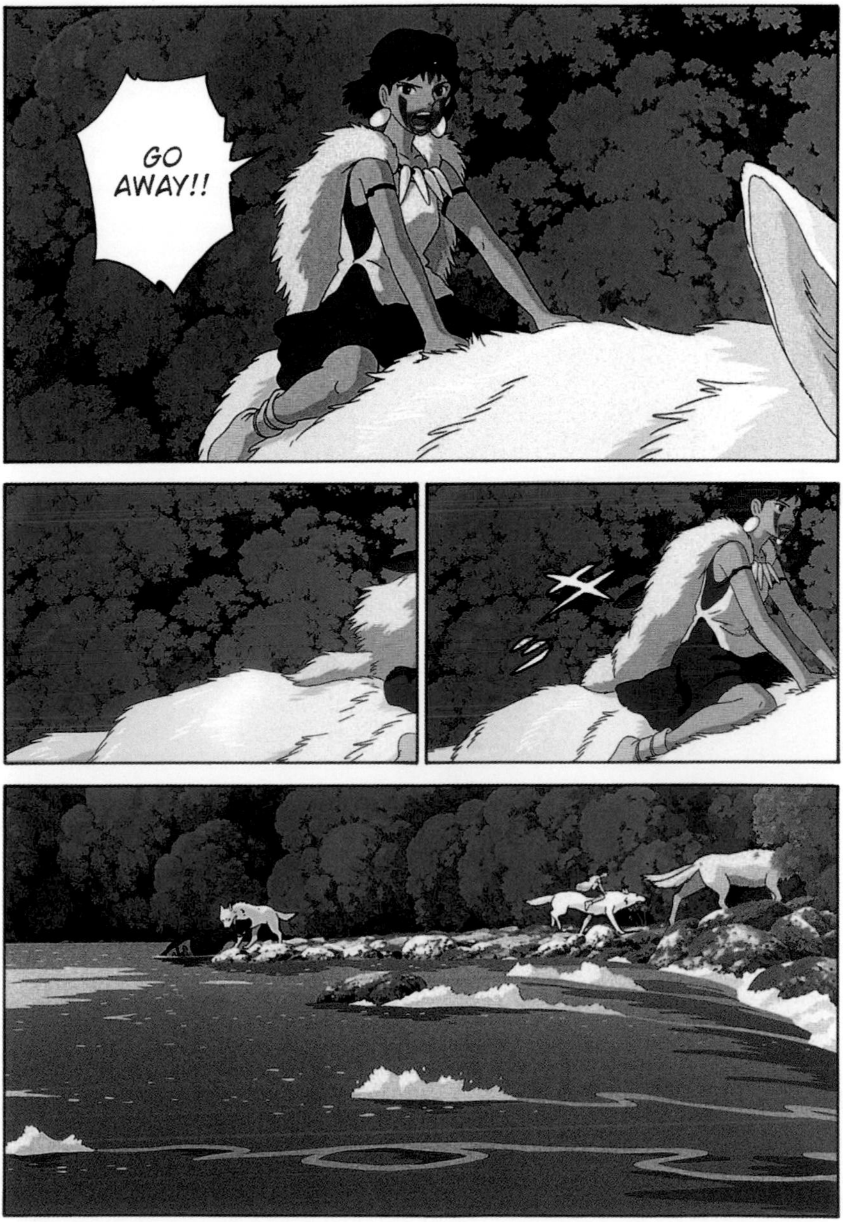
GO AWAY!!

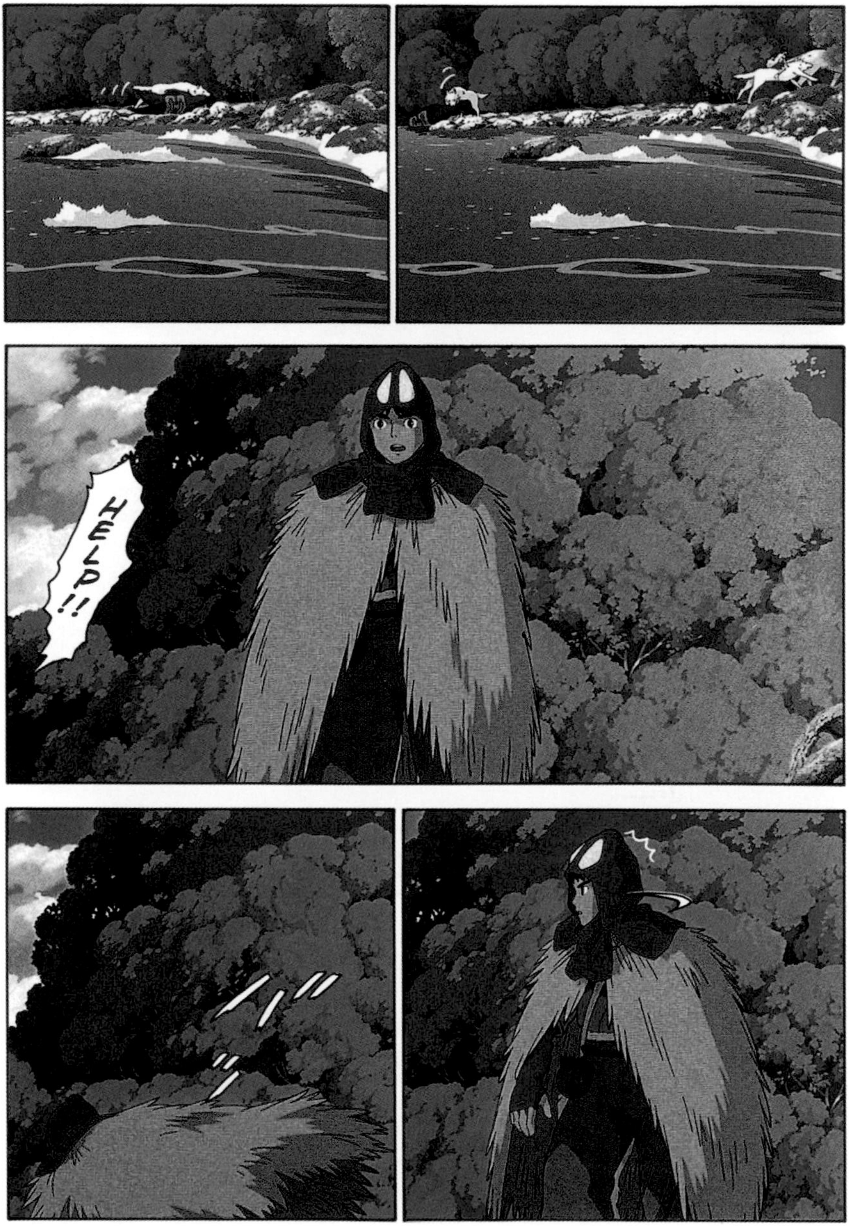
HELP!!

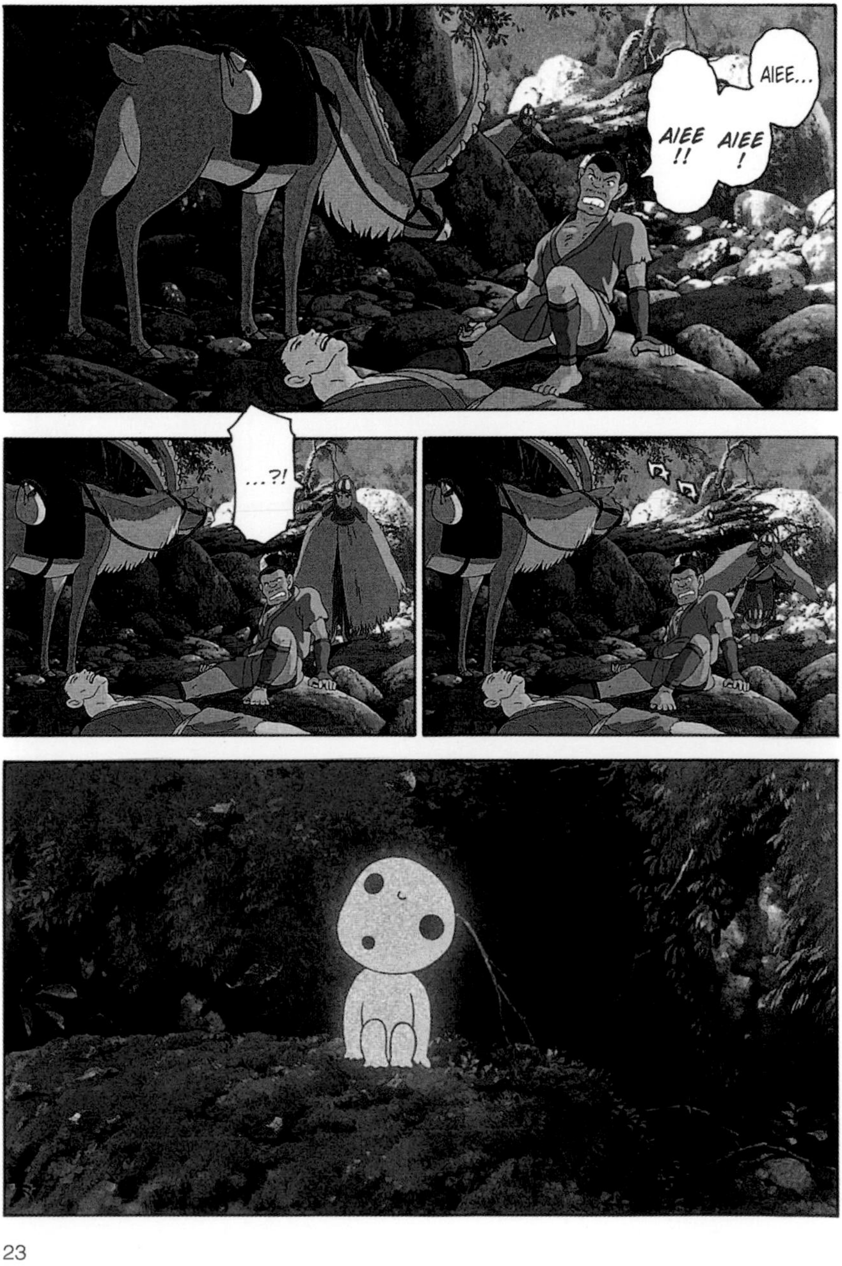
AIEE...
AIEE !
AIEE !!
...?!

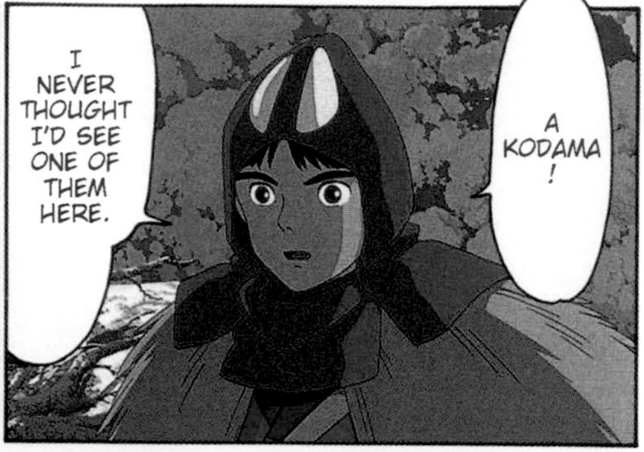
A KODAMA!
I NEVER THOUGHT I'D SEE ONE OF THEM HERE.

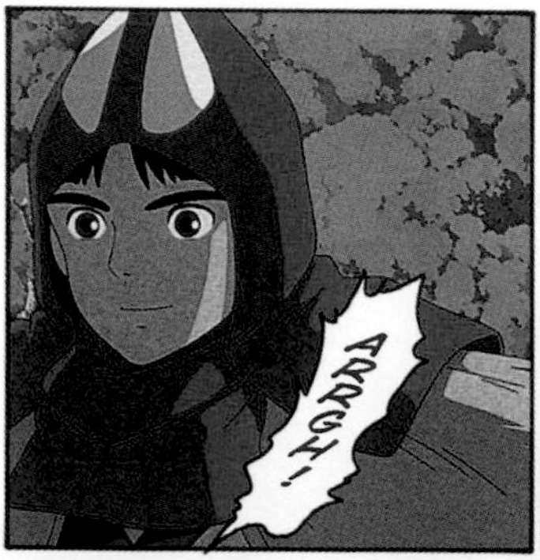
ARRGH!

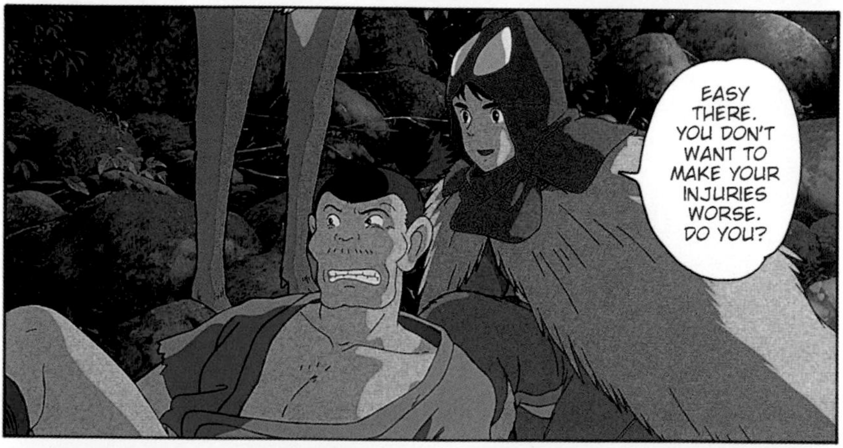
EASY THERE. YOU DON'T WANT TO MAKE YOUR INJURIES WORSE. DO YOU?

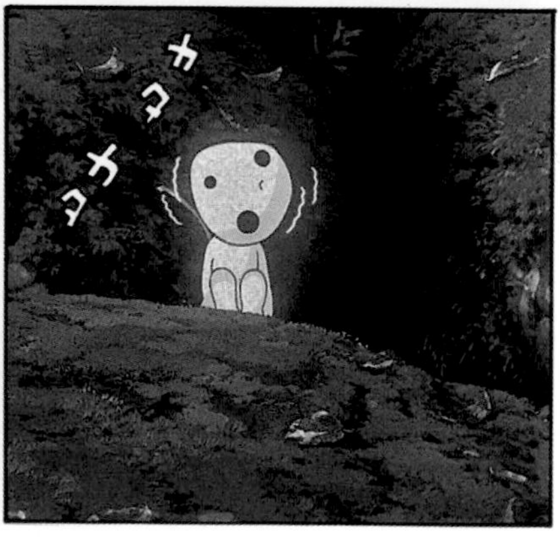

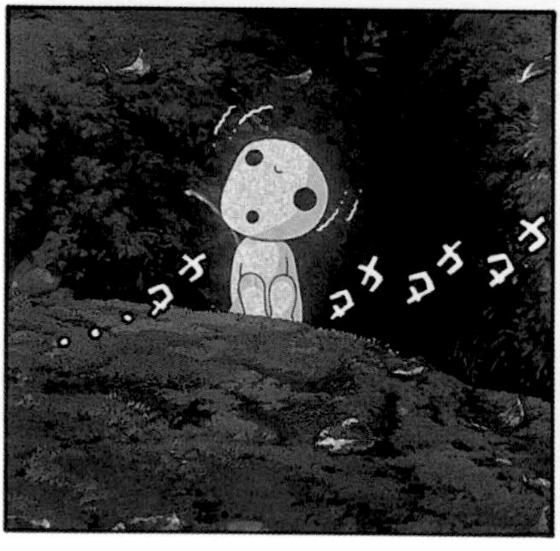

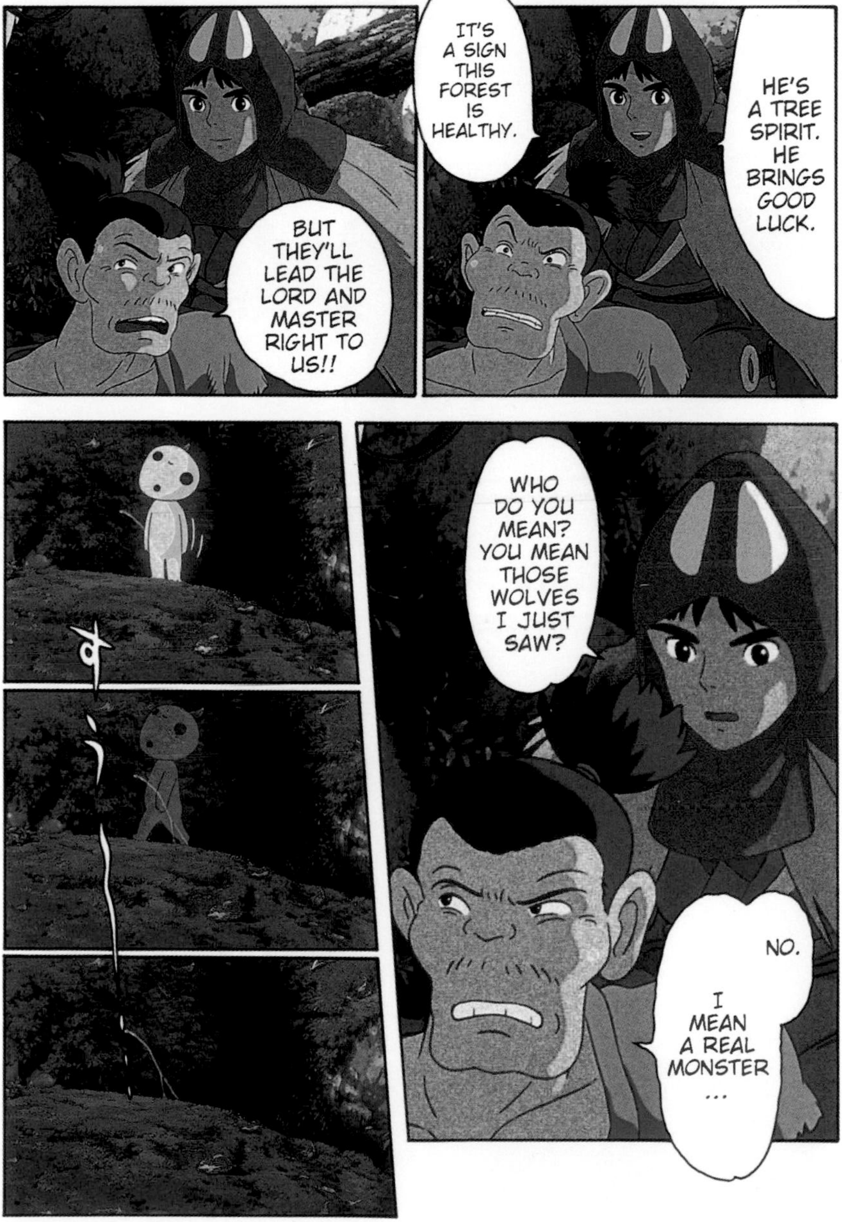
HE'S A TREE SPIRIT. HE BRINGS GOOD LUCK.
IT'S A SIGN THIS FOREST IS HEALTHY.
BUT THEY'LL LEAD THE LORD AND MASTER RIGHT TO US!!
WHO DO YOU MEAN? YOU MEAN THOSE WOLVES I JUST SAW?
NO.
I MEAN A REAL MONSTER ...
す

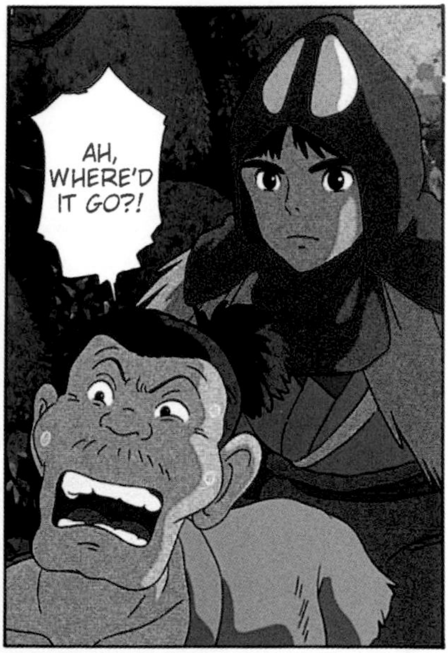
AH, WHERE'D IT GO?!
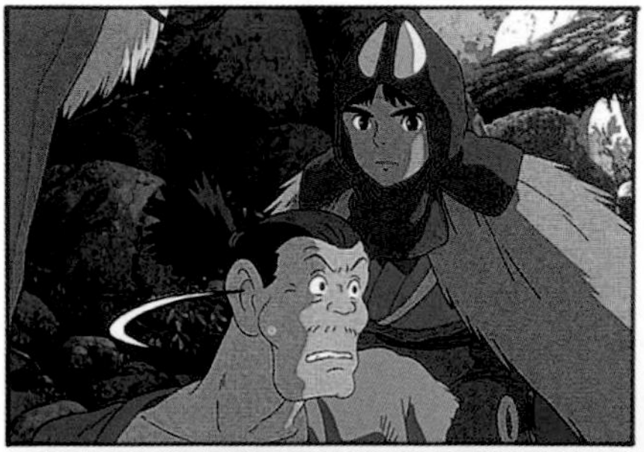
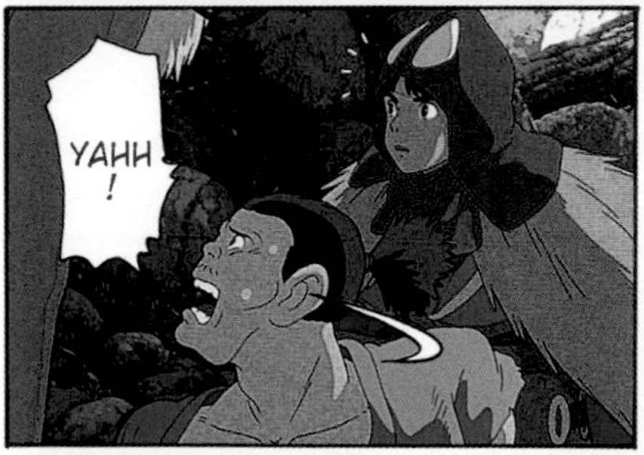
YAHH!
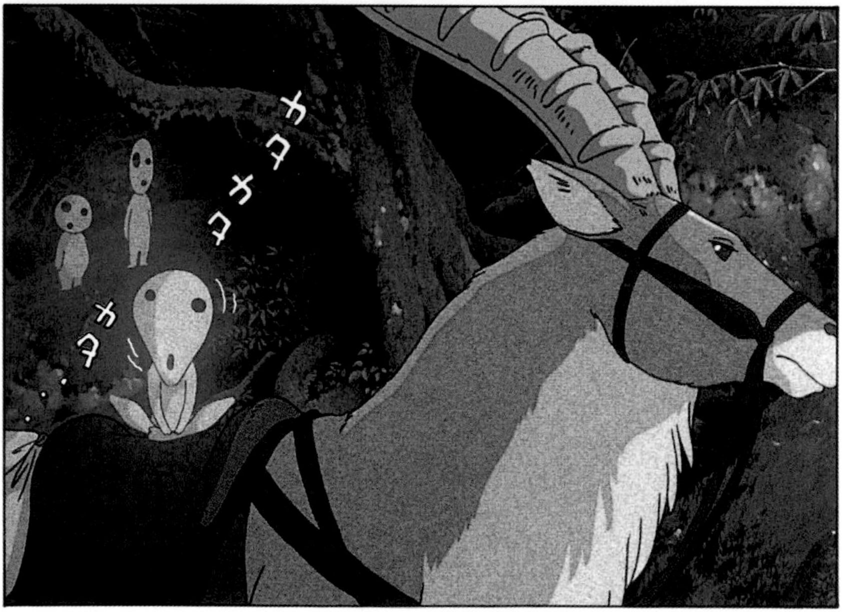
カタカタ
カタ

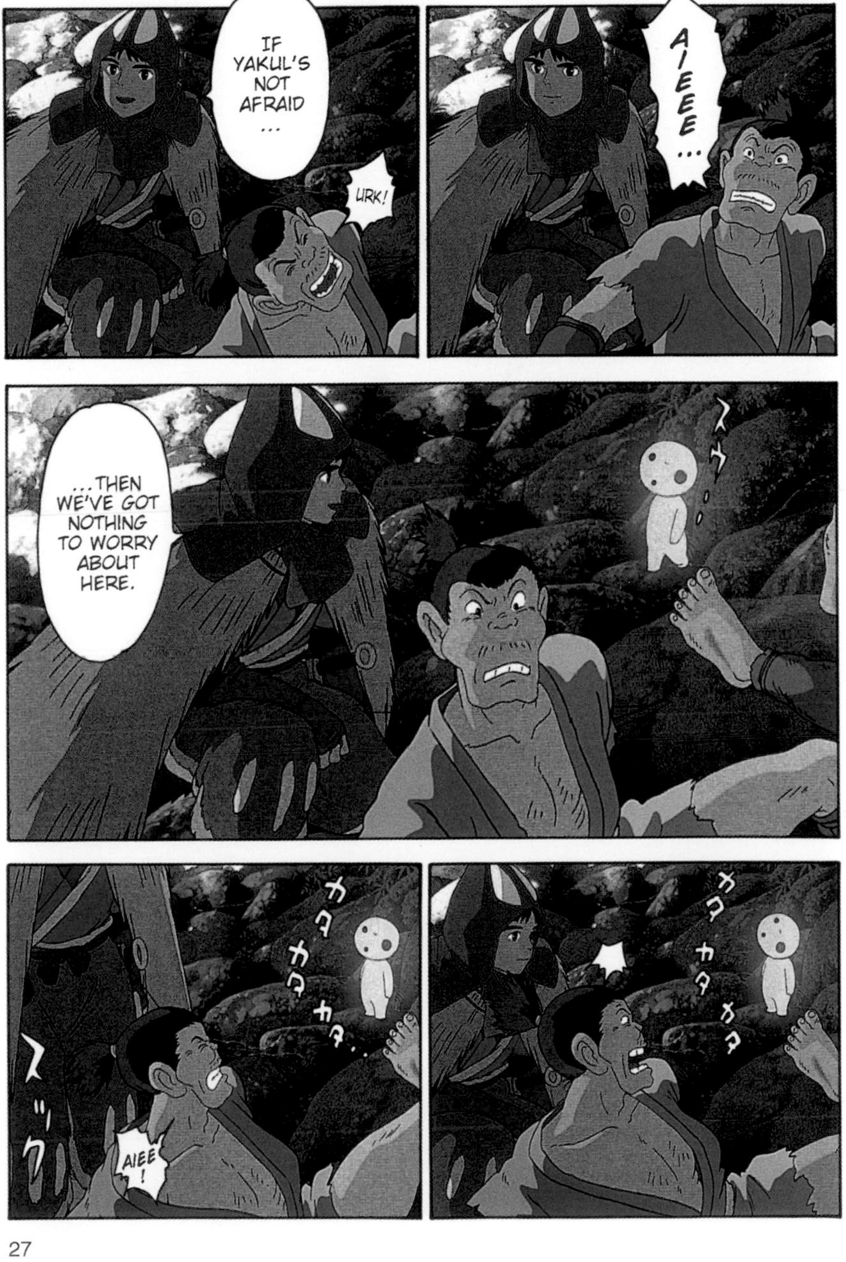
IF YAKUL'S NOT AFRAID ...
URK!
AIEEE ...
...THEN WE'VE GOT NOTHING TO WORRY ABOUT HERE.
スゥ...
スック
カタカタカタ...
AIEE!
カタカタカタ

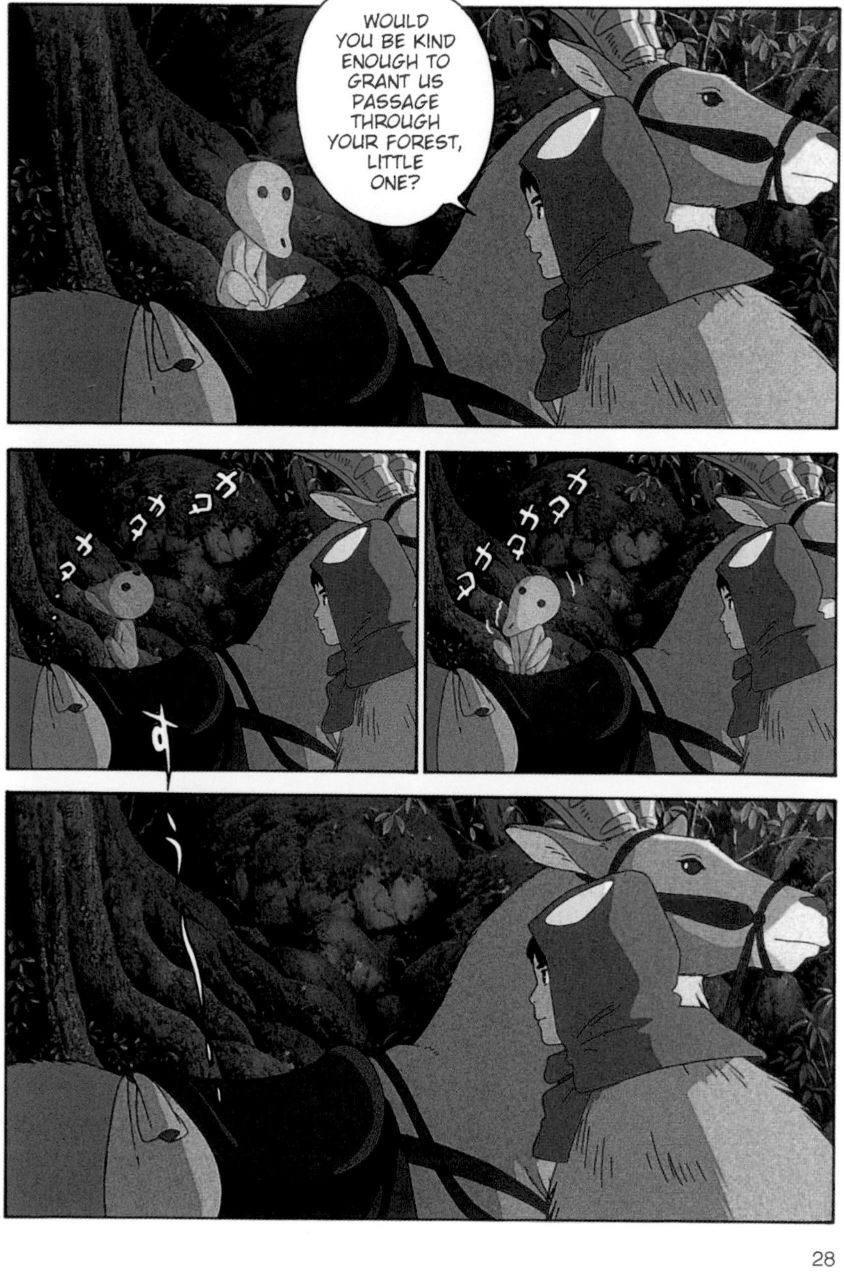
WOULD YOU BE KIND ENOUGH TO GRANT US PASSAGE THROUGH YOUR FOREST, LITTLE ONE?

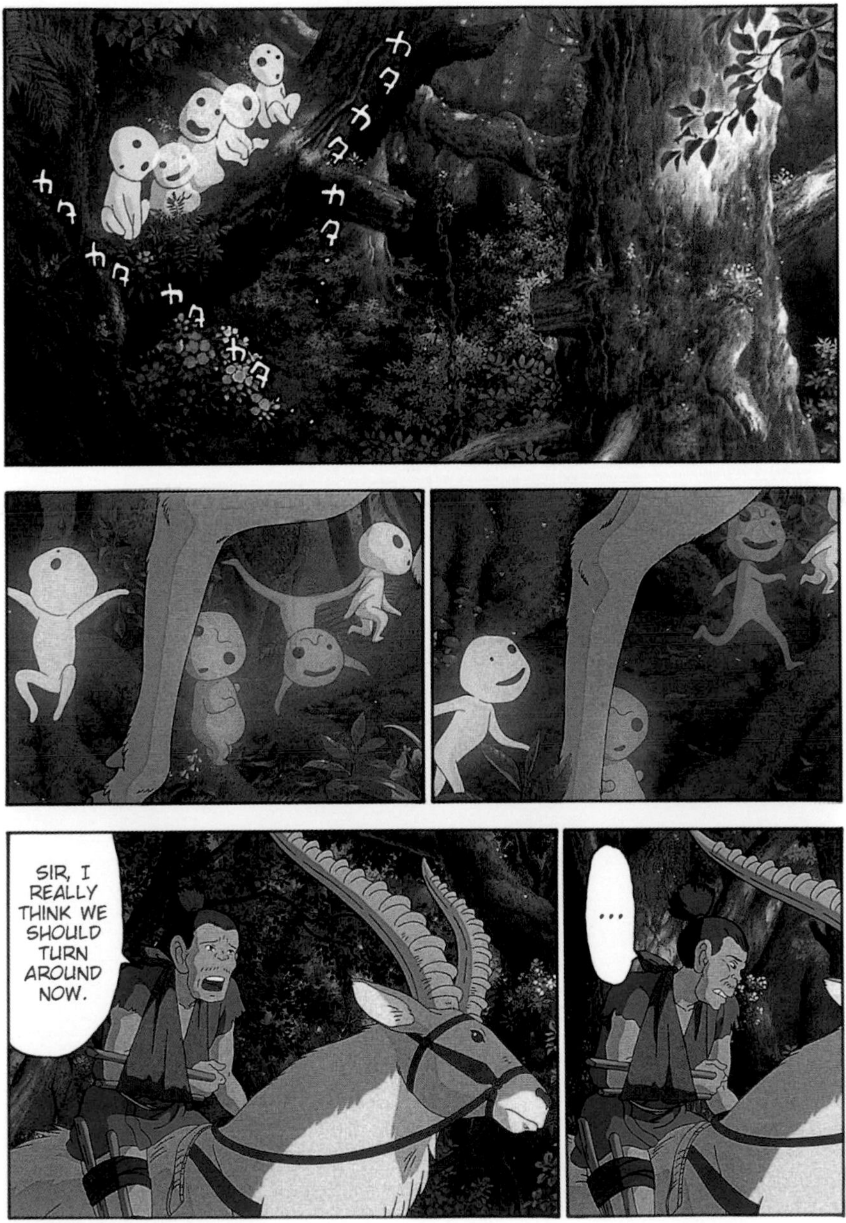
カタカタカタ
カタカタカタカタ
SIR, I REALLY THINK WE SHOULD TURN AROUND NOW.
...

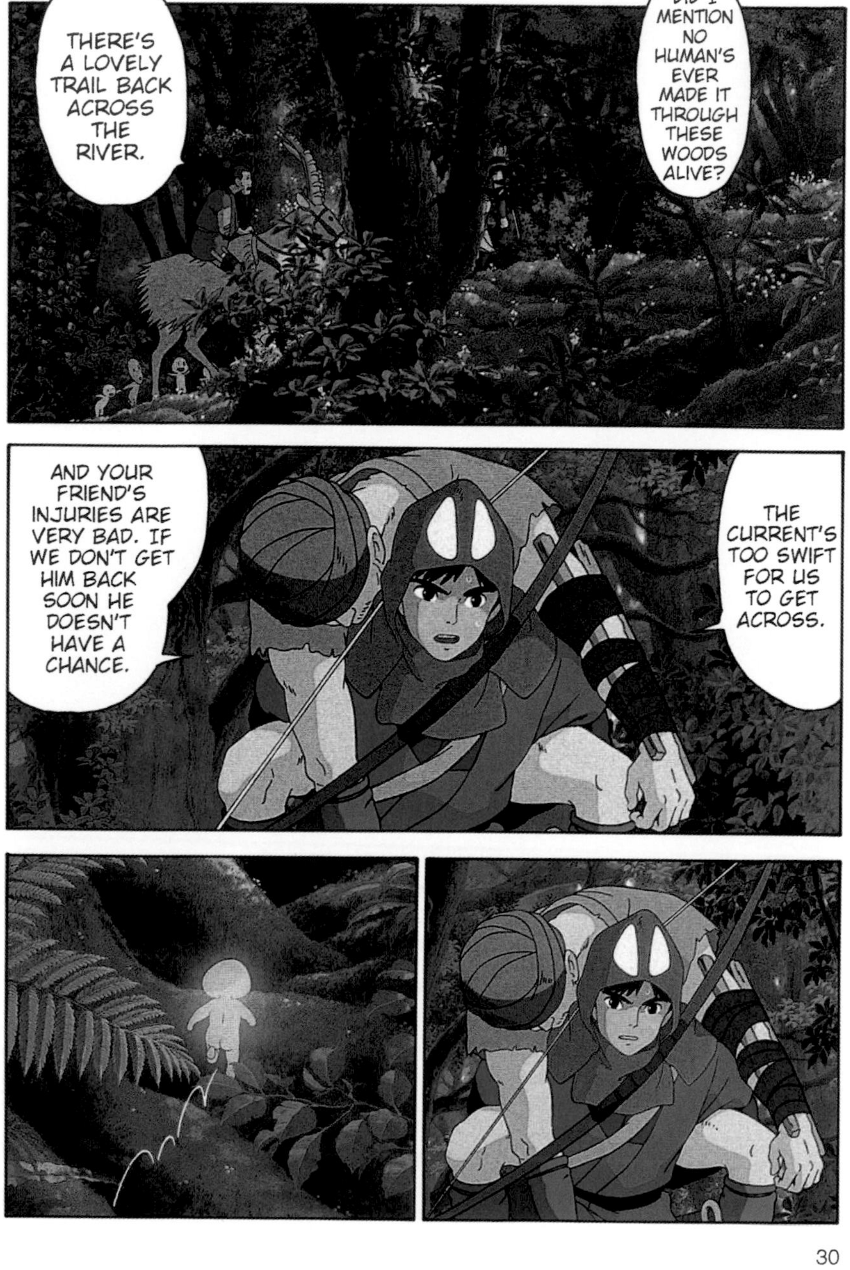
DID I MENTION NO HUMAN'S EVER MADE IT THROUGH THESE WOODS ALIVE?
THERE'S A LOVELY TRAIL BACK ACROSS THE RIVER.
THE CURRENT'S TOO SWIFT FOR US TO GET ACROSS.
AND YOUR FRIEND'S INJURIES ARE VERY BAD. IF WE DON'T GET HIM BACK SOON HE DOESN'T HAVE A CHANCE.

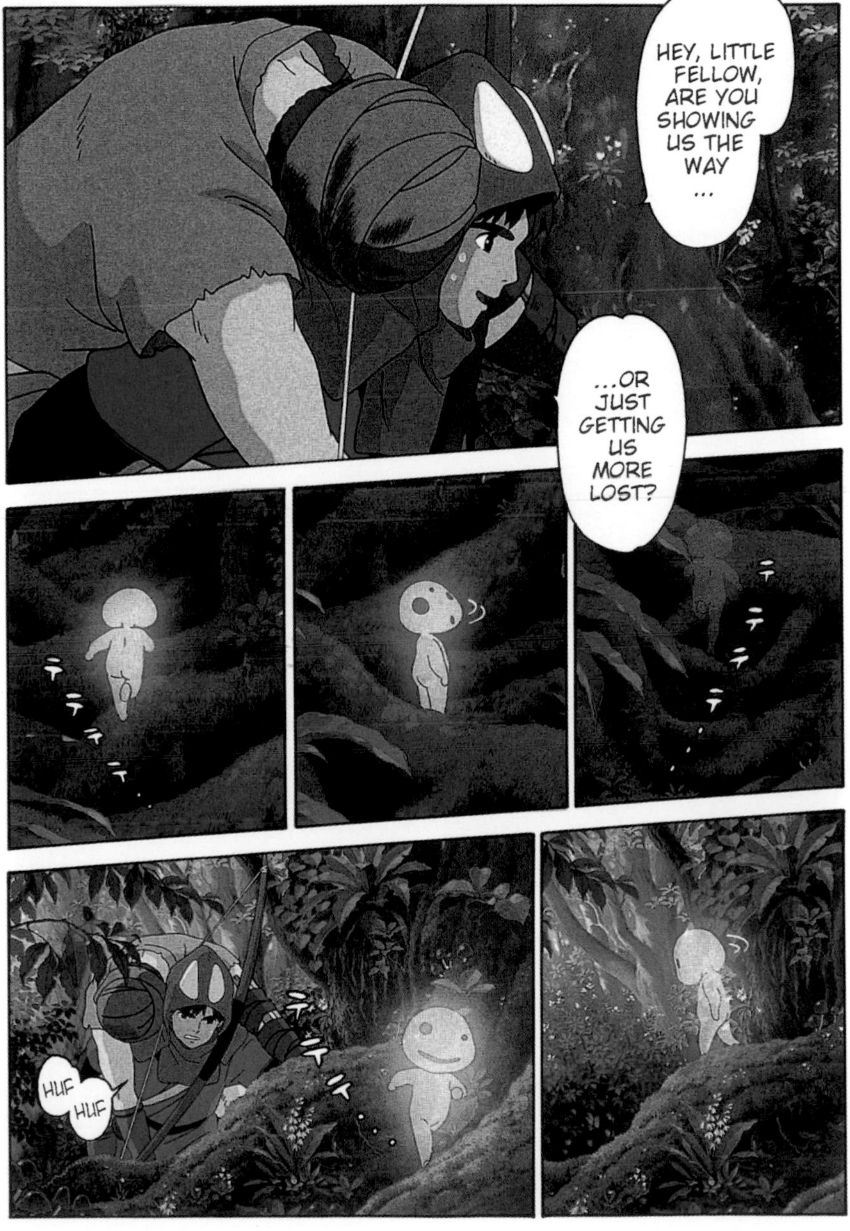

HEY, LITTLE FELLOW, ARE YOU SHOWING US THE WAY ...
...OR JUST GETTING US MORE LOST?
HUF
HUF

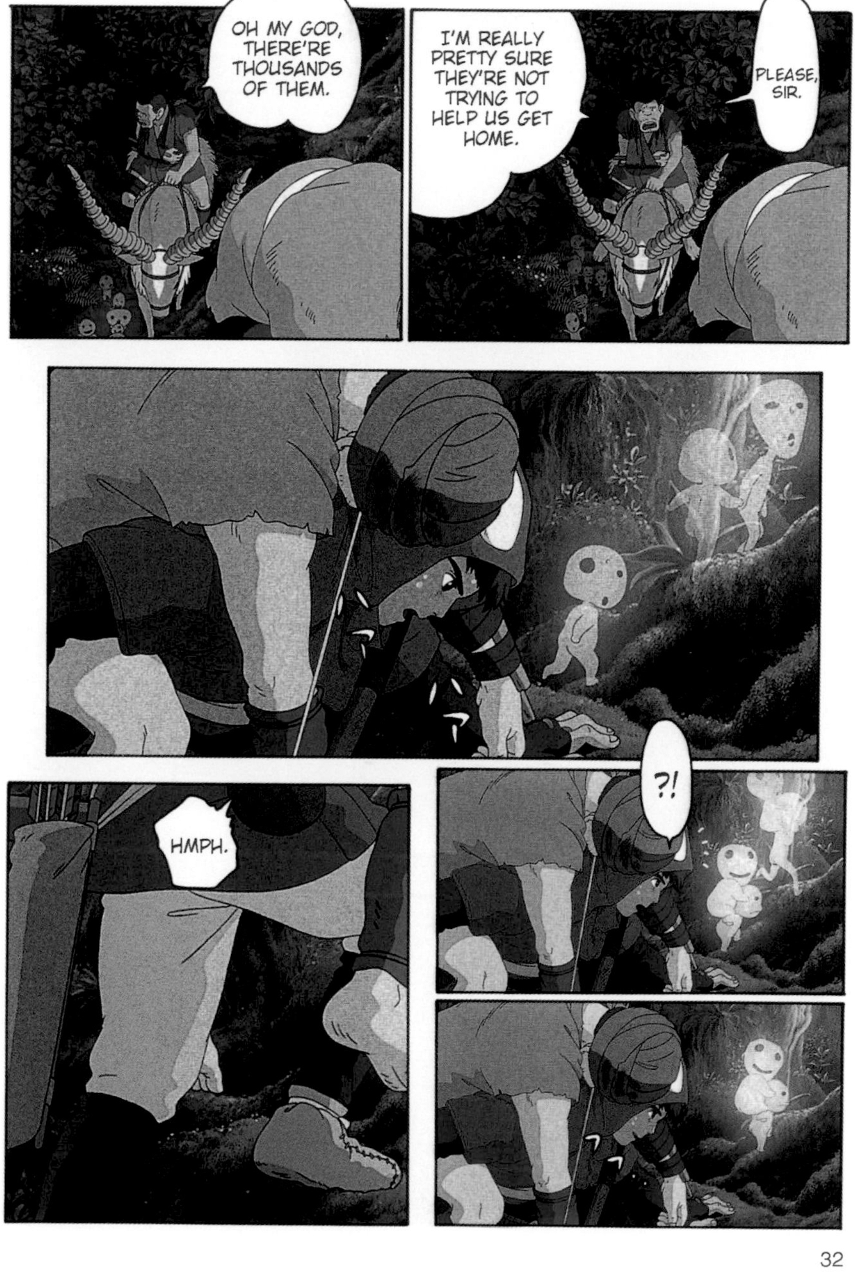
OH MY GOD, THERE'RE THOUSANDS OF THEM.
I'M REALLY PRETTY SURE THEY'RE NOT TRYING TO HELP US GET HOME.
PLEASE, SIR.
HMPH.
?!

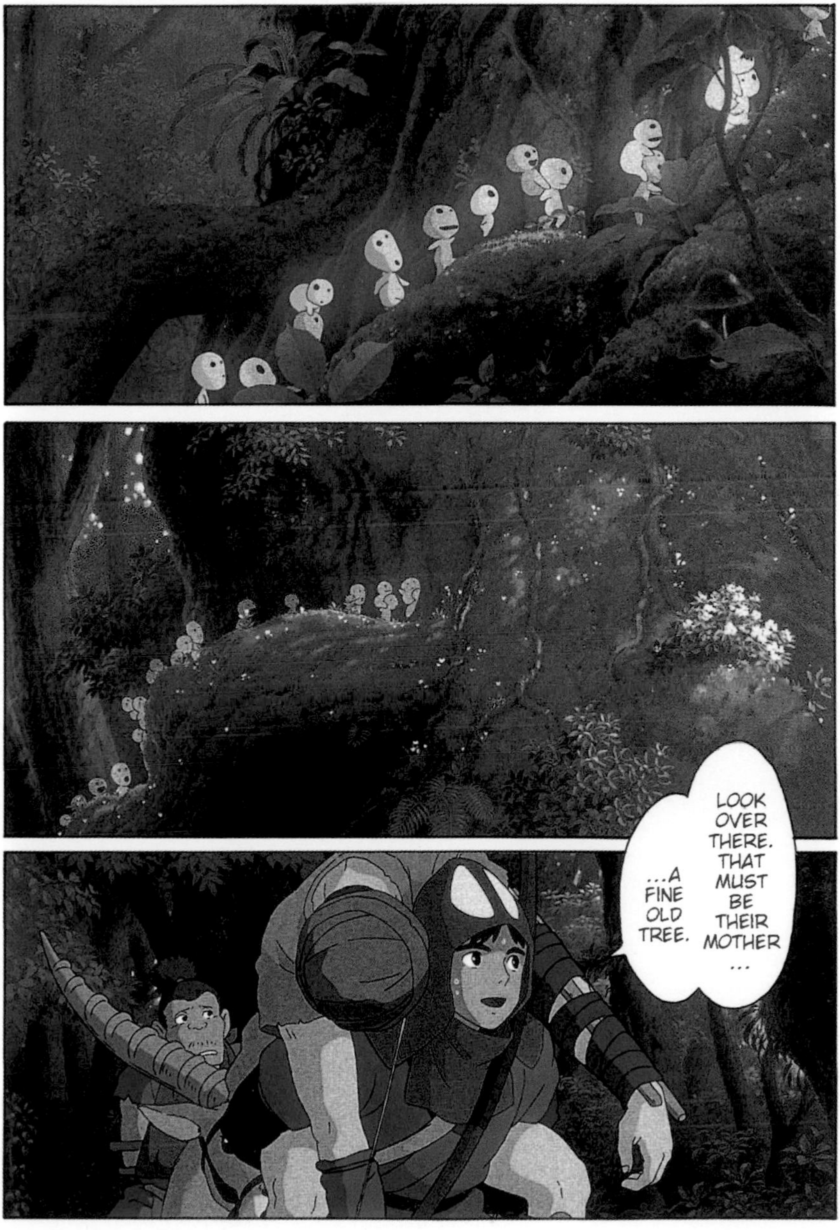
LOOK OVER THERE. THAT MUST BE THEIR MOTHER...
...A FINE OLD TREE.

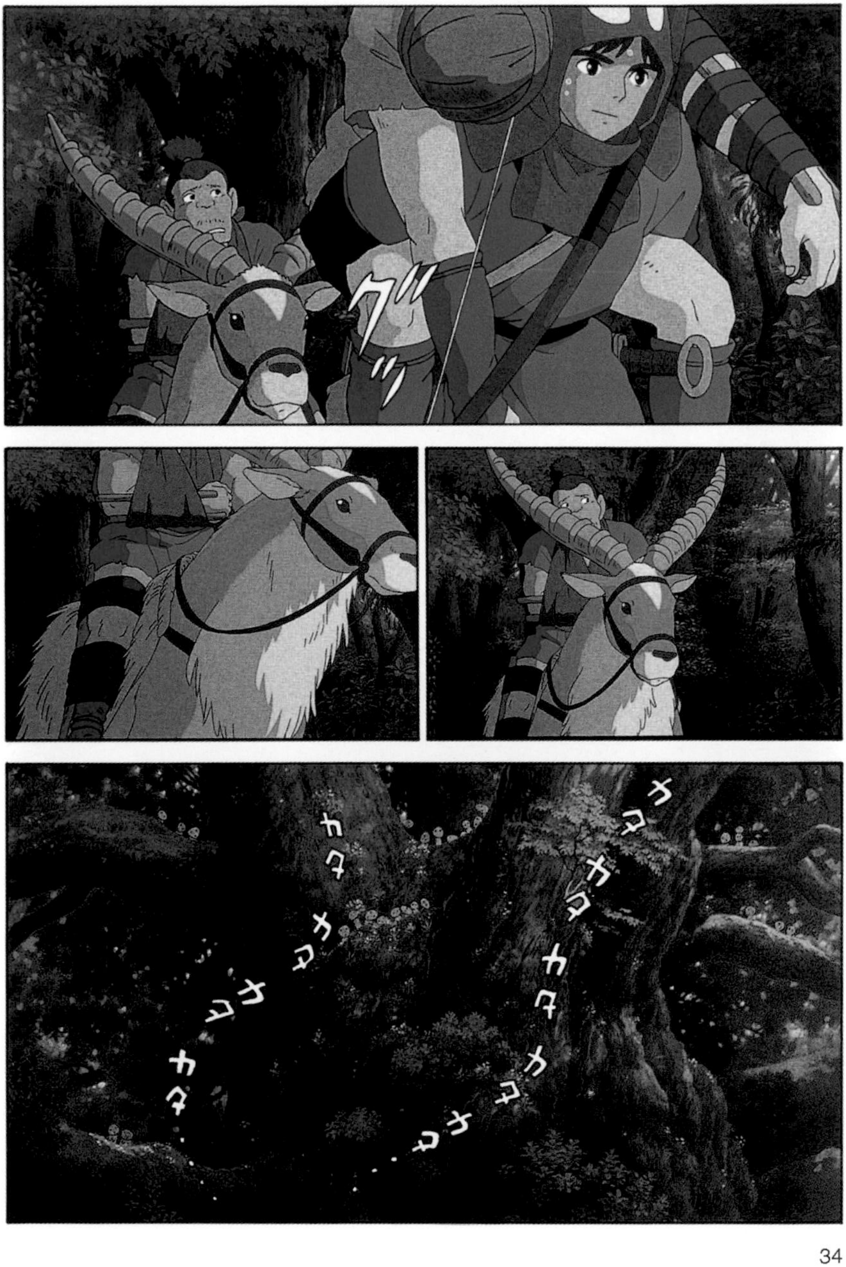
グッ
カタカタカタカタカタ…
カタカタカタカタ…

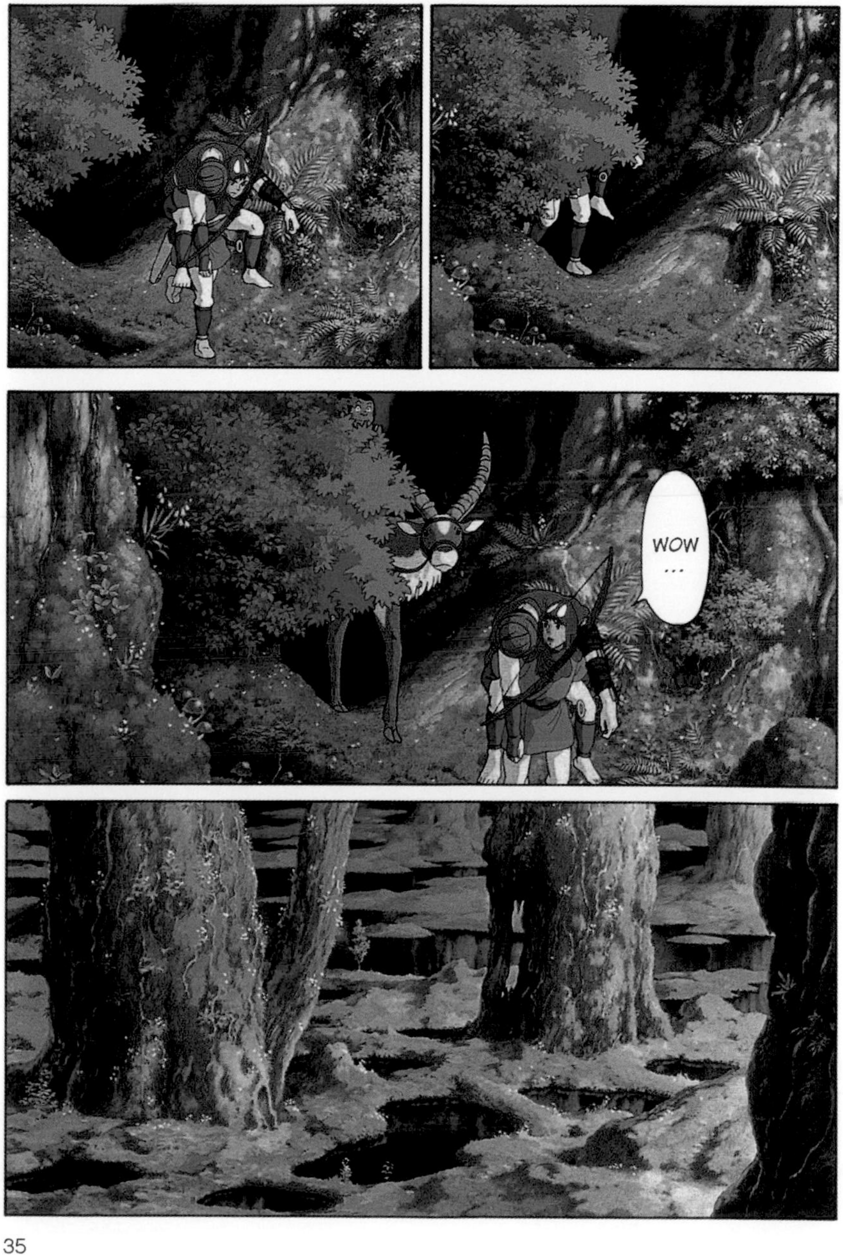
WOW ...

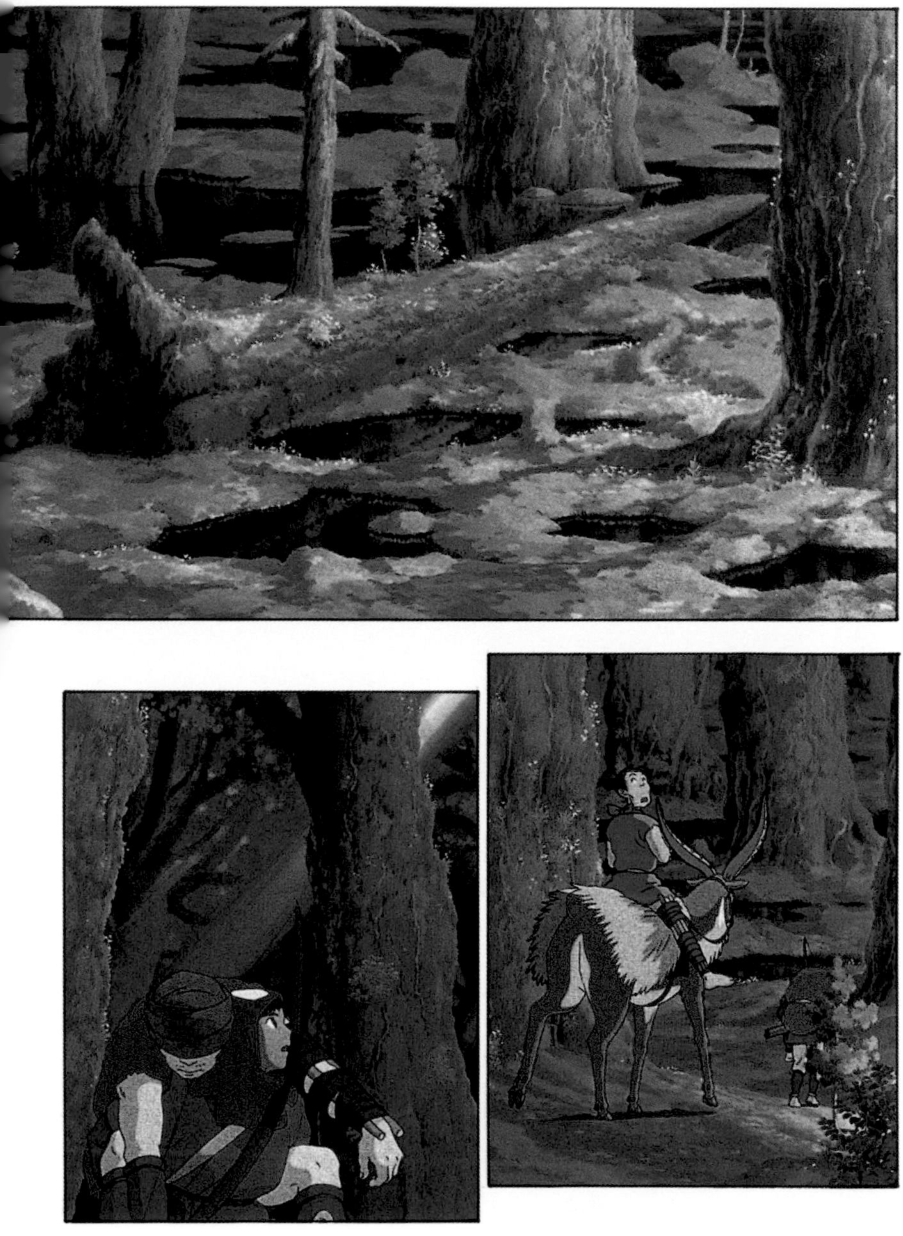

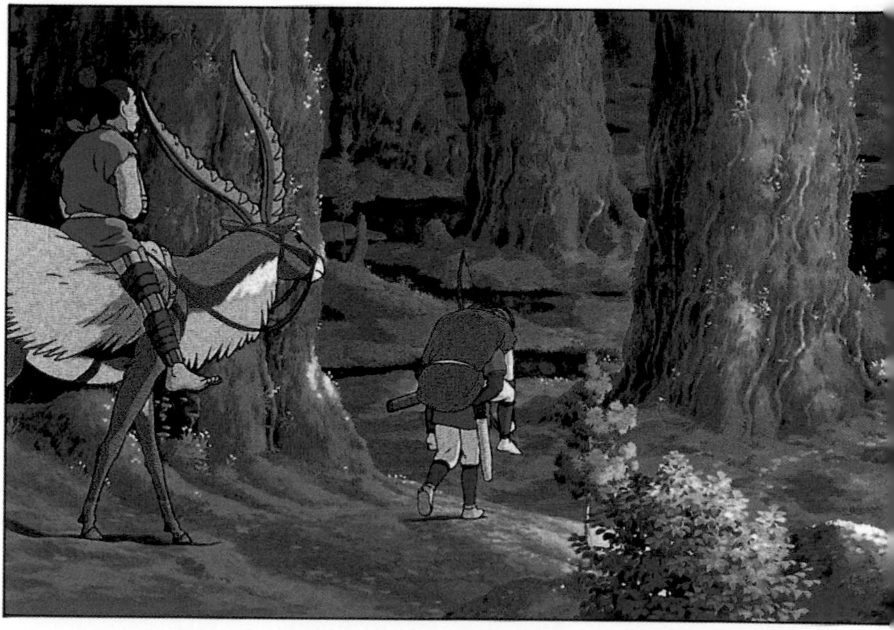

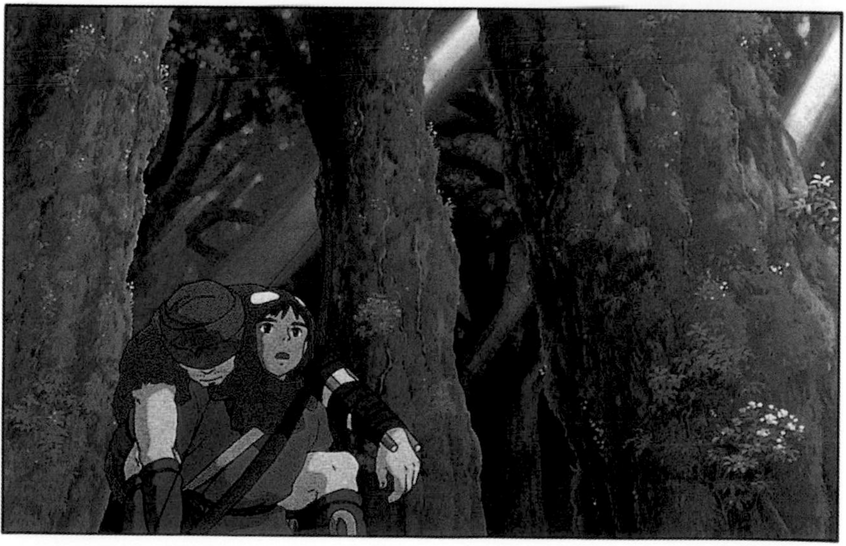

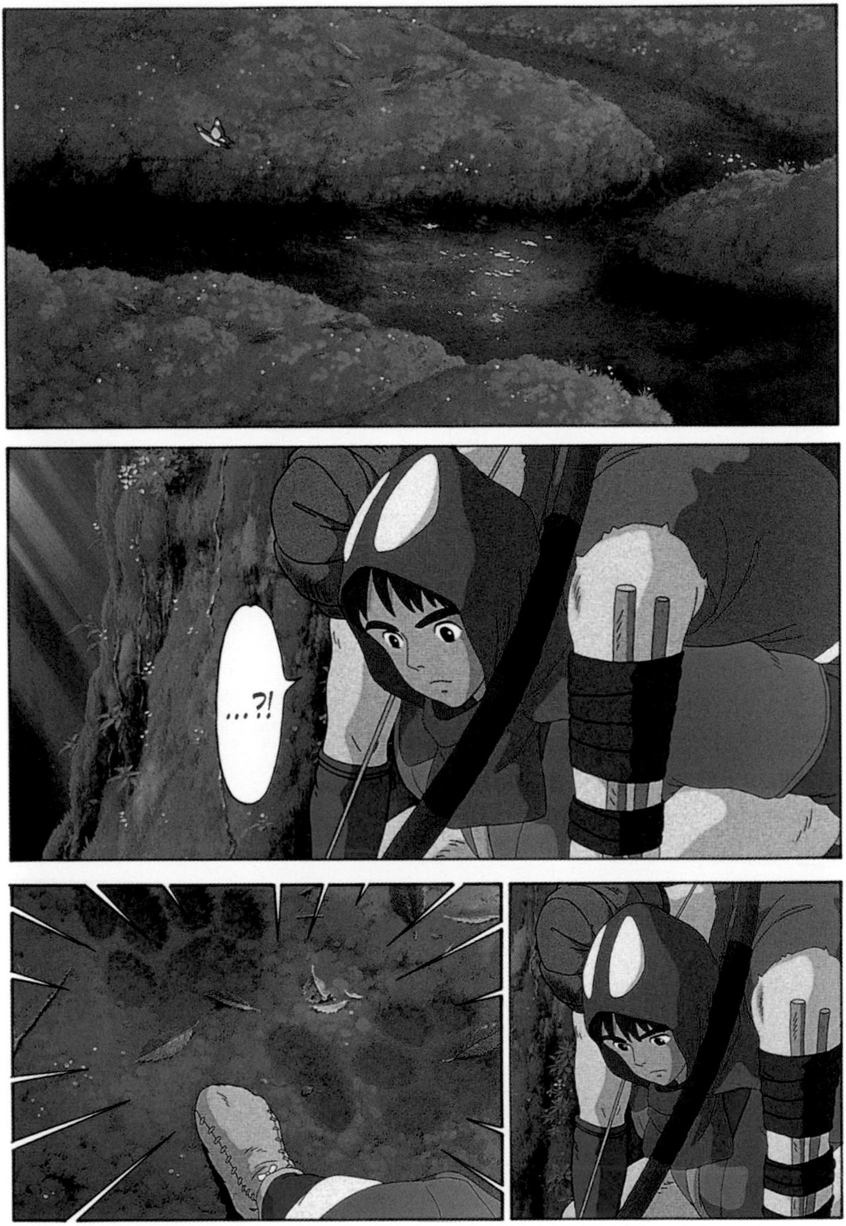
...?!

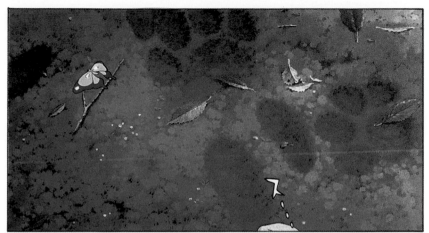

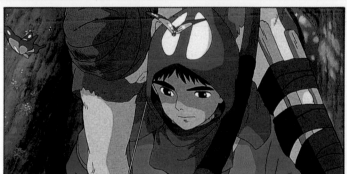

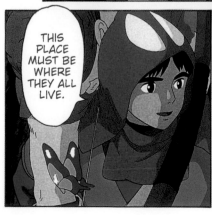

ス
THE TRACKS OF THOSE WOLVES AND THE GIRL WITH THEM.
THIS PLACE MUST BE WHERE THEY ALL LIVE.

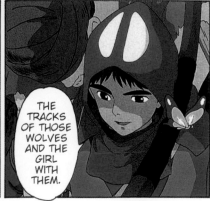

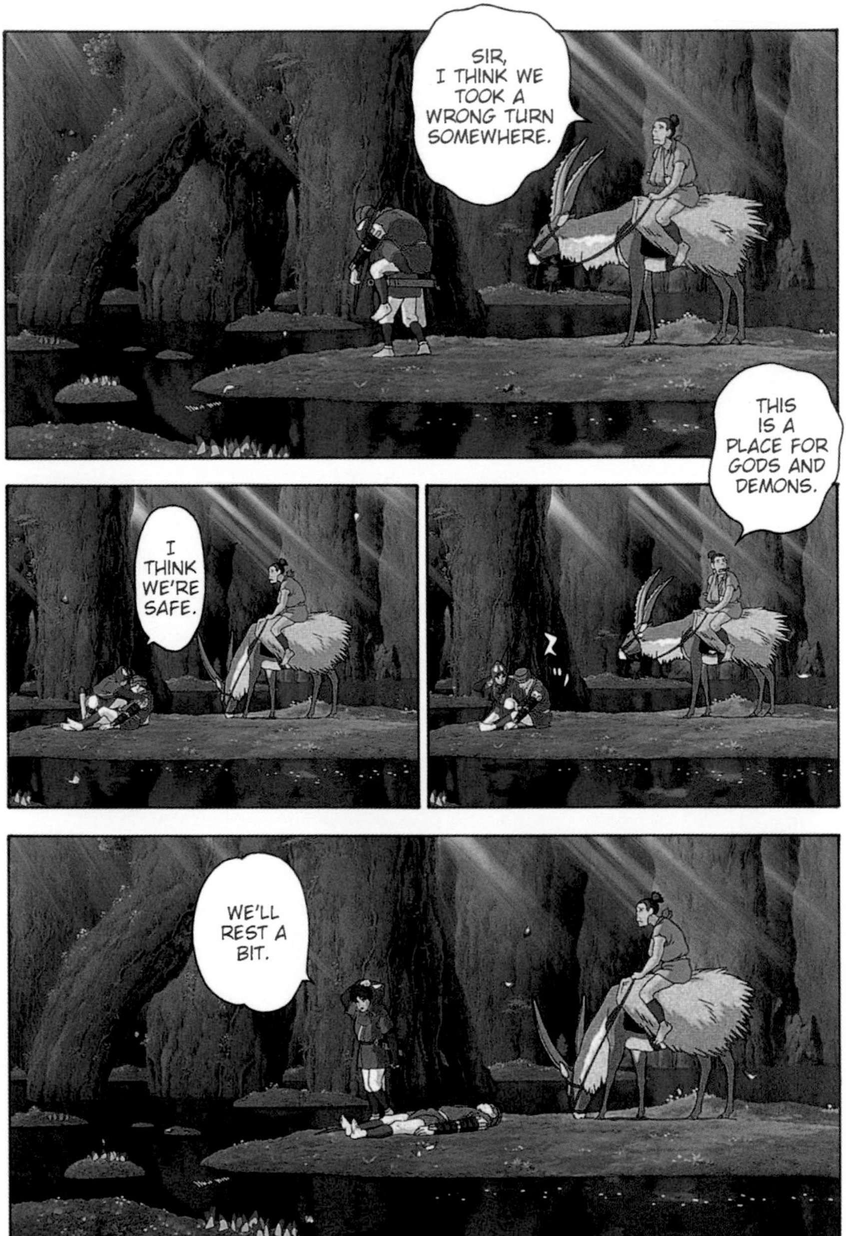
SIR, I THINK WE TOOK A WRONG TURN SOMEWHERE.
THIS IS A PLACE FOR GODS AND DEMONS.
I THINK WE'RE SAFE.
WE'LL REST A BIT.

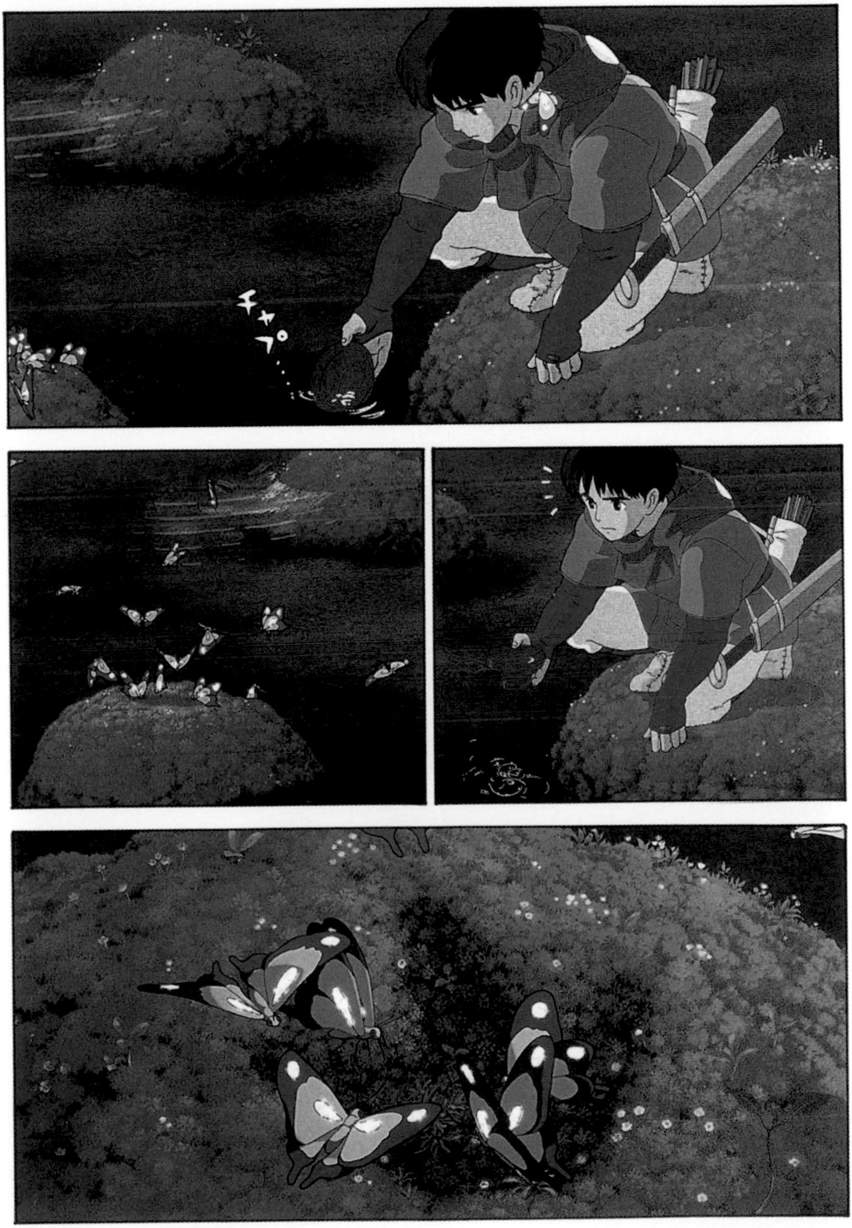
チャプ…

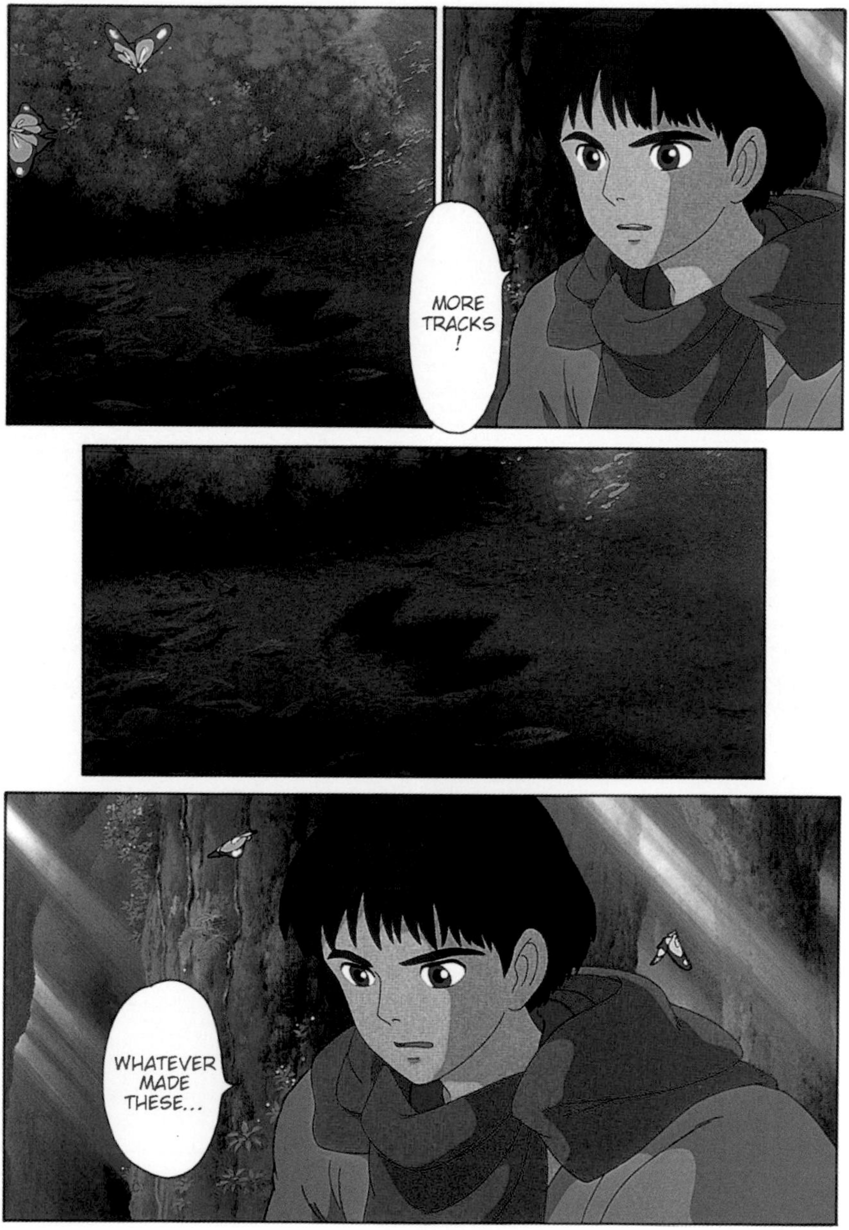
MORE TRACKS!
WHATEVER MADE THESE...

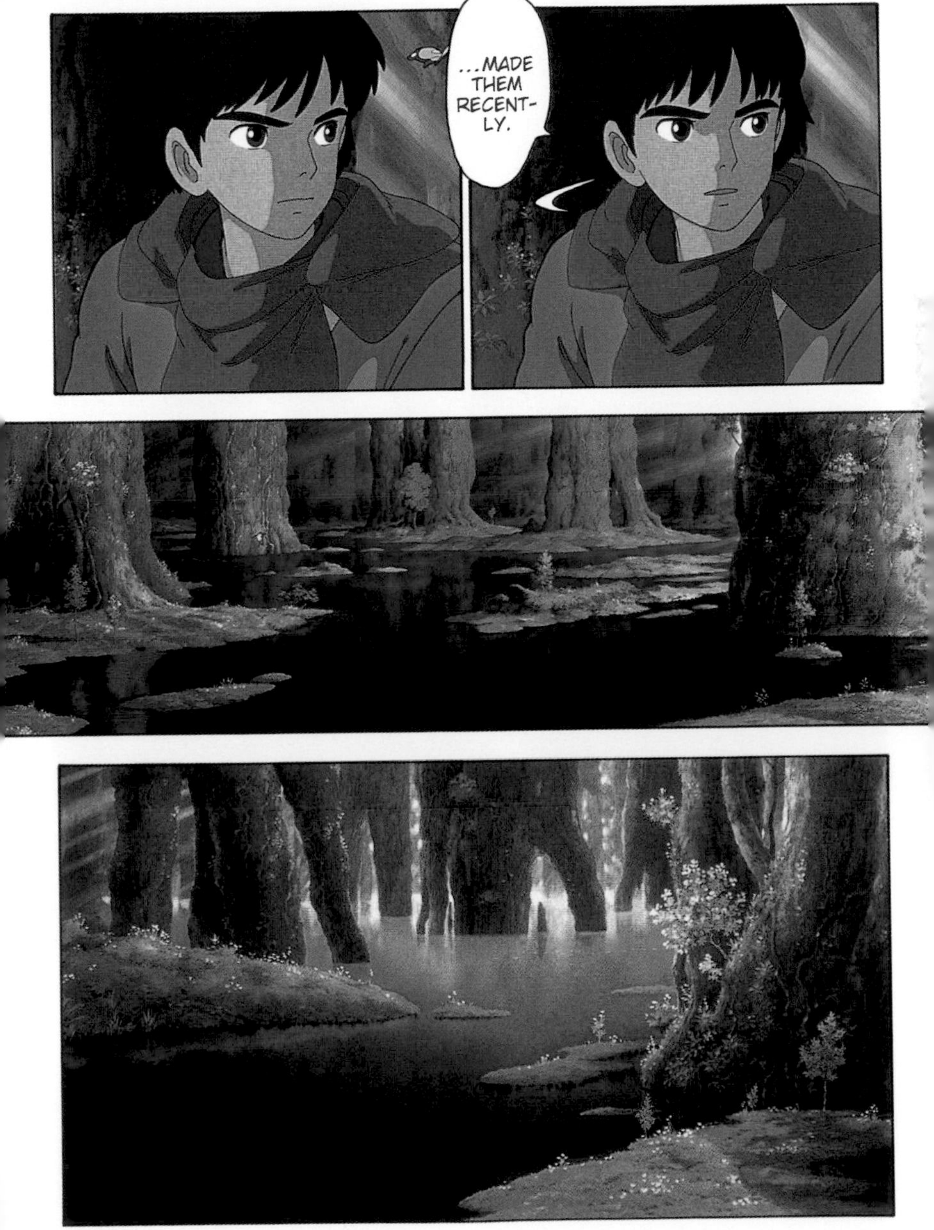
...MADE THEM RECENT-LY.

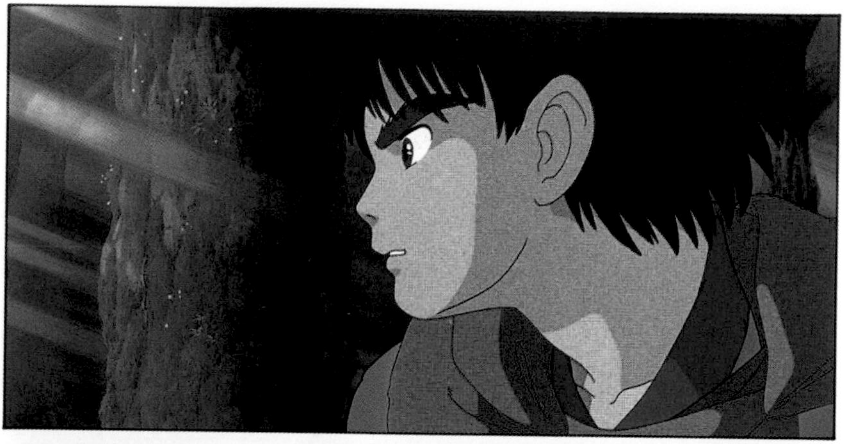
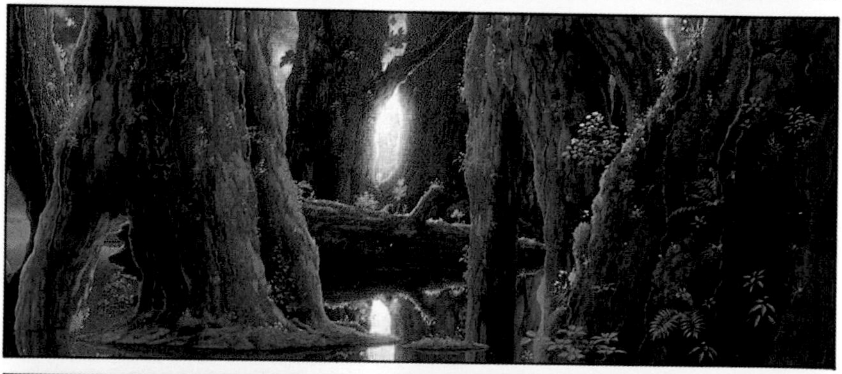
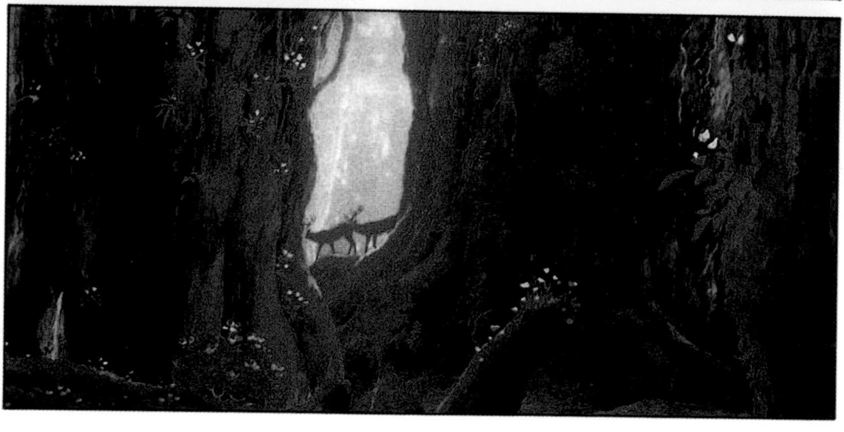

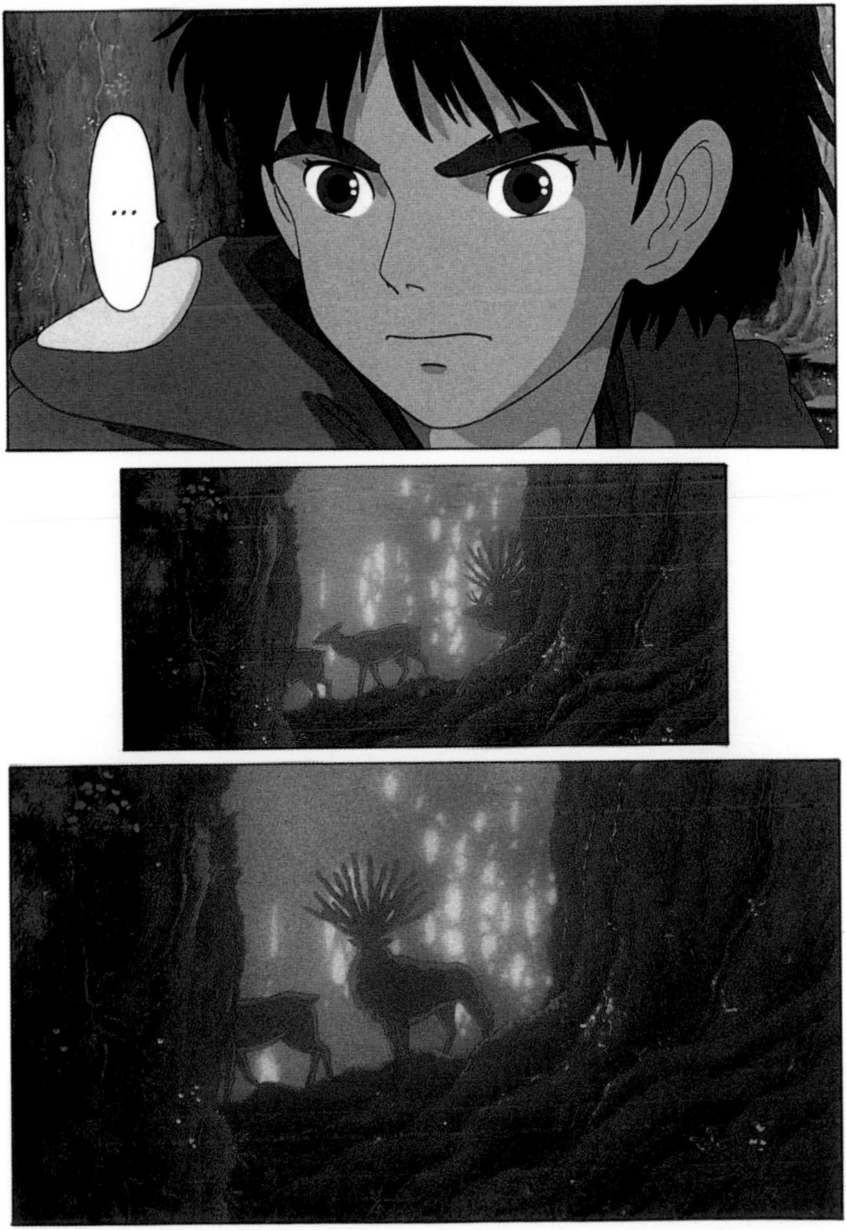
...

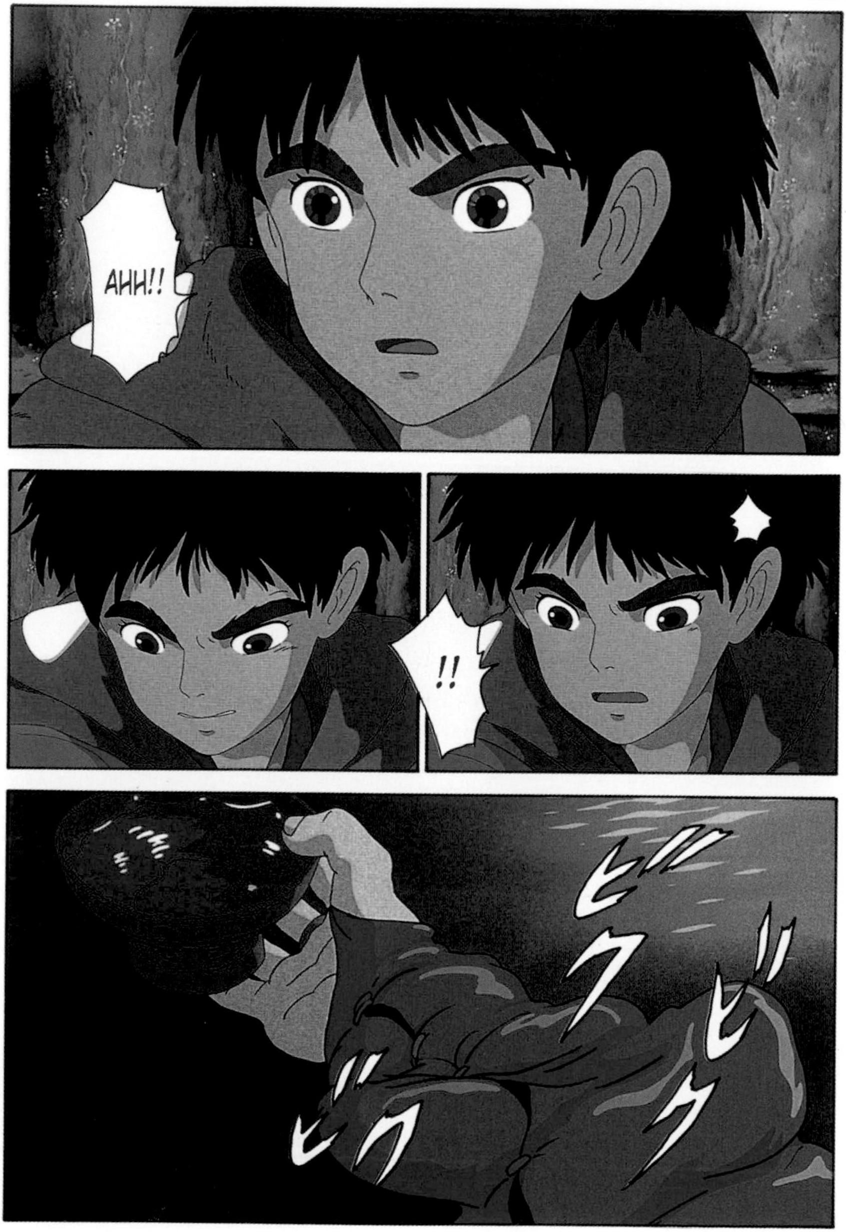
AHH!!
!!
ビク ビク ビク

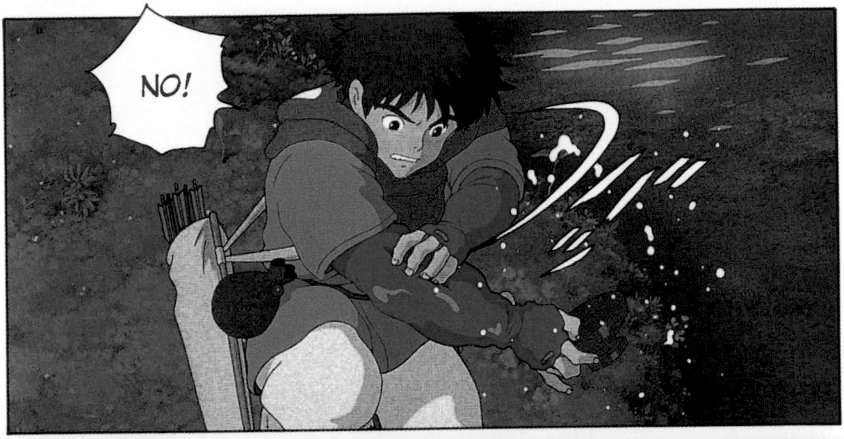
NO!

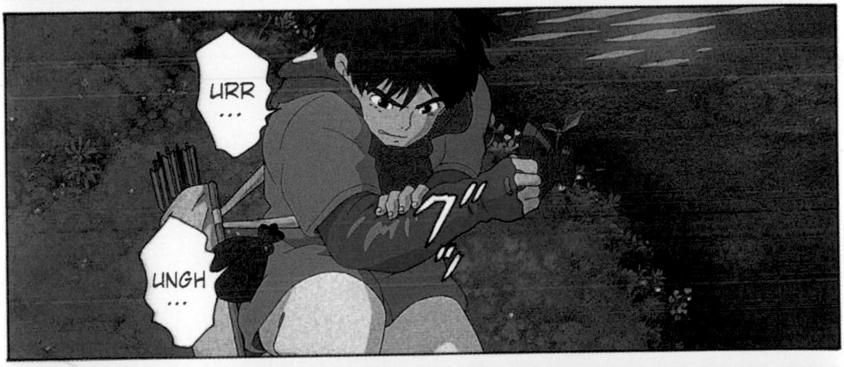
URR ...
UNGH ...

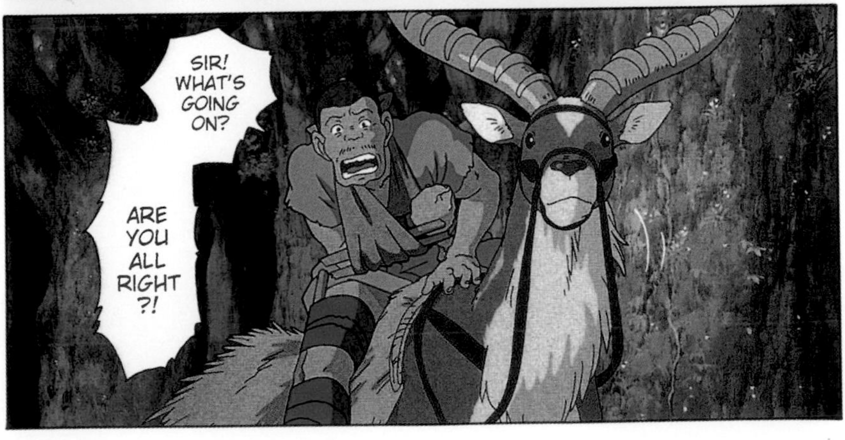
SIR! WHAT'S GOING ON?
ARE YOU ALL RIGHT ?!

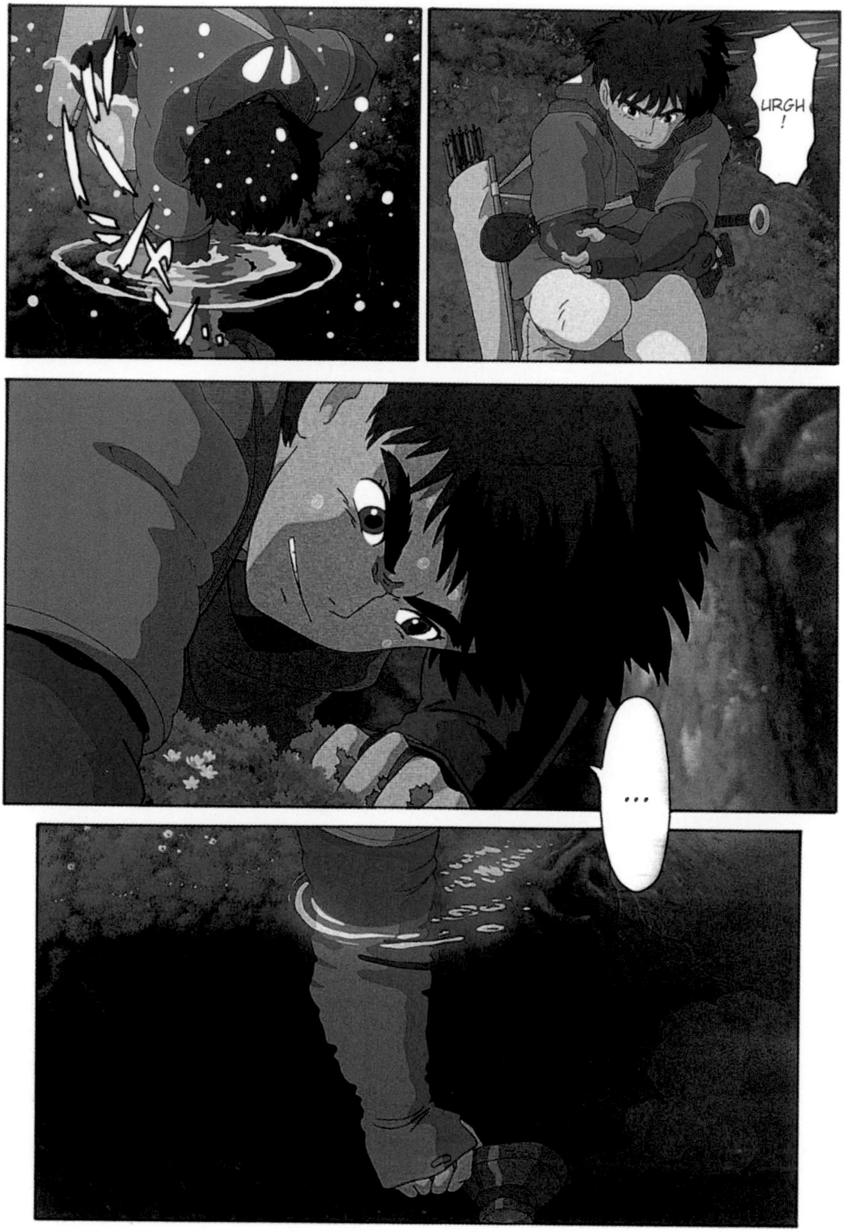
URGH!
...

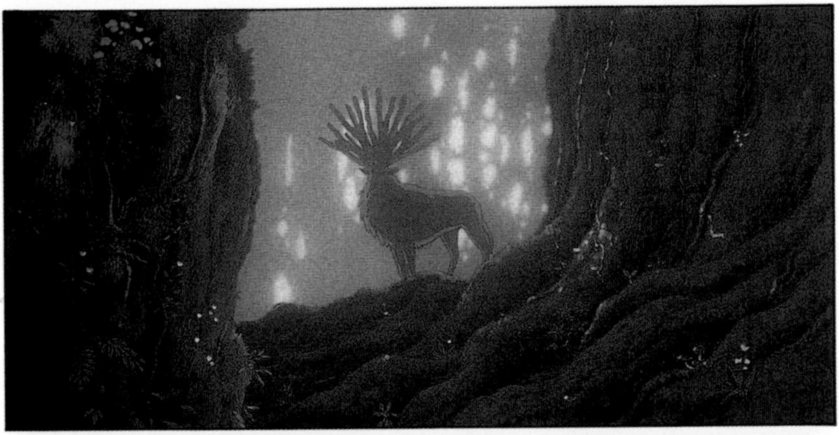
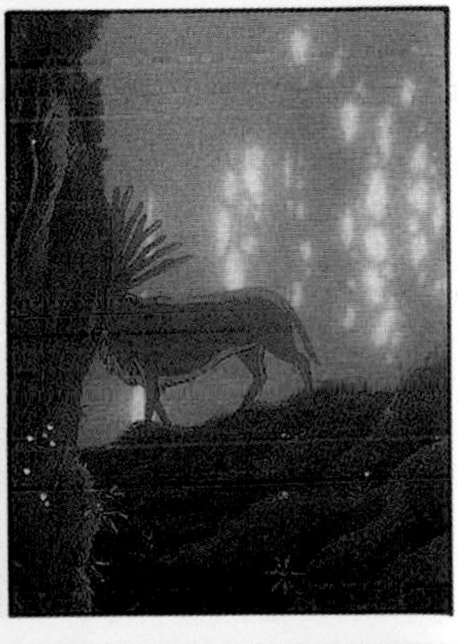
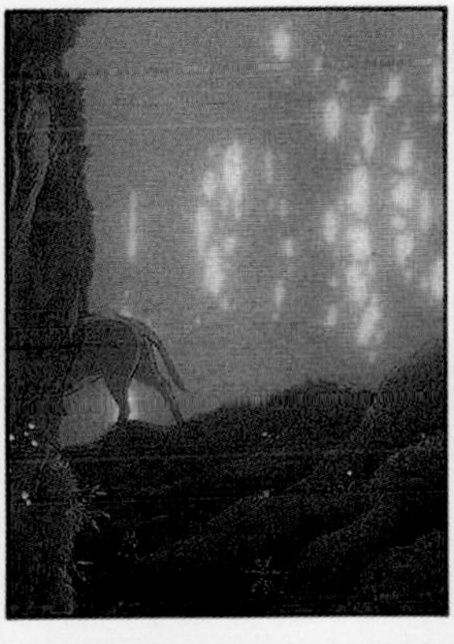
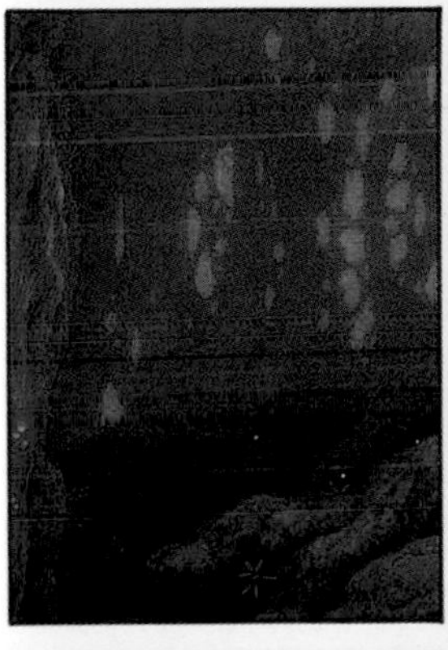
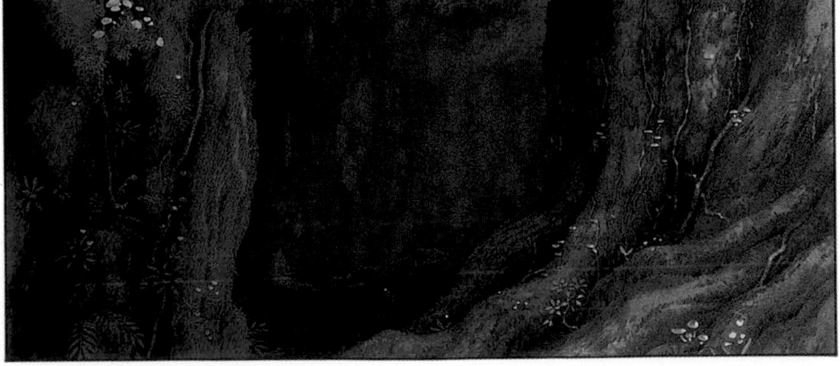

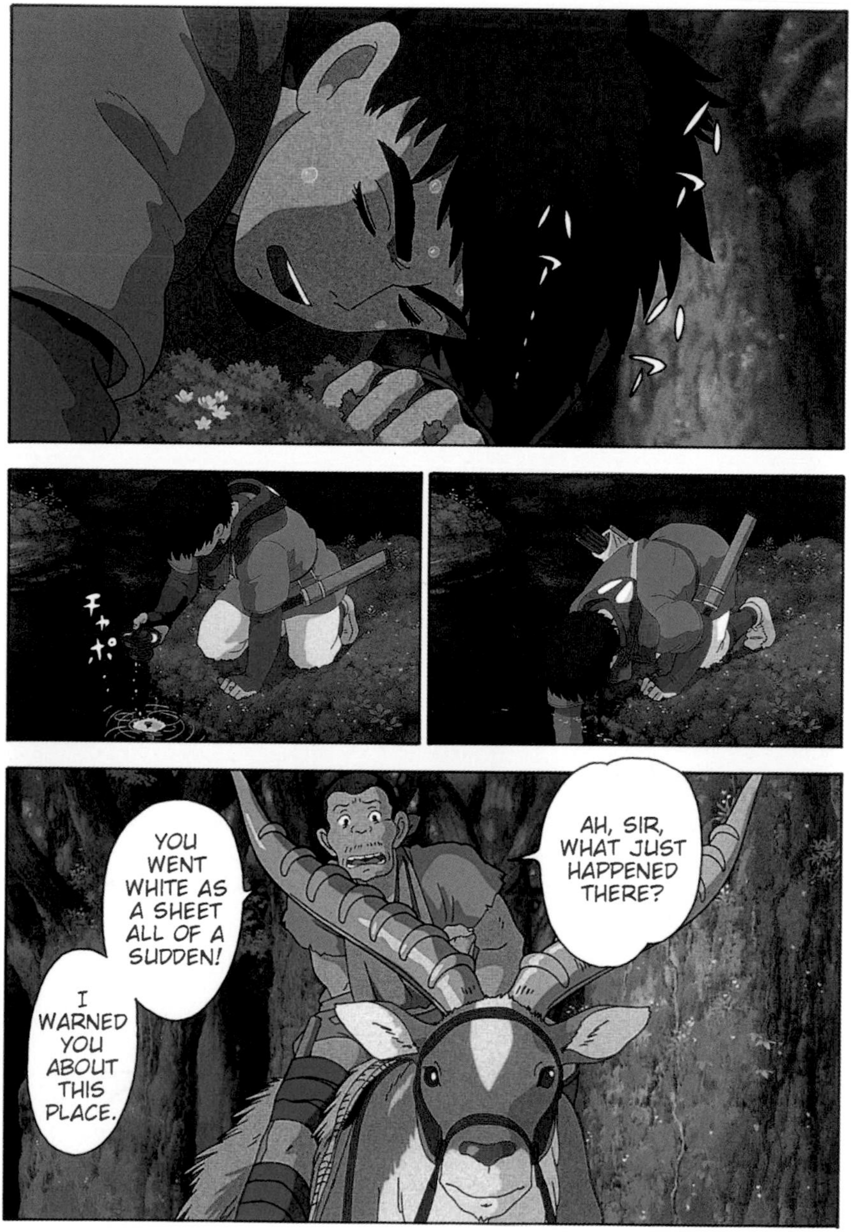
チャポ
AH, SIR, WHAT JUST HAPPENED THERE?
YOU WENT WHITE AS A SHEET ALL OF A SUDDEN!
I WARNED YOU ABOUT THIS PLACE.

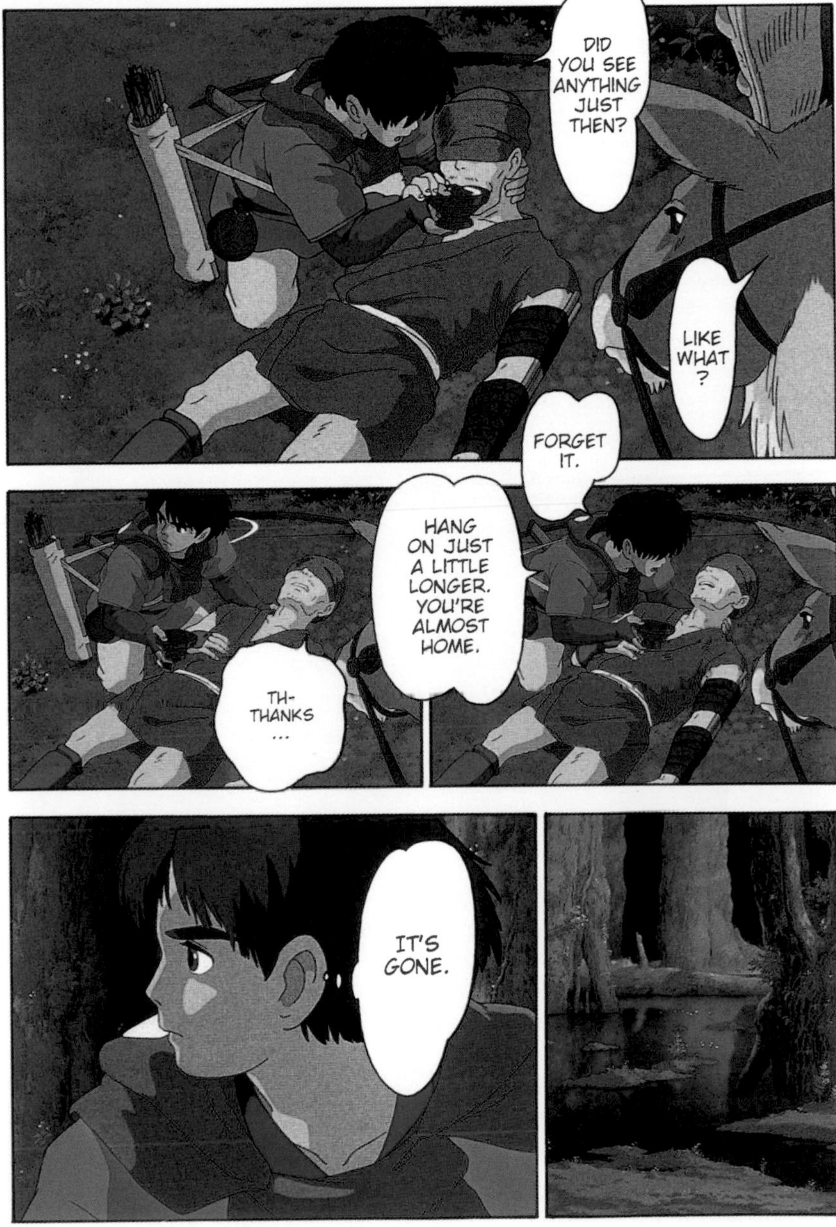
DID YOU SEE ANYTHING JUST THEN?
LIKE WHAT?
FORGET IT.
HANG ON JUST A LITTLE LONGER. YOU'RE ALMOST HOME.
TH-THANKS...
IT'S GONE.

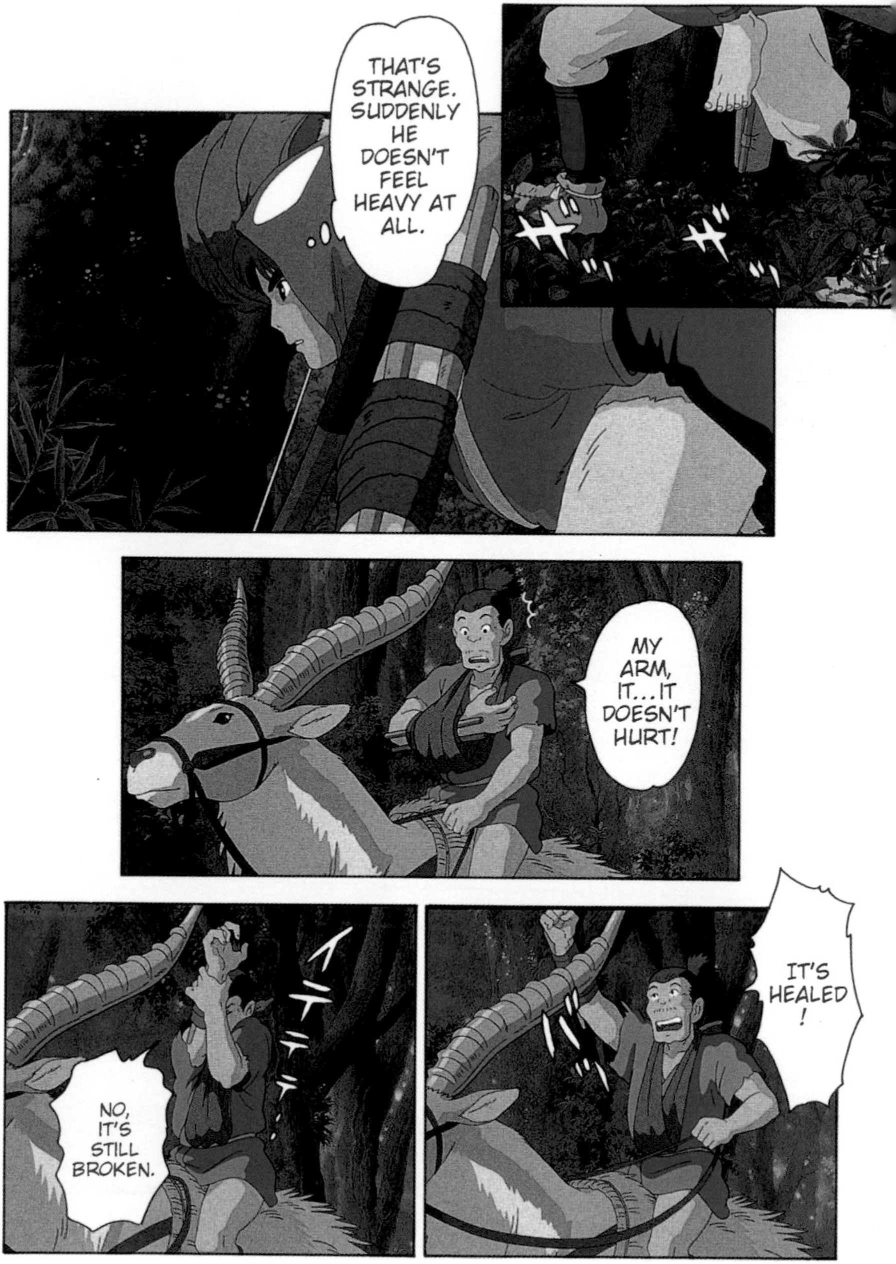
ザッ ザッ
THAT'S STRANGE. SUDDENLY HE DOESN'T FEEL HEAVY AT ALL.
MY ARM, IT...IT DOESN'T HURT!
IT'S HEALED!
イテテテ
NO, IT'S STILL BROKEN.

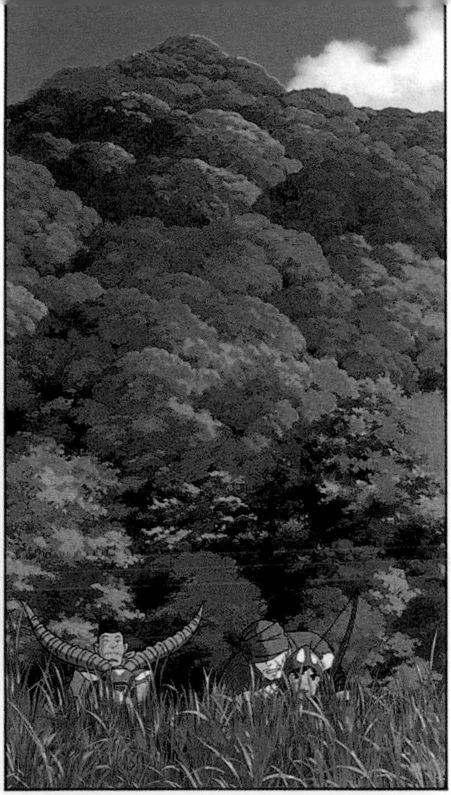

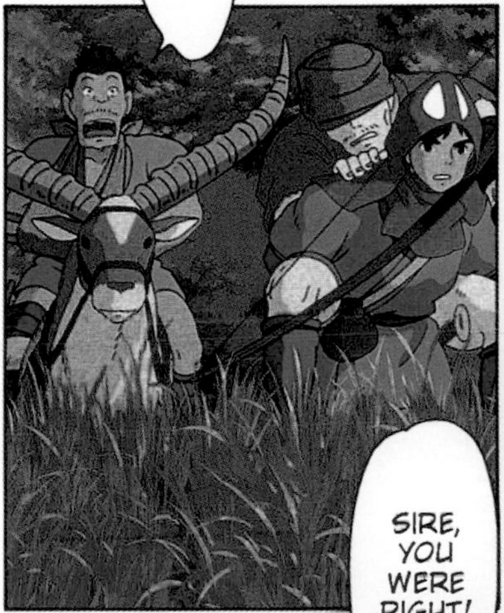
WOW.

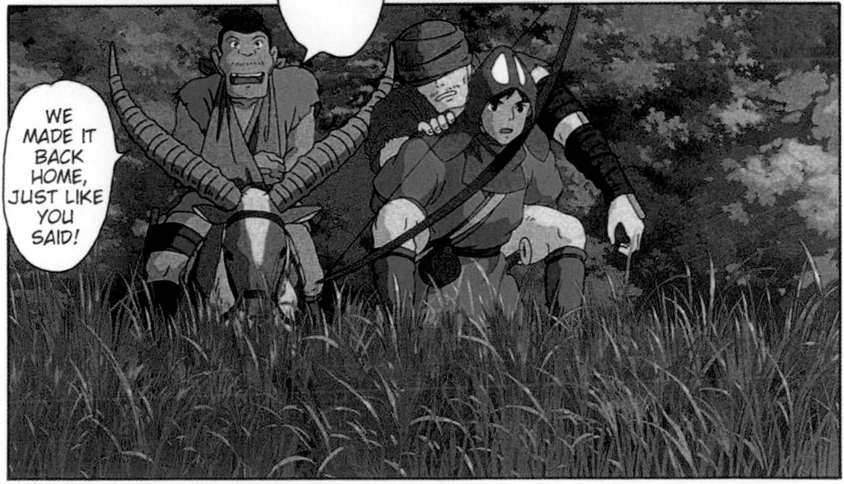
SIRE, YOU WERE RIGHT!
WE MADE IT BACK HOME, JUST LIKE YOU SAID!

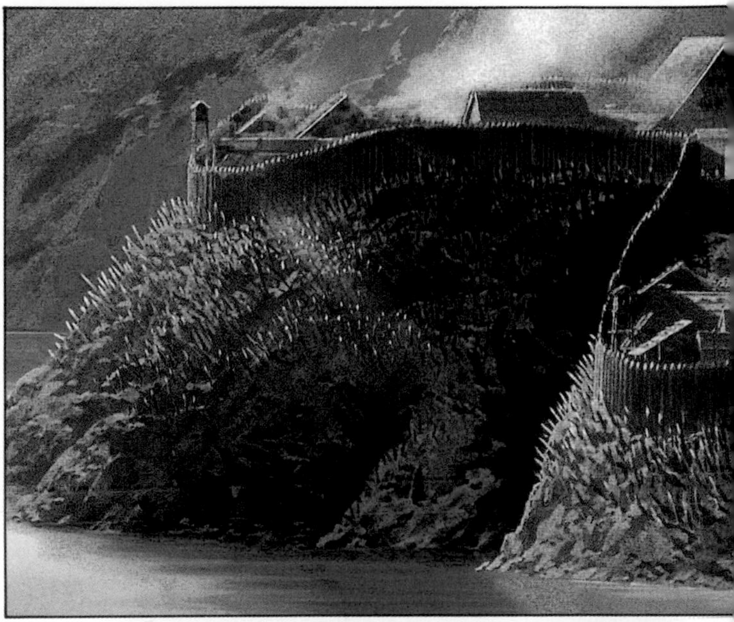

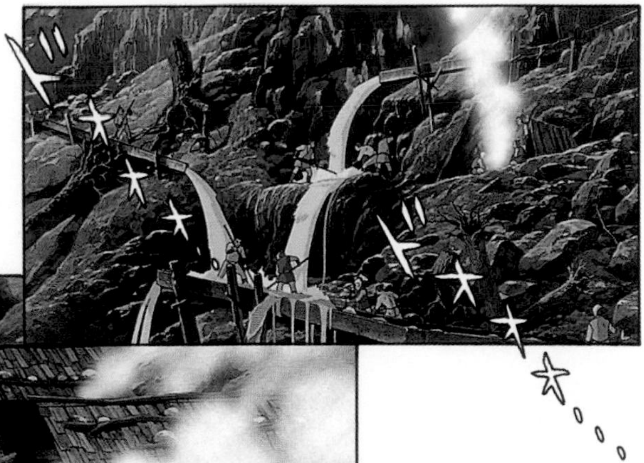

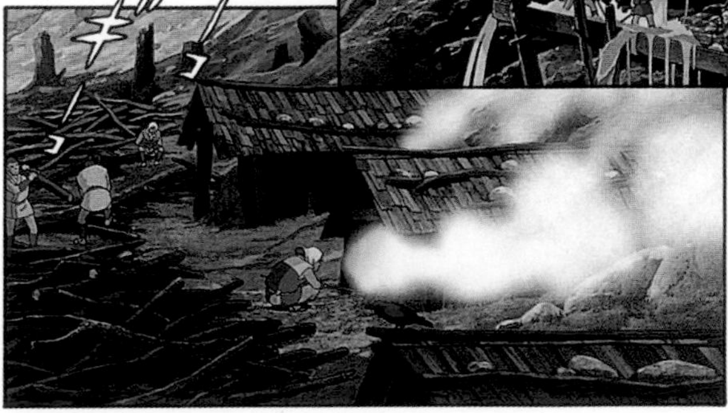

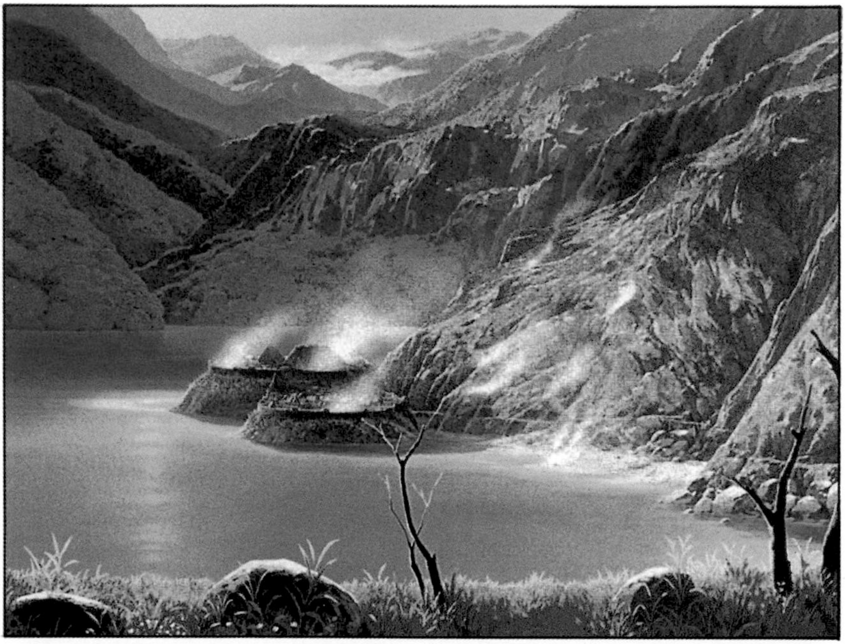

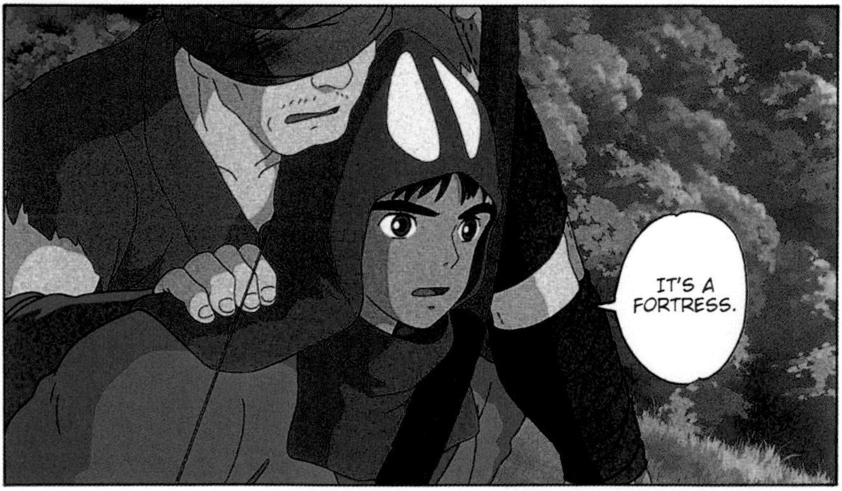
IT'S A FORTRESS.

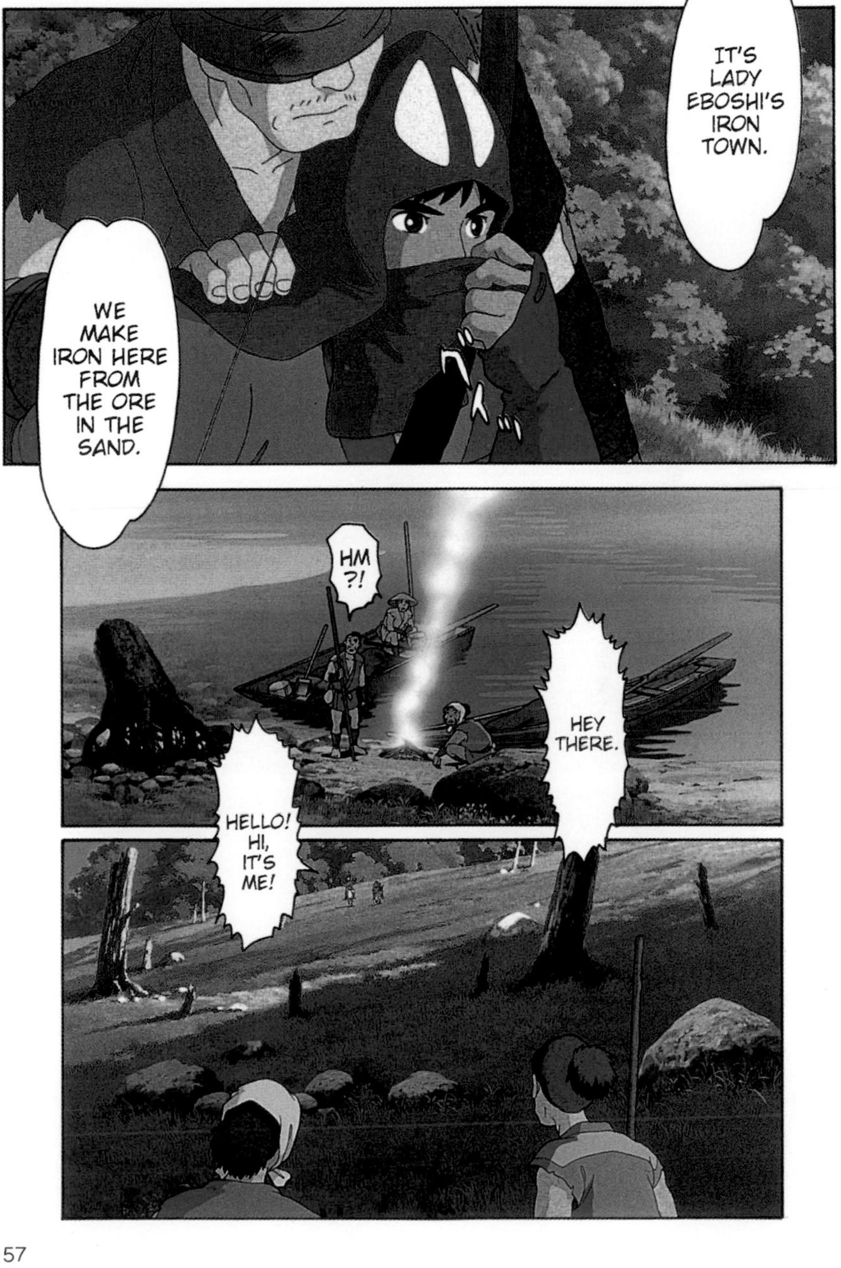
IT'S LADY EBOSHI'S IRON TOWN.
WE MAKE IRON HERE FROM THE ORE IN THE SAND.
HM?!
HEY THERE.
HELLO! HI, IT'S ME!

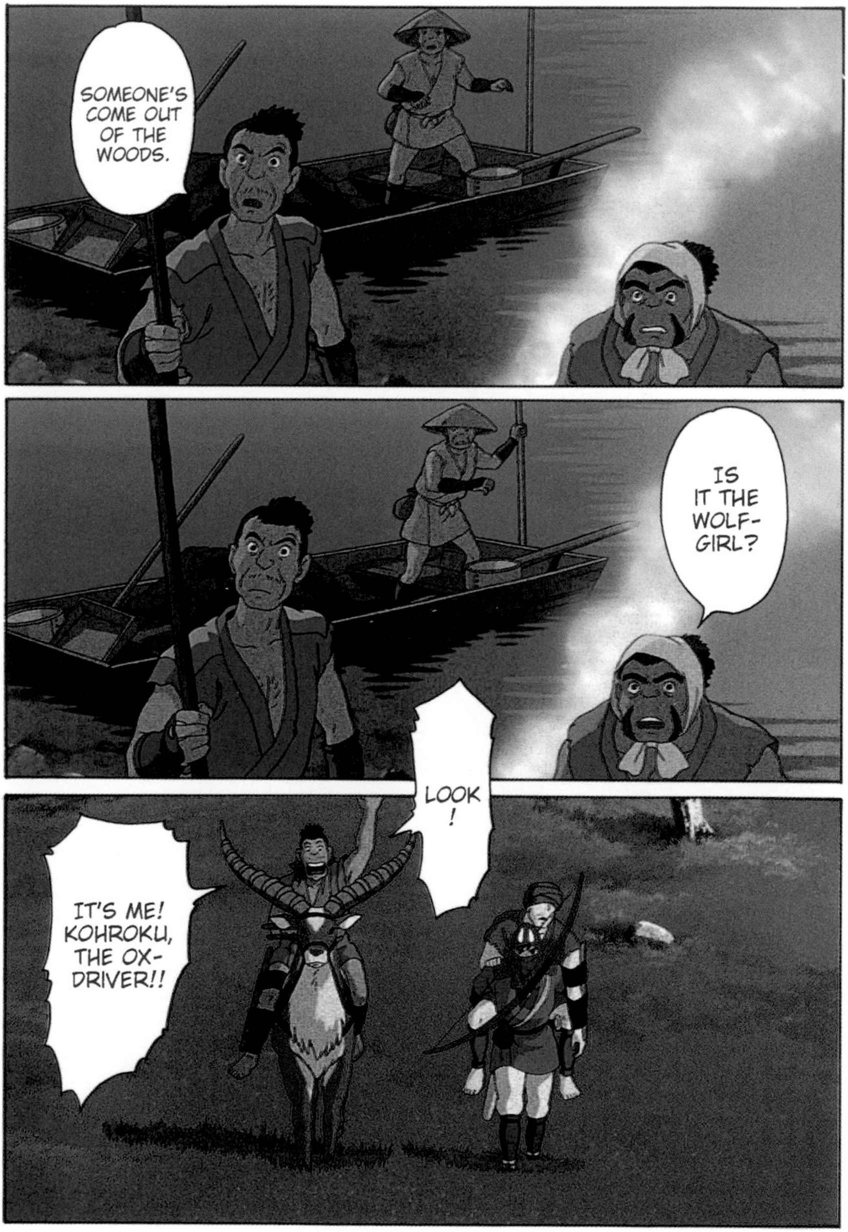
SOMEONE'S COME OUT OF THE WOODS.
IS IT THE WOLF-GIRL?
LOOK!
IT'S ME! KOHROKU, THE OX-DRIVER!!

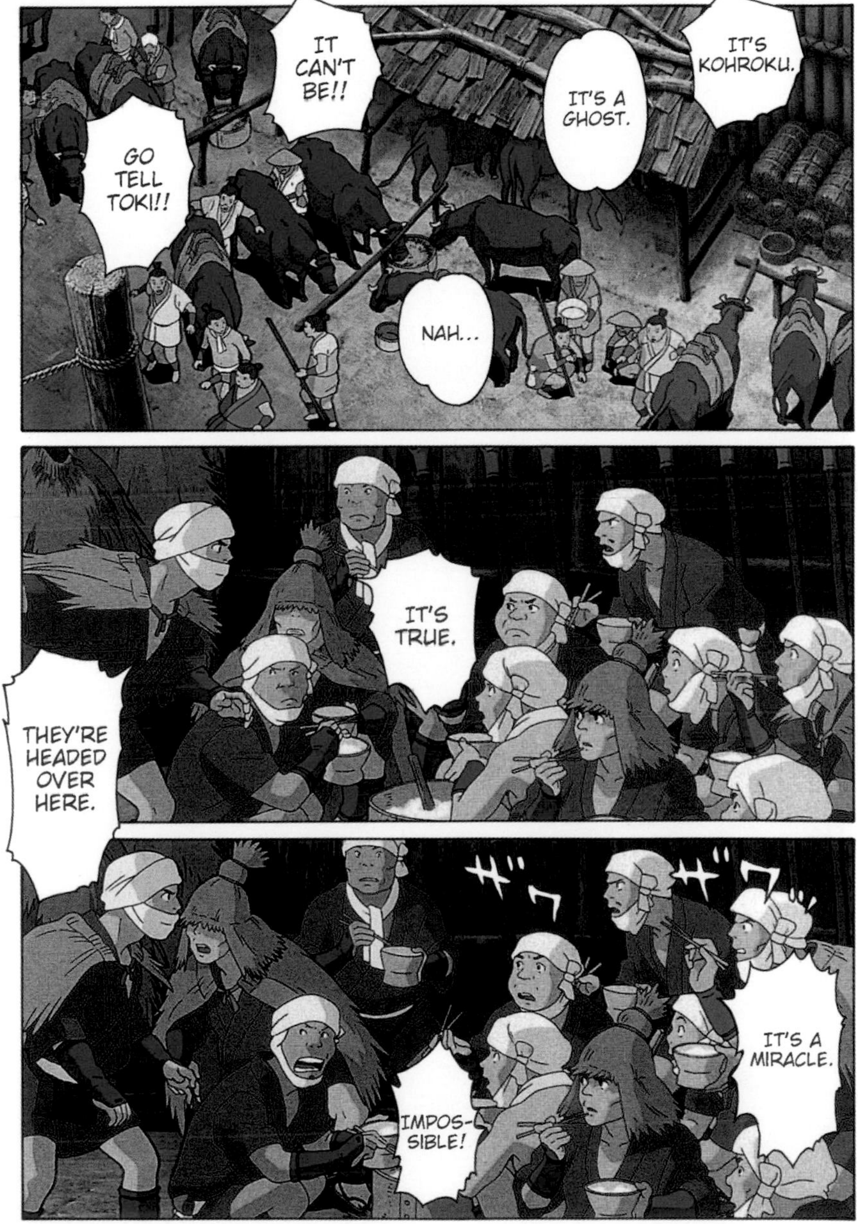
IT'S KOHROKU.
IT'S A GHOST.
IT CAN'T BE!!
GO TELL TOKI!!
NAH...
IT'S TRUE.
THEY'RE HEADED OVER HERE.
ザワッ
ザワ..
IT'S A MIRACLE.
IMPOS-SIBLE!

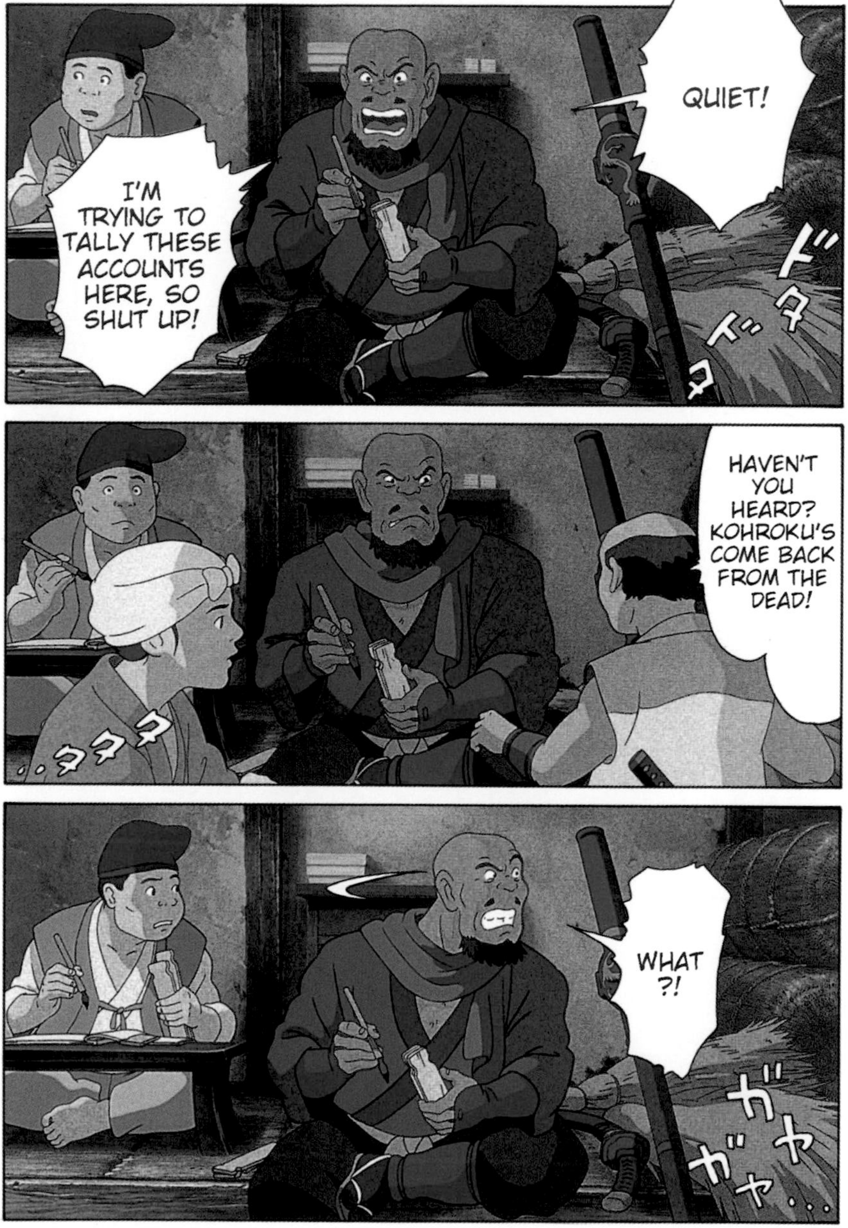
QUIET!
I'M TRYING TO TALLY THESE ACCOUNTS HERE, SO SHUT UP!
ドタドタ
HAVEN'T YOU HEARD? KOHROKU'S COME BACK FROM THE DEAD!
..タタタ
WHAT ?!
ガヤガヤ...

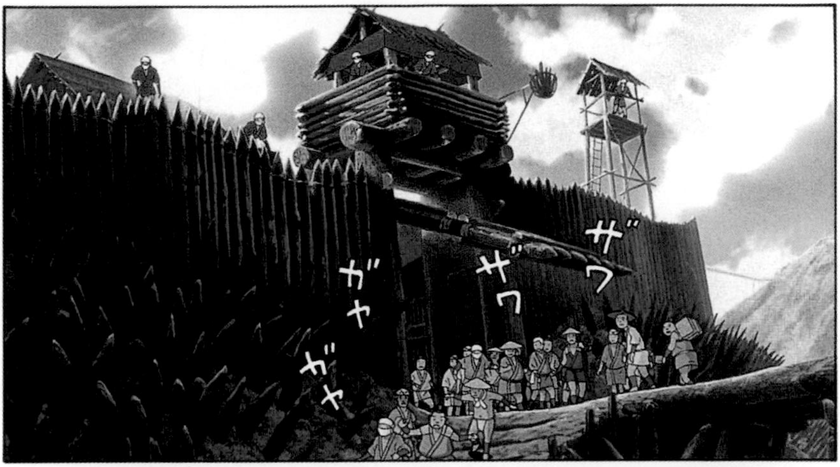
ザワ
ザワ
ガヤ
ガヤ
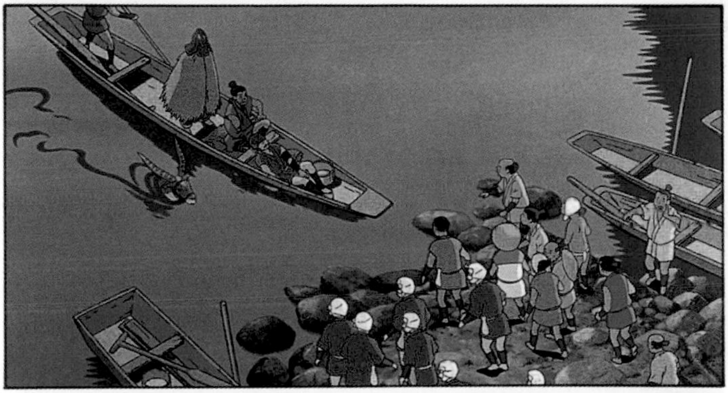
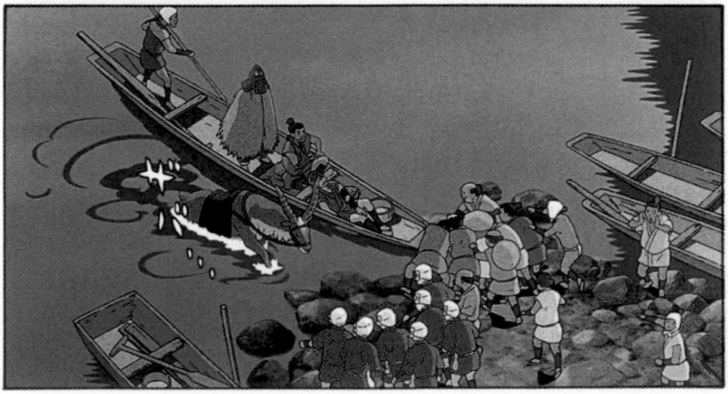
ザ

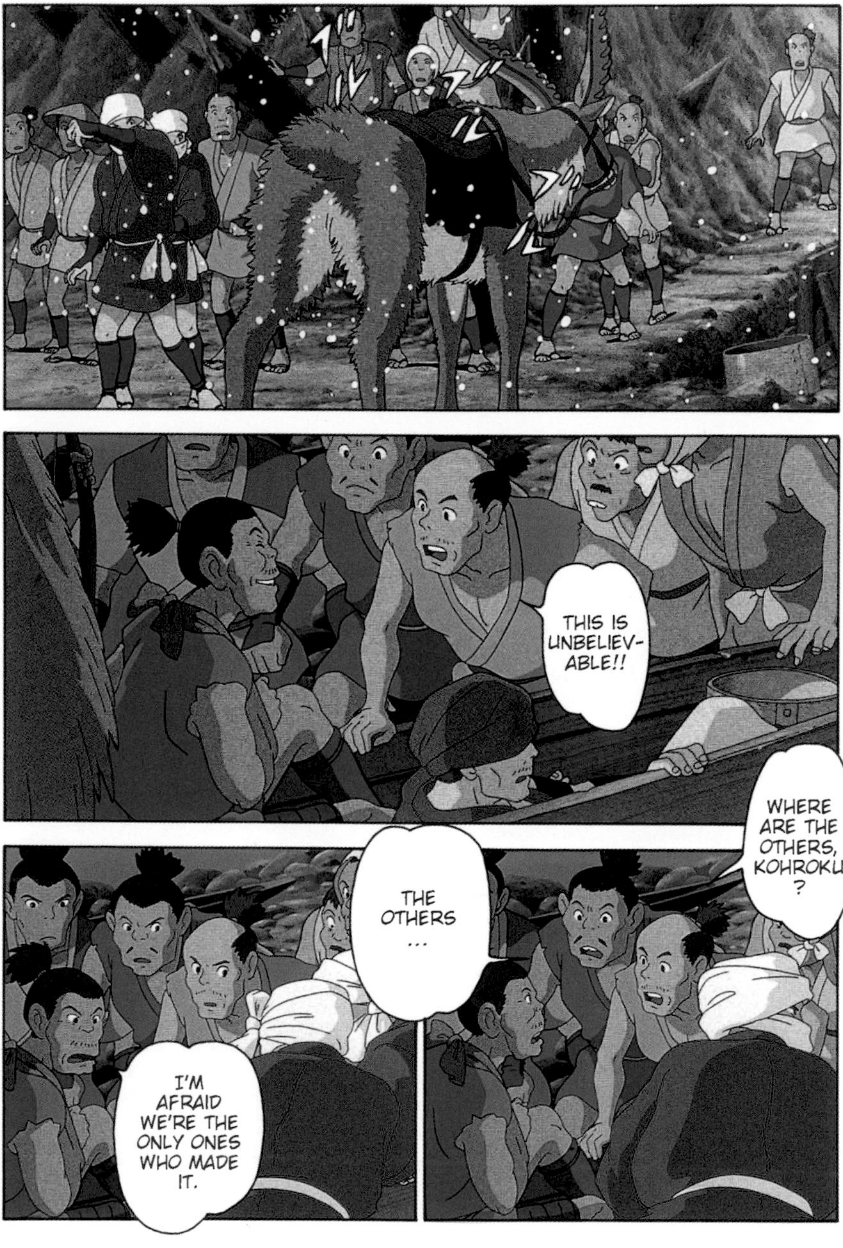
THIS IS UNBELIEVABLE!!
WHERE ARE THE OTHERS, KOHROKU?
THE OTHERS ...
I'M AFRAID WE'RE THE ONLY ONES WHO MADE IT.

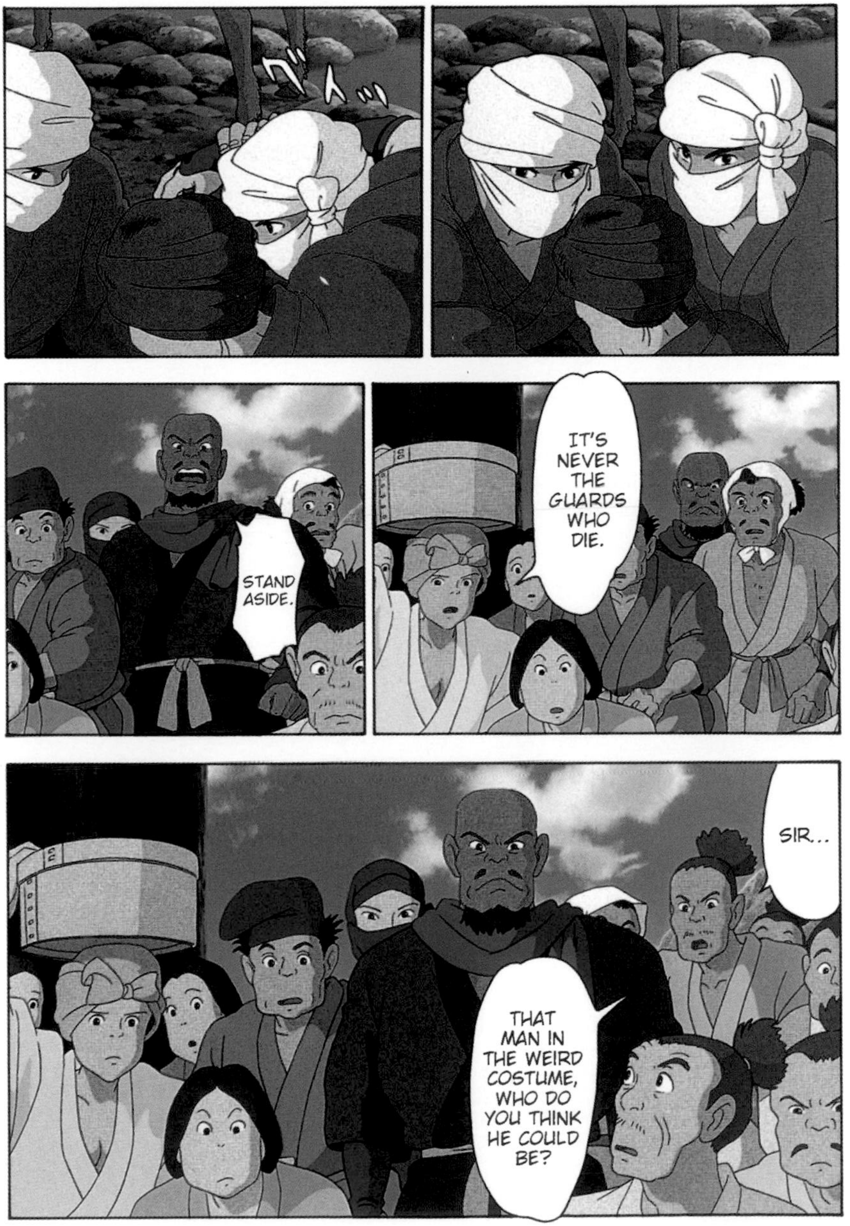
IT'S NEVER THE GUARDS WHO DIE.
STAND ASIDE.
SIR...
THAT MAN IN THE WEIRD COSTUME, WHO DO YOU THINK HE COULD BE?

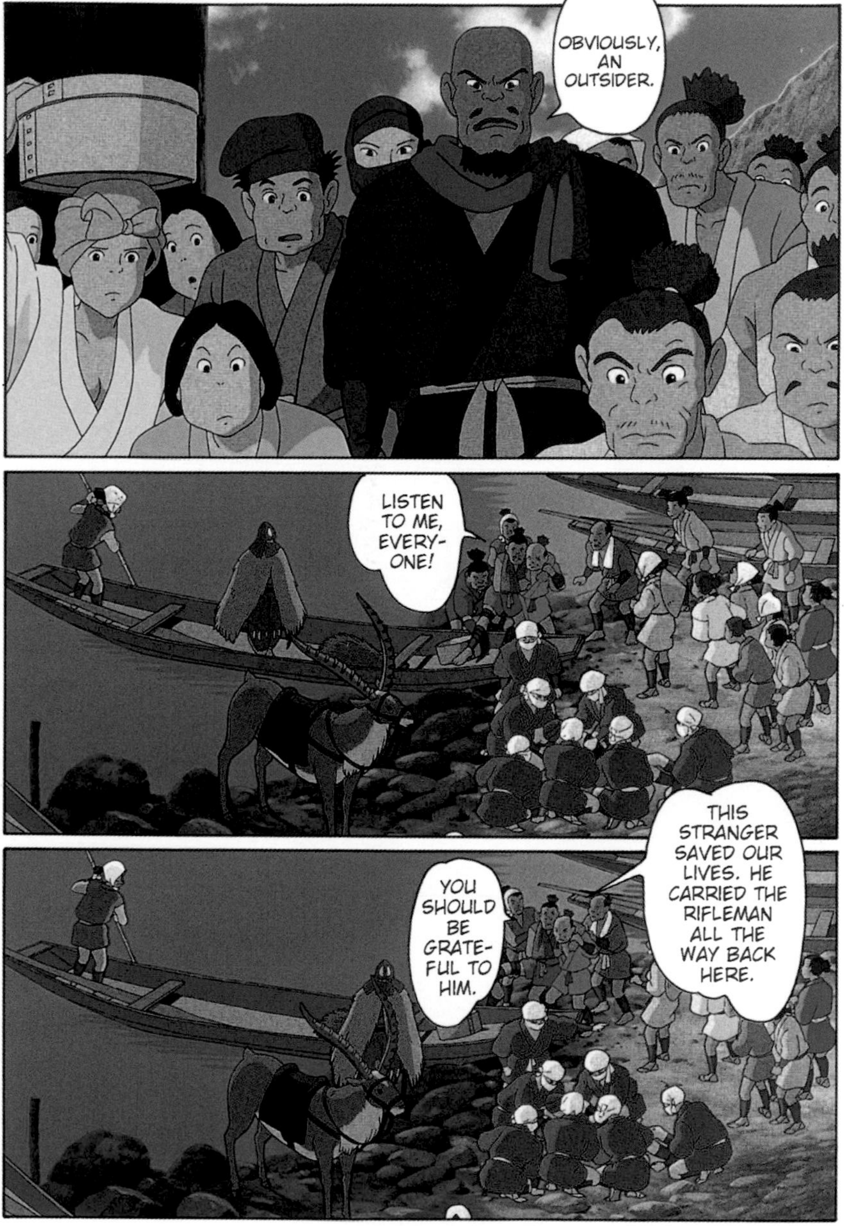
OBVIOUSLY, AN OUTSIDER.
LISTEN TO ME, EVERY-ONE!
THIS STRANGER SAVED OUR LIVES. HE CARRIED THE RIFLEMAN ALL THE WAY BACK HERE.
YOU SHOULD BE GRATE-FUL TO HIM.

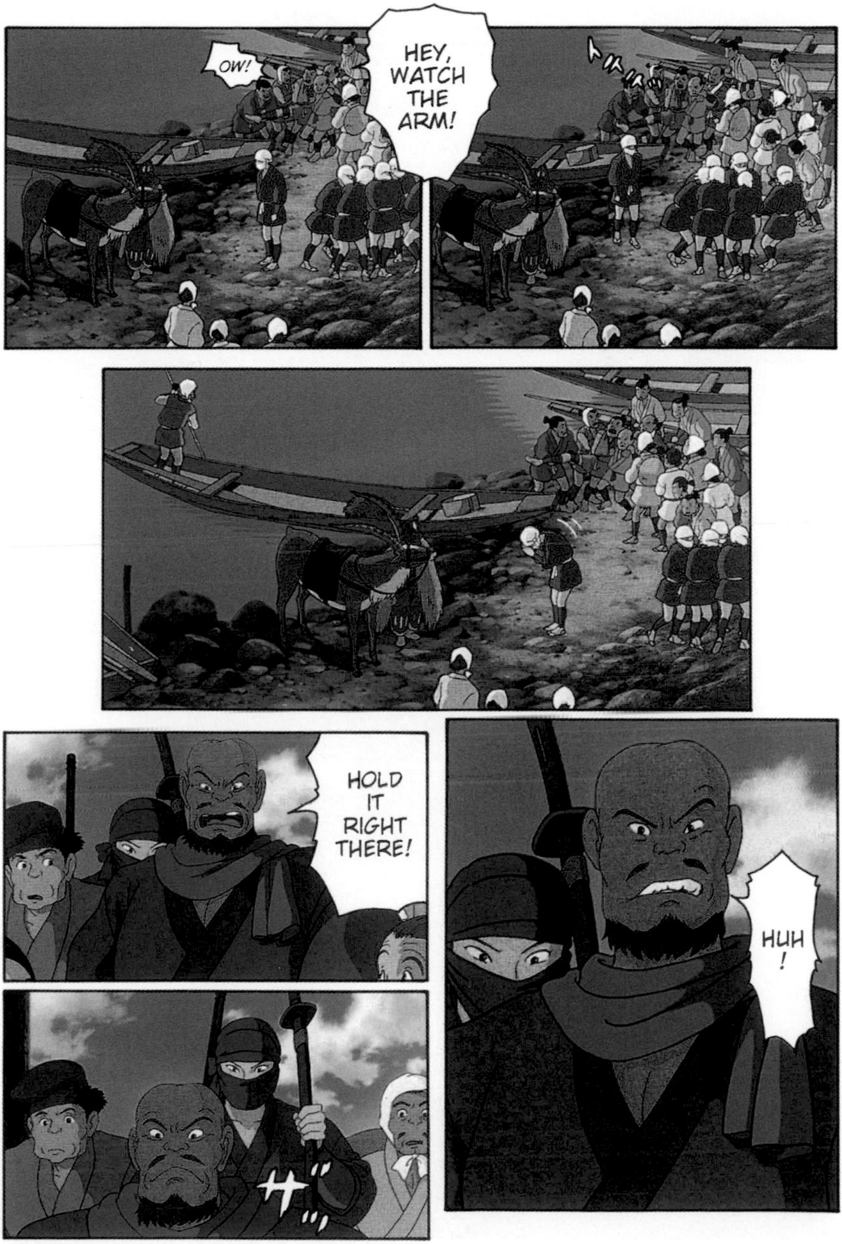
OW!
HEY, WATCH THE ARM!
HOLD IT RIGHT THERE!
ザッ
HUH!

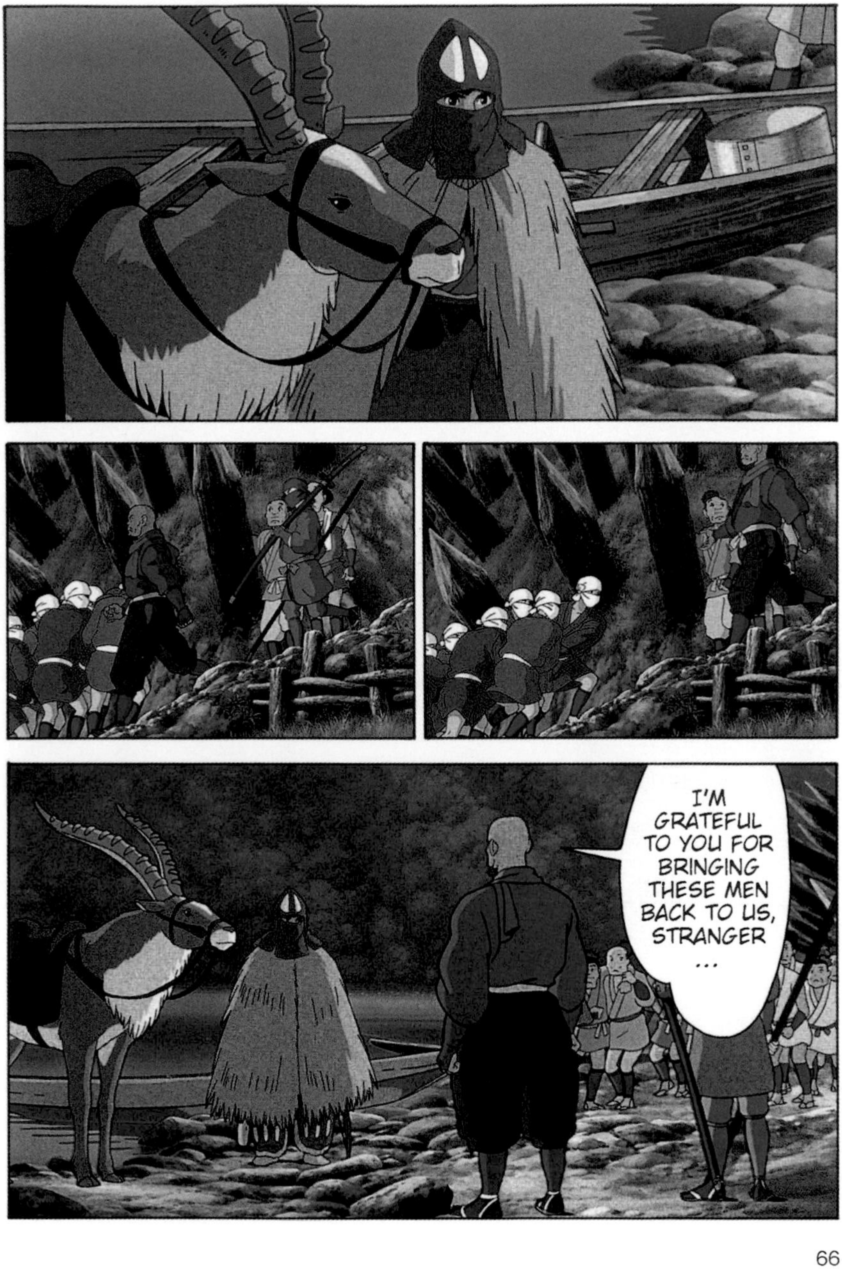
I'M GRATEFUL TO YOU FOR BRINGING THESE MEN BACK TO US, STRANGER ...

YOU GOT BACK HERE ALMOST AS FAST AS WE DID, AND THROUGH THE FORBIDDEN FOREST...
BUT SOME-THING DOESN'T SMELL RIGHT.
ON TOP OF THAT, YOU DID IT WITH TWO BADLY INJURED MEN! AND YOU WANT ME TO BELIEVE THAT...
TOKI, MY LOVE!
KOH-ROKU!
YOU'RE ALIVE!!

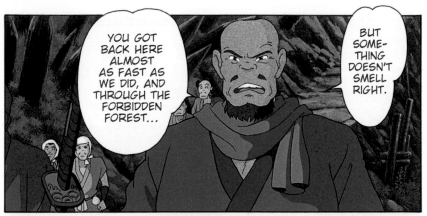

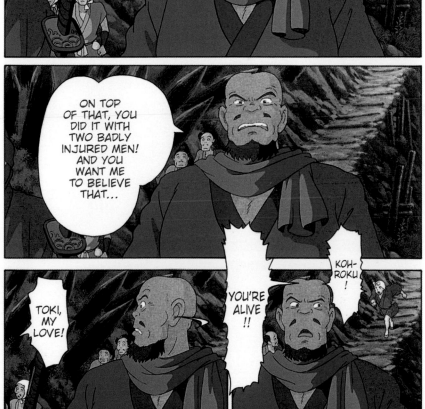

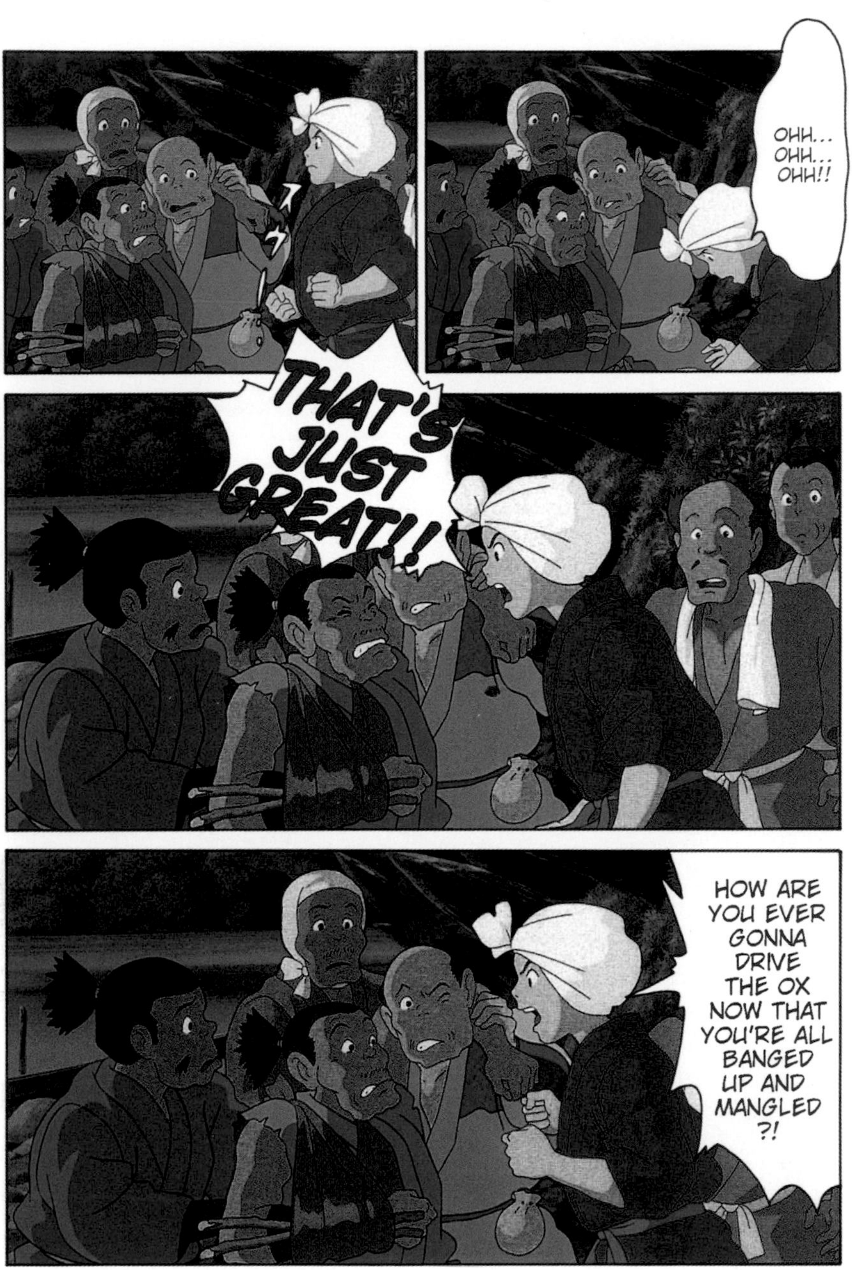
OHH... OHH... OHH!!
THAT'S JUST GREAT!!
HOW ARE YOU EVER GONNA DRIVE THE OX NOW THAT YOU'RE ALL BANGED UP AND MANGLED ?!

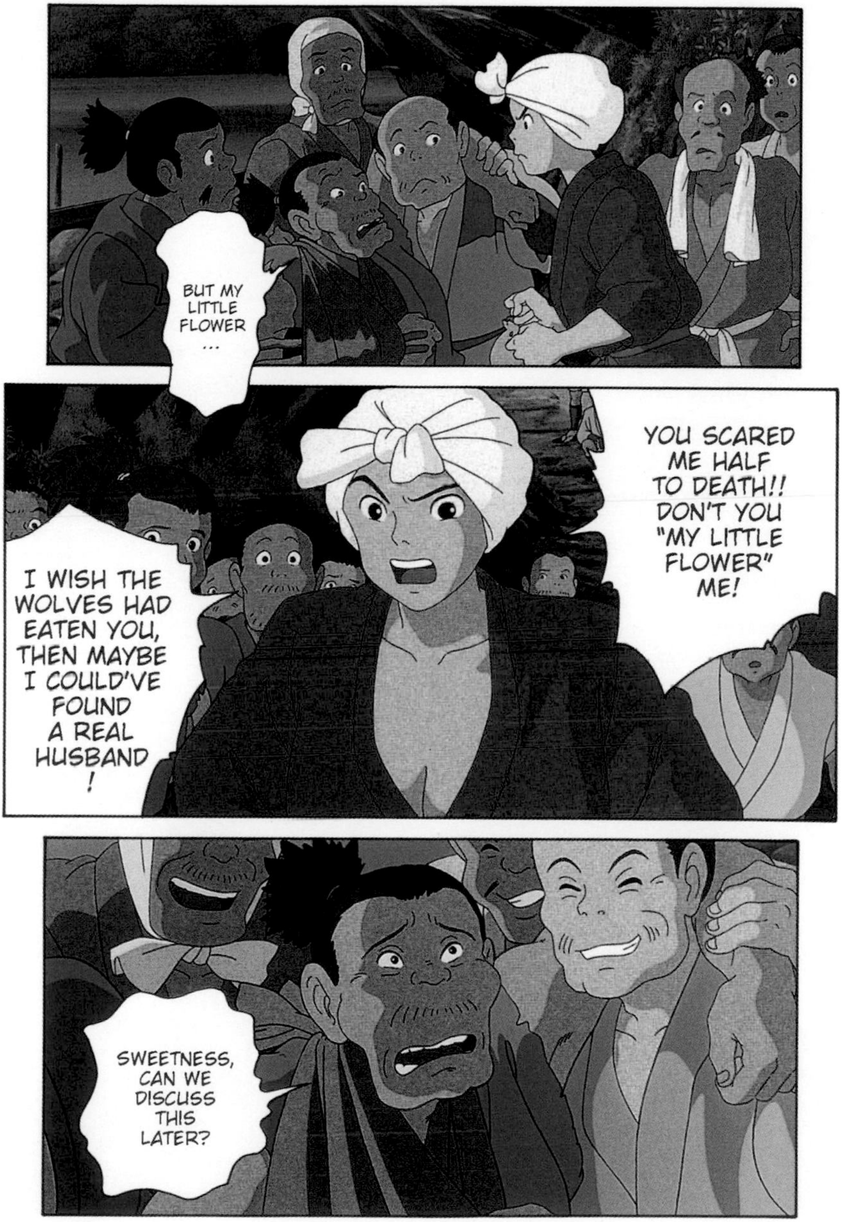
BUT MY LITTLE FLOWER ...
YOU SCARED ME HALF TO DEATH!! DON'T YOU "MY LITTLE FLOWER" ME!
I WISH THE WOLVES HAD EATEN YOU, THEN MAYBE I COULD'VE FOUND A REAL HUSBAND!
SWEETNESS, CAN WE DISCUSS THIS LATER?

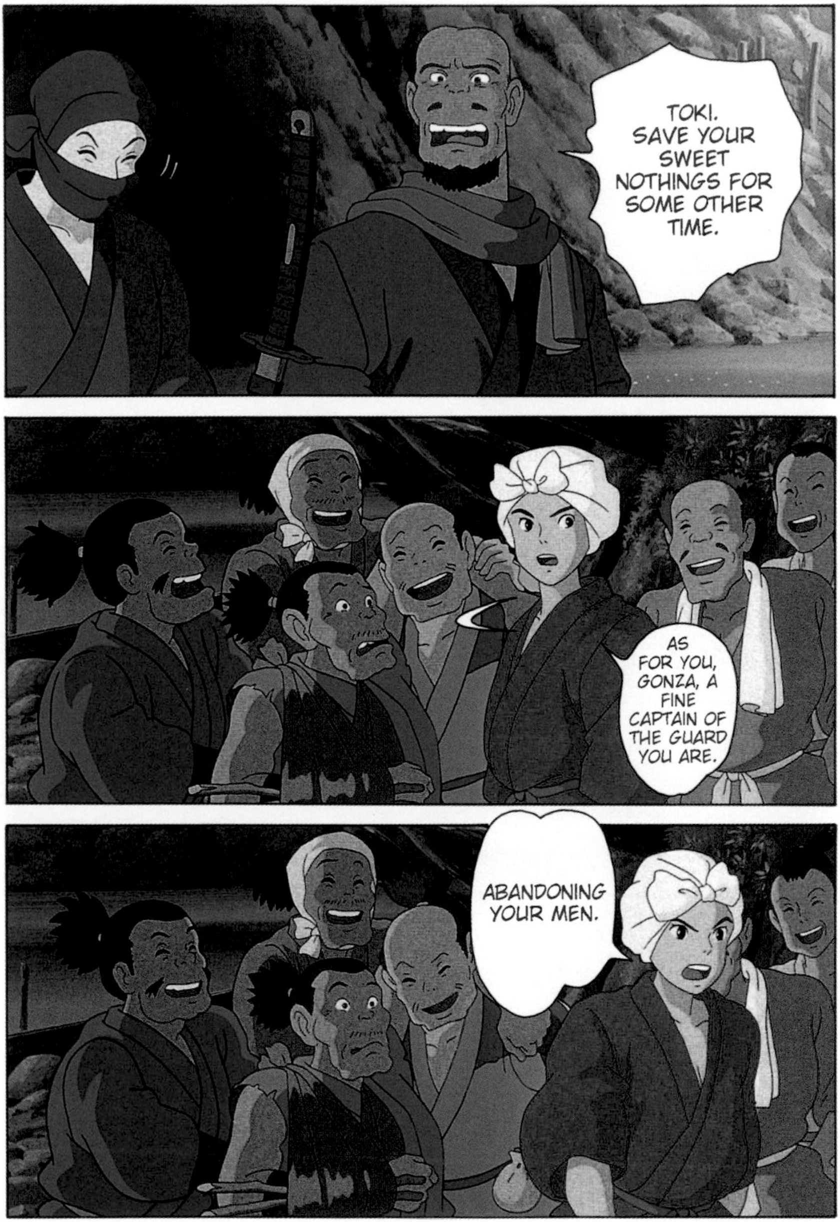
TOKI. SAVE YOUR SWEET NOTHINGS FOR SOME OTHER TIME.
AS FOR YOU, GONZA, A FINE CAPTAIN OF THE GUARD YOU ARE.
ABANDONING YOUR MEN.

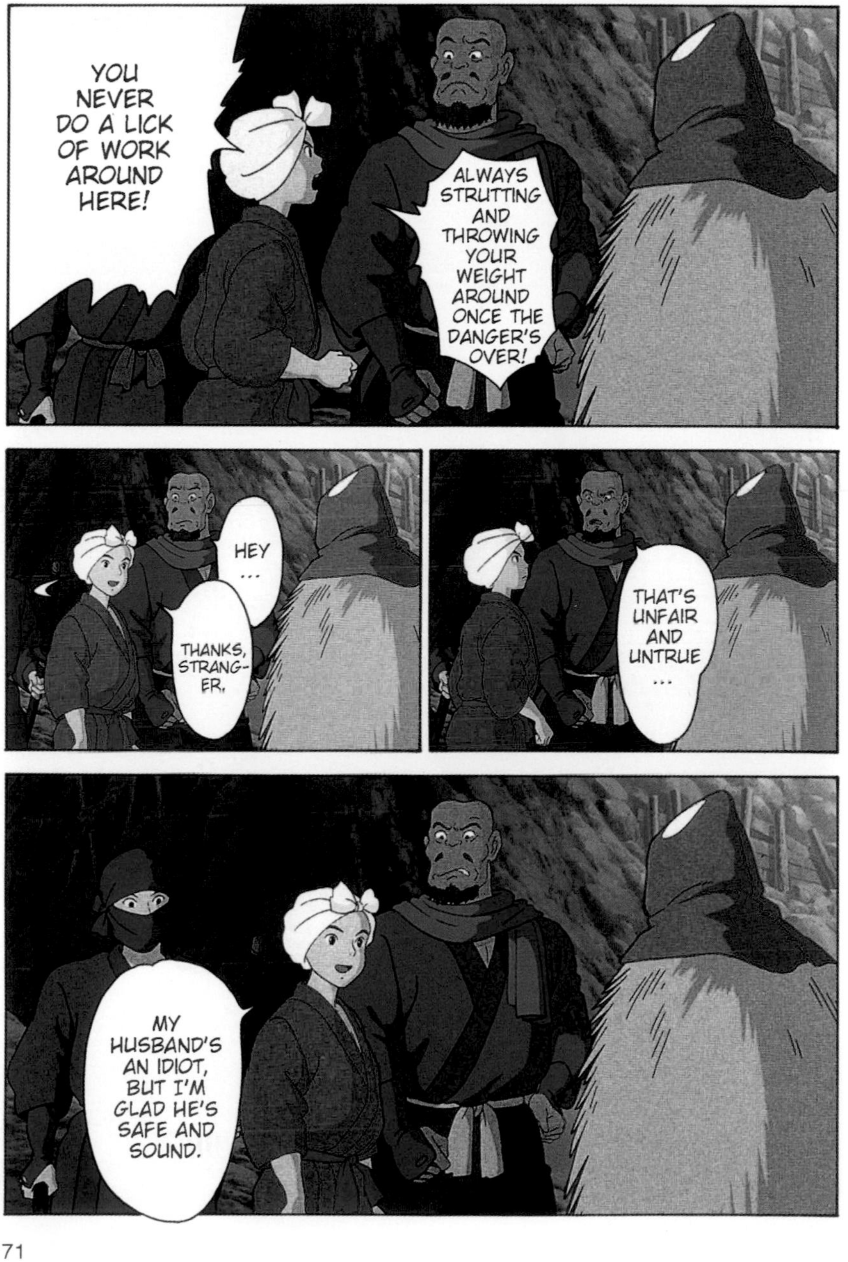
YOU NEVER DO A LICK OF WORK AROUND HERE!
ALWAYS STRUTTING AND THROWING YOUR WEIGHT AROUND ONCE THE DANGER'S OVER!
HEY...
THANKS, STRANGER.
THAT'S UNFAIR AND UNTRUE...
MY HUSBAND'S AN IDIOT, BUT I'M GLAD HE'S SAFE AND SOUND.

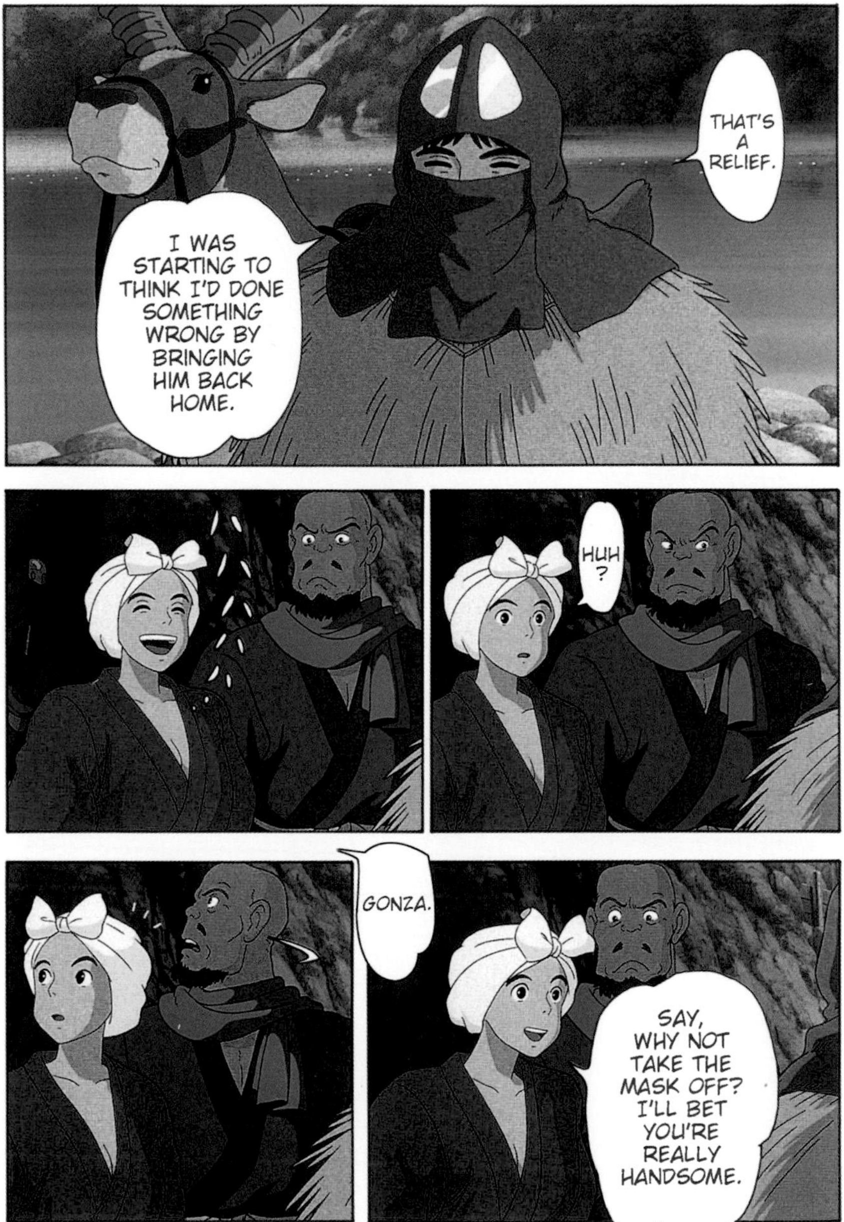
THAT'S A RELIEF.
I WAS STARTING TO THINK I'D DONE SOMETHING WRONG BY BRINGING HIM BACK HOME.
HUH?
GONZA.
SAY, WHY NOT TAKE THE MASK OFF? I'LL BET YOU'RE REALLY HANDSOME.

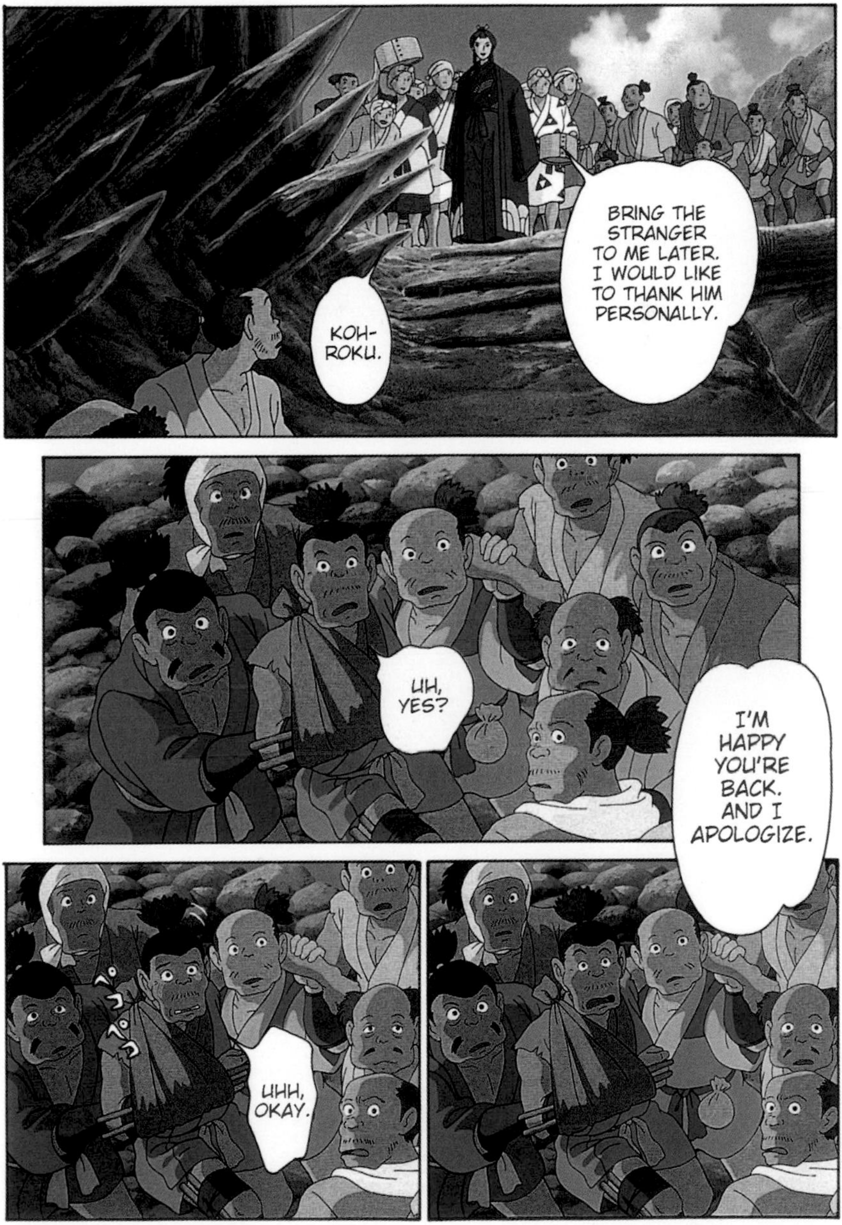
KOH-ROKU.
BRING THE STRANGER TO ME LATER. I WOULD LIKE TO THANK HIM PERSONALLY.
UH, YES?
I'M HAPPY YOU'RE BACK. AND I APOLOGIZE.
UHH, OKAY.

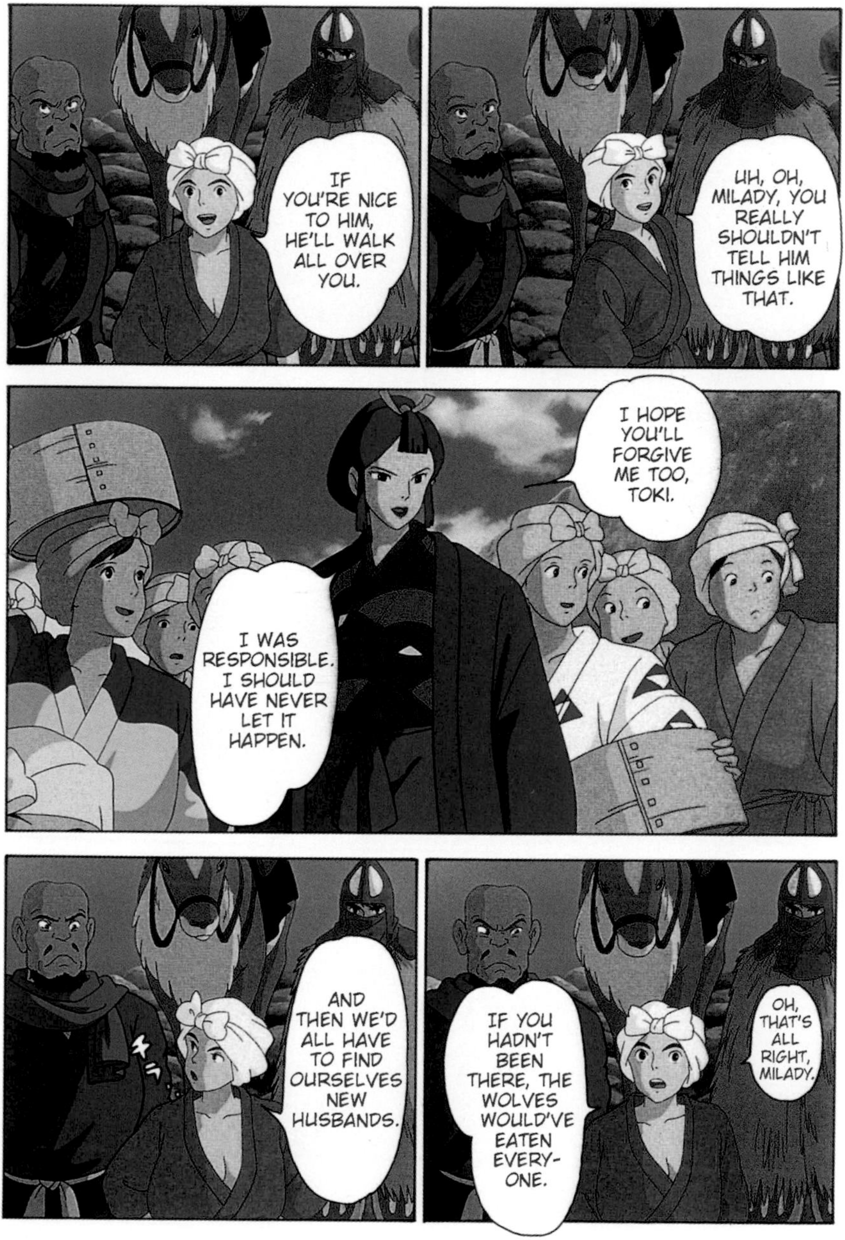
UH, OH, MILADY, YOU REALLY SHOULDN'T TELL HIM THINGS LIKE THAT.
IF YOU'RE NICE TO HIM, HE'LL WALK ALL OVER YOU.
I HOPE YOU'LL FORGIVE ME TOO, TOKI.
I WAS RESPONSIBLE. I SHOULD HAVE NEVER LET IT HAPPEN.
OH, THAT'S ALL RIGHT, MILADY.
IF YOU HADN'T BEEN THERE, THE WOLVES WOULD'VE EATEN EVERY-ONE.
AND THEN WE'D ALL HAVE TO FIND OURSELVES NEW HUSBANDS.

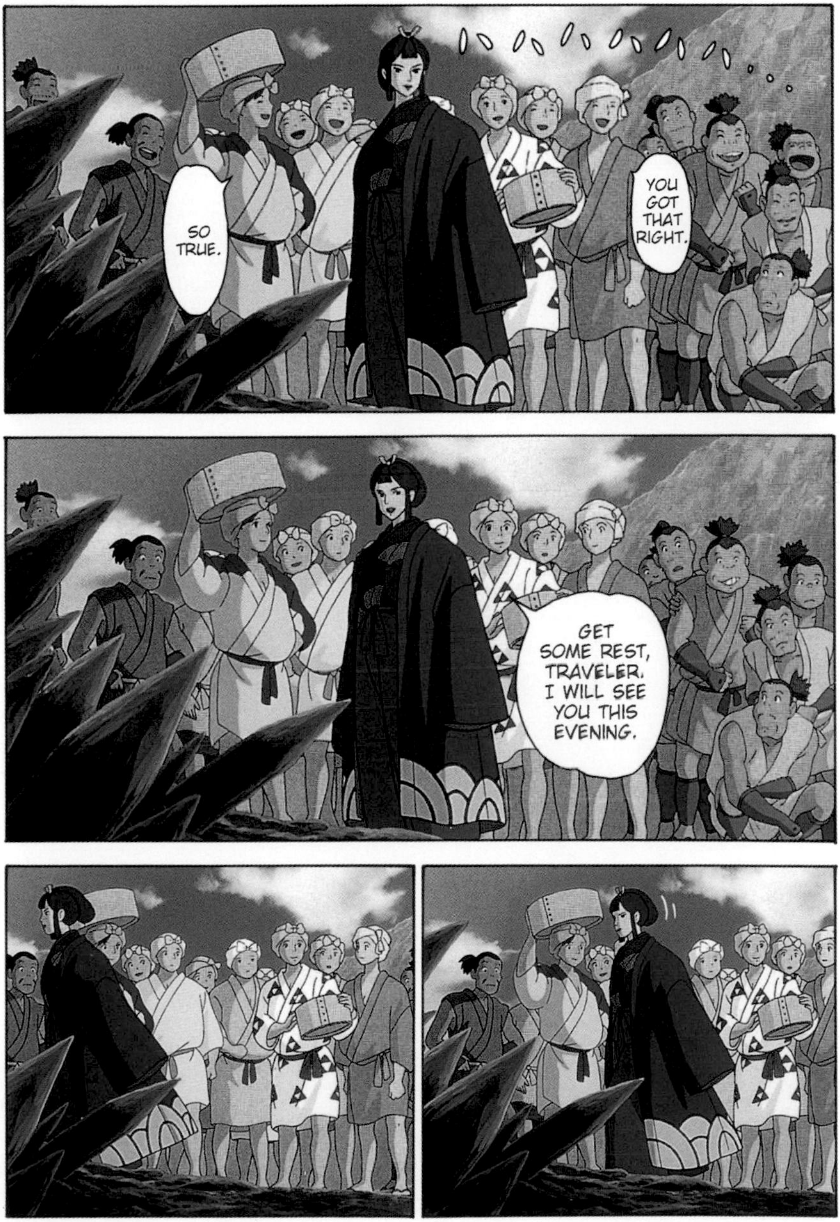
YOU GOT THAT RIGHT.
SO TRUE.
GET SOME REST, TRAVELER. I WILL SEE YOU THIS EVENING.

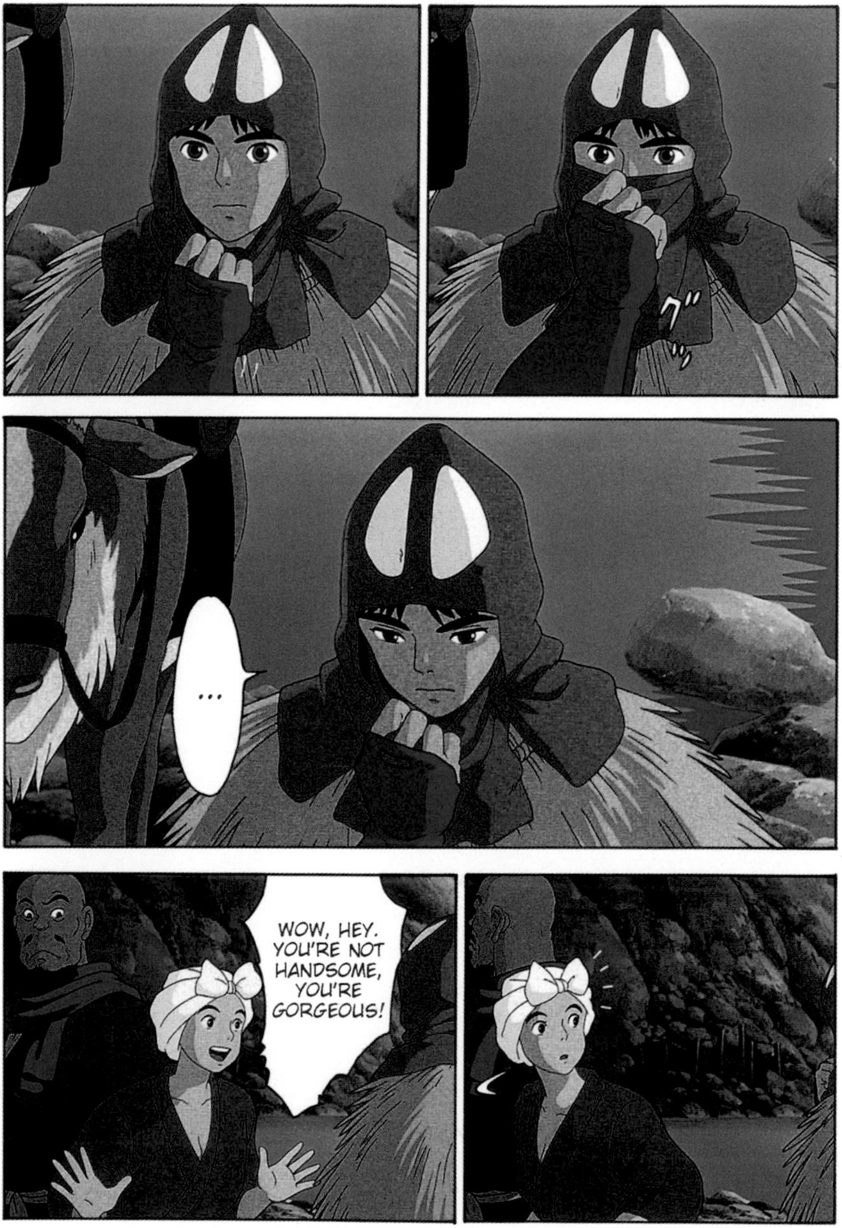
グ
...
WOW, HEY. YOU'RE NOT HANDSOME, YOU'RE GORGEOUS!

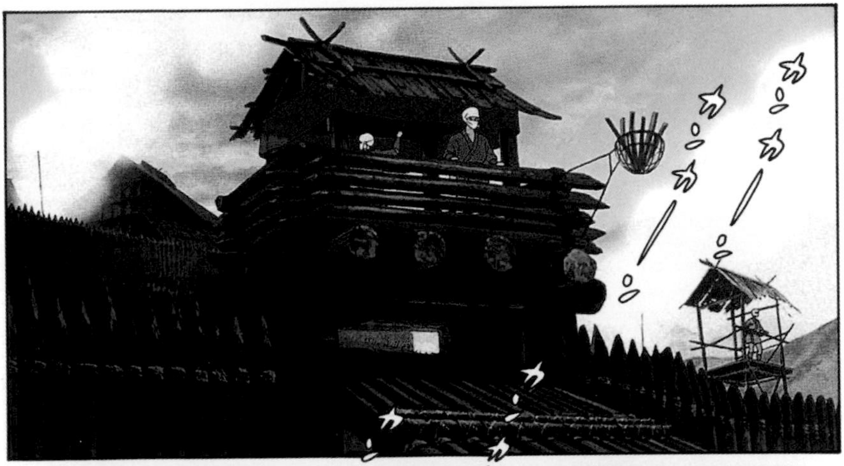
カンカーン
カンカーン
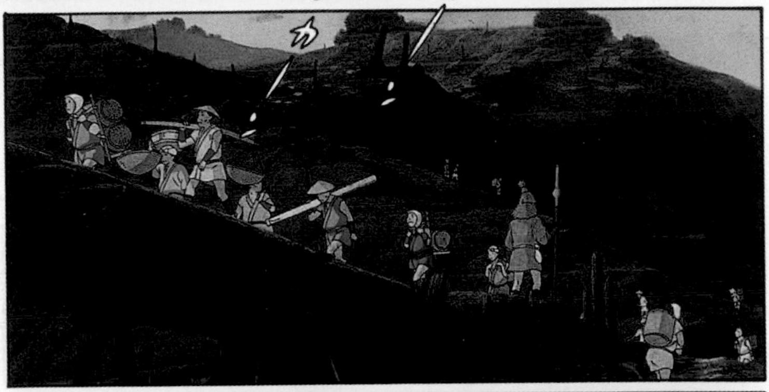
カンカーン
カンカーン
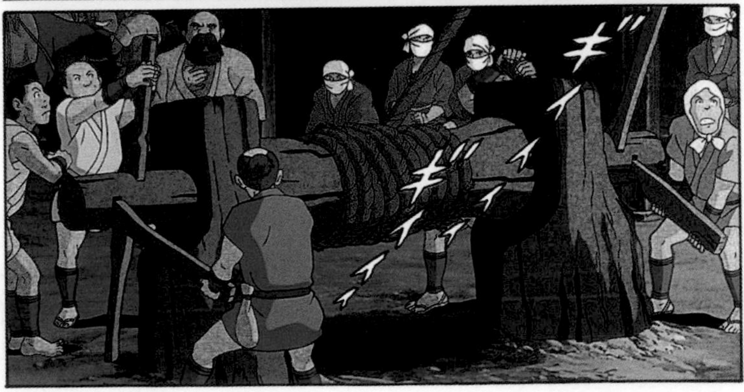
ギイイイ
ギイイイイ

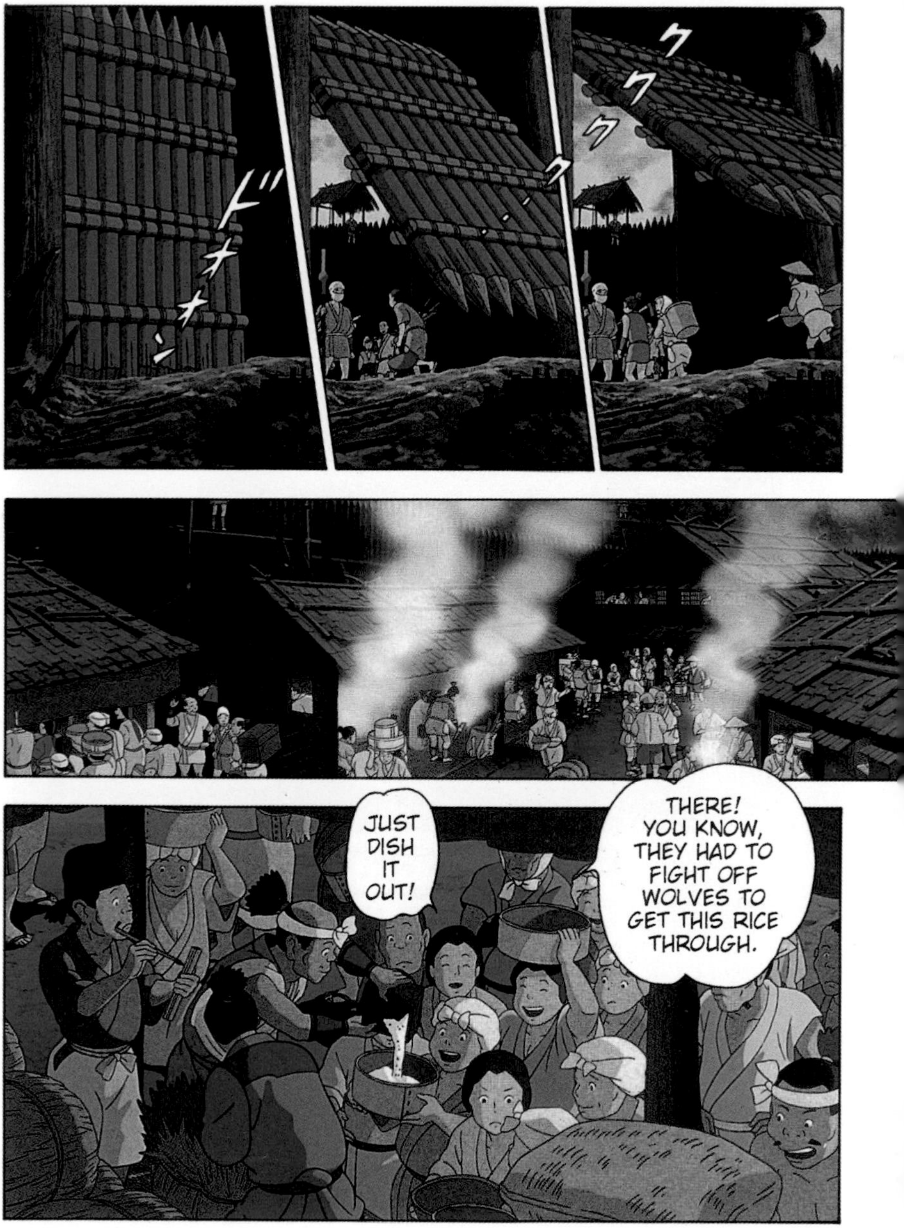
ククククク
ドオオン
THERE! YOU KNOW, THEY HAD TO FIGHT OFF WOLVES TO GET THIS RICE THROUGH.
JUST DISH IT OUT!

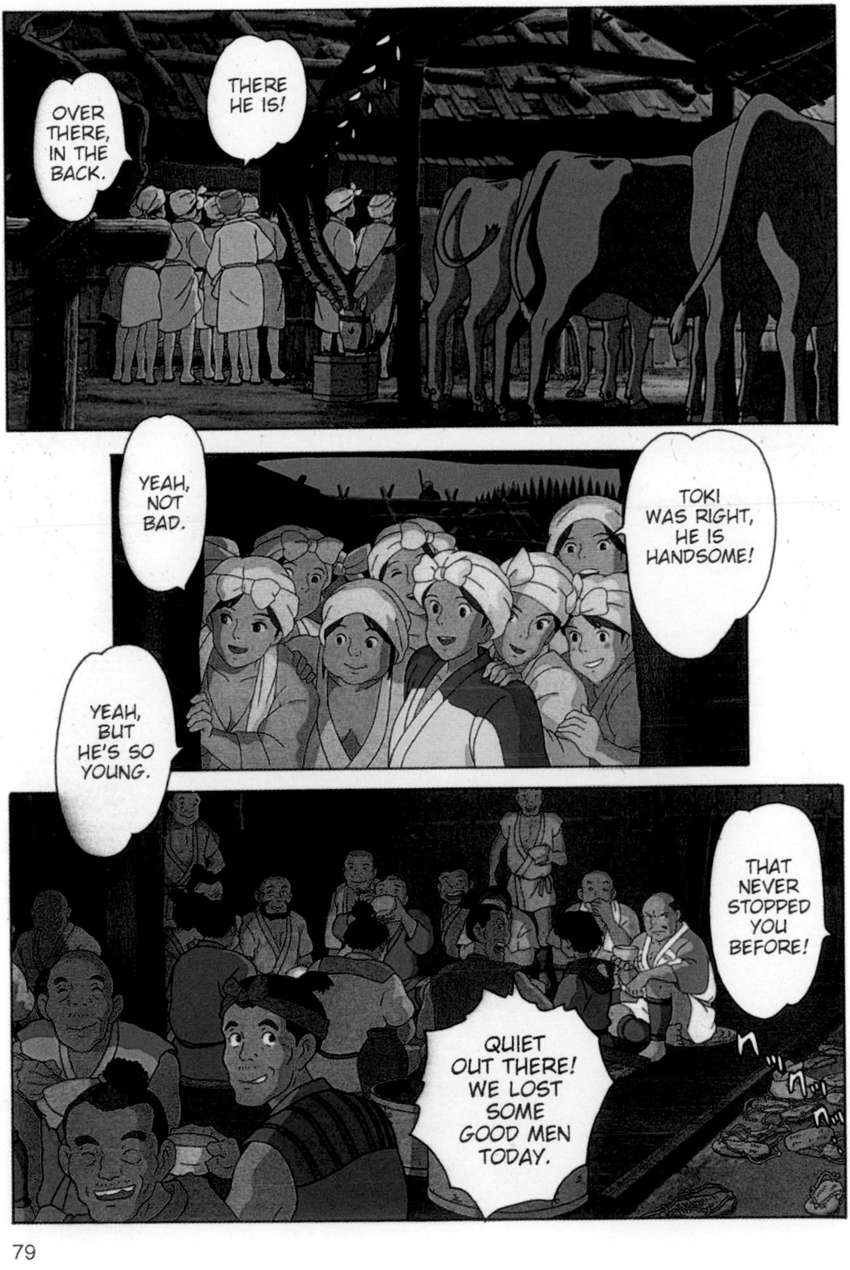
THERE HE IS!
OVER THERE, IN THE BACK.
TOKI WAS RIGHT, HE IS HANDSOME!
YEAH, NOT BAD.
YEAH, BUT HE'S SO YOUNG.
THAT NEVER STOPPED YOU BEFORE!
QUIET OUT THERE! WE LOST SOME GOOD MEN TODAY.

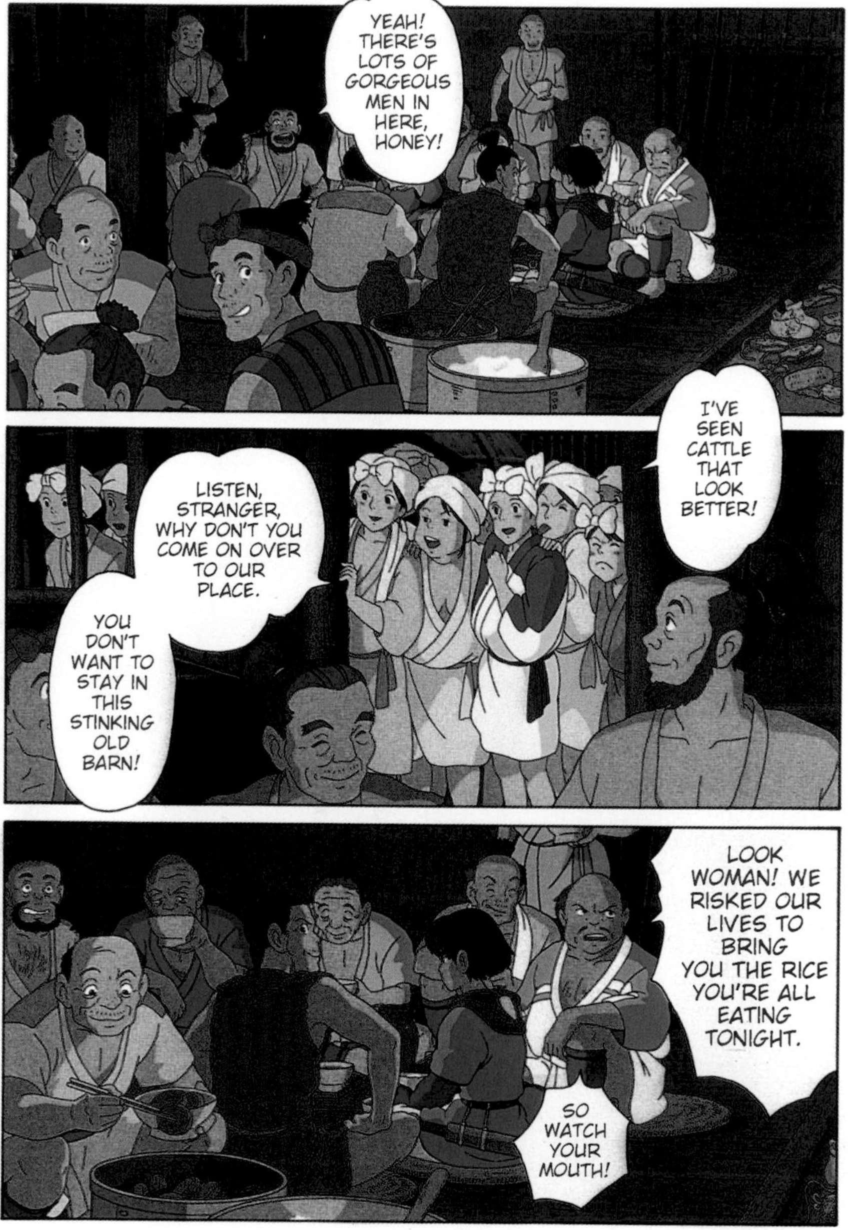
YEAH! THERE'S LOTS OF GORGEOUS MEN IN HERE, HONEY!
I'VE SEEN CATTLE THAT LOOK BETTER!
LISTEN, STRANGER, WHY DON'T YOU COME ON OVER TO OUR PLACE.
YOU DON'T WANT TO STAY IN THIS STINKING OLD BARN!
LOOK WOMAN! WE RISKED OUR LIVES TO BRING YOU THE RICE YOU'RE ALL EATING TONIGHT.
SO WATCH YOUR MOUTH!

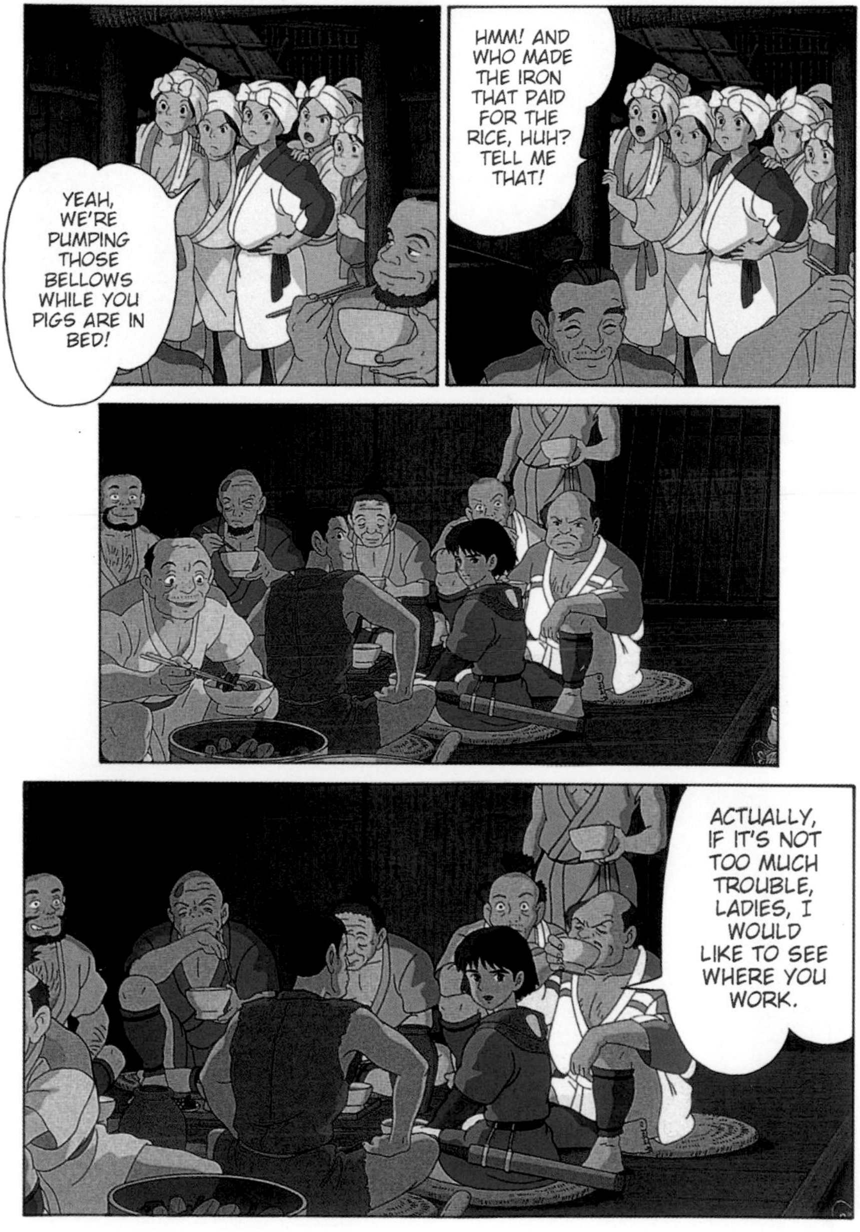
YEAH, WE'RE PUMPING THOSE BELLOWS WHILE YOU PIGS ARE IN BED!
HMM! AND WHO MADE THE IRON THAT PAID FOR THE RICE, HUH? TELL ME THAT!
ACTUALLY, IF IT'S NOT TOO MUCH TROUBLE, LADIES, I WOULD LIKE TO SEE WHERE YOU WORK.

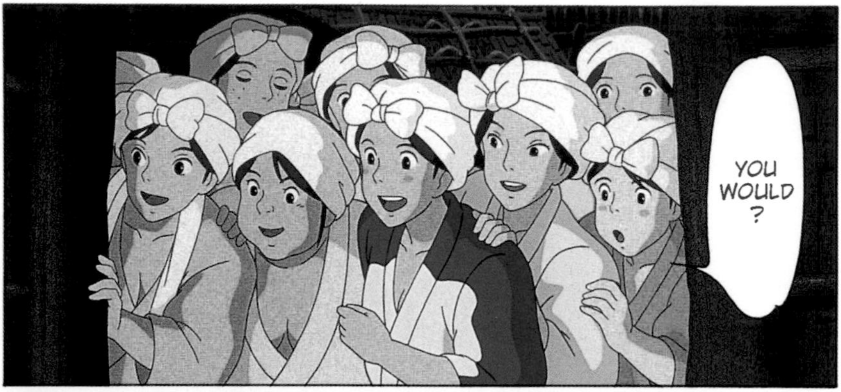
YOU WOULD ?
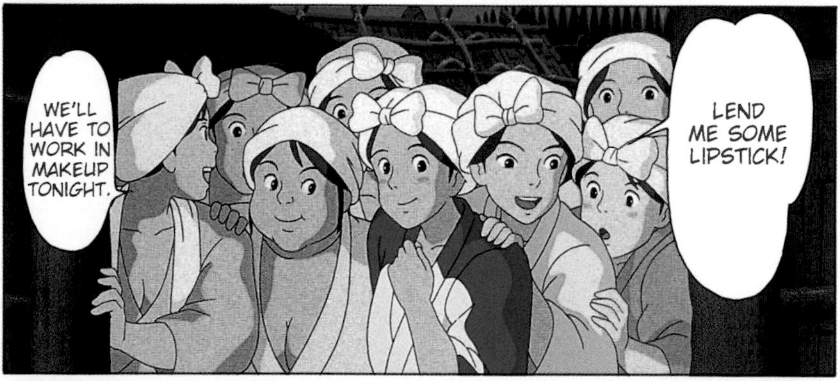
LEND ME SOME LIPSTICK!
WE'LL HAVE TO WORK IN MAKEUP TONIGHT.
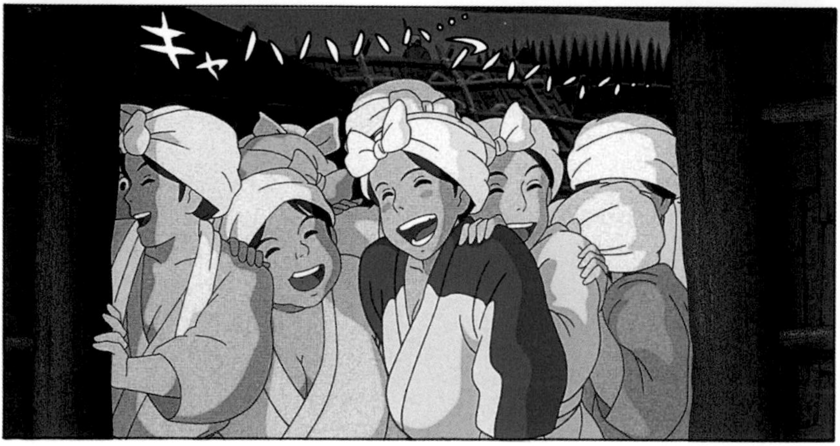

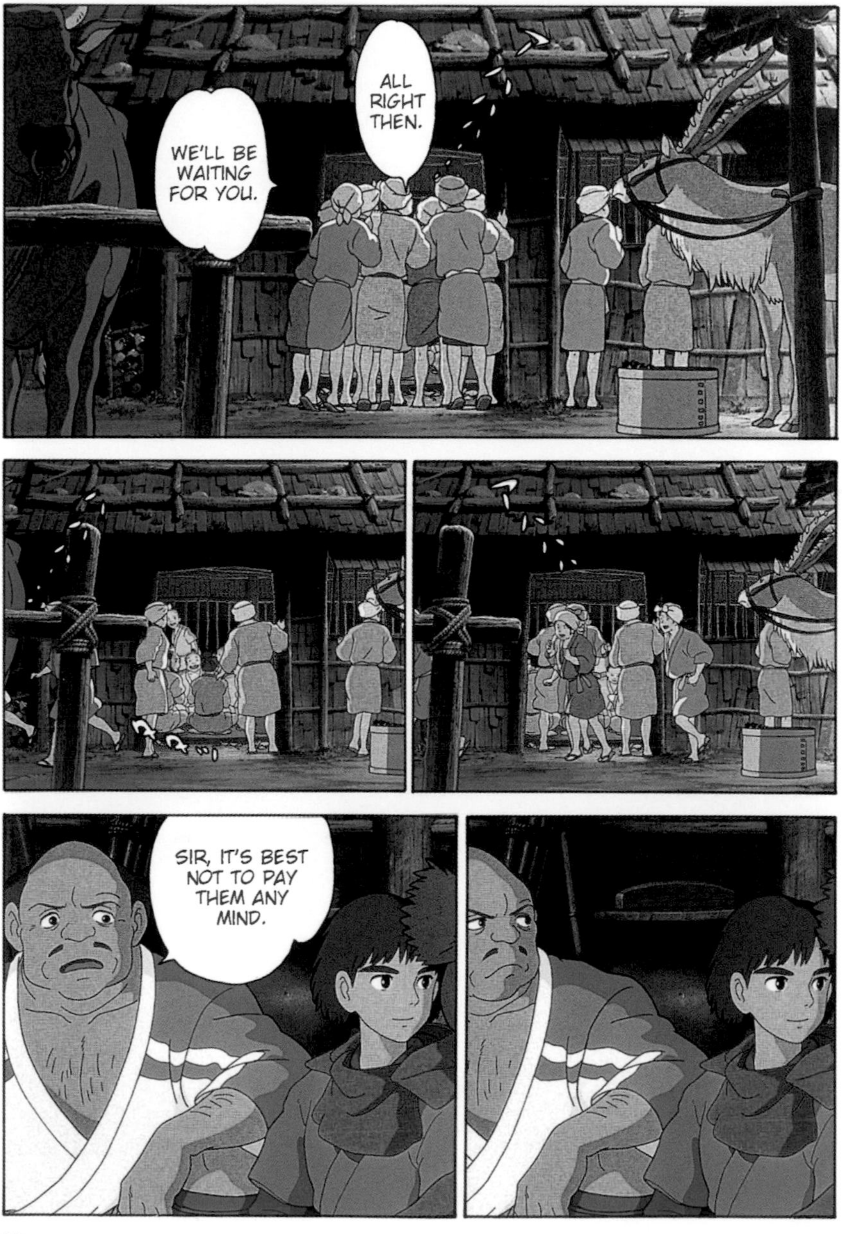
ALL RIGHT THEN.
WE'LL BE WAITING FOR YOU.
SIR, IT'S BEST NOT TO PAY THEM ANY MIND.

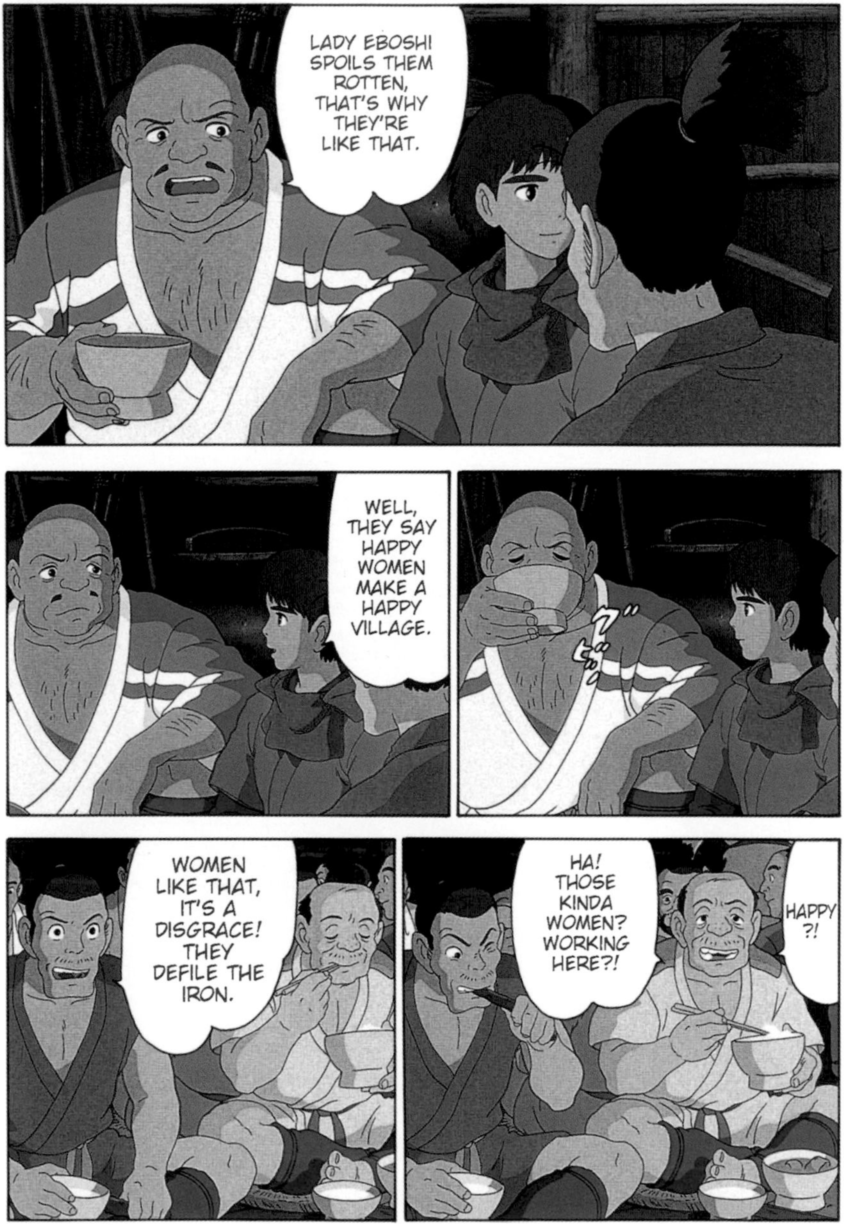
LADY EBOSHI SPOILS THEM ROTTEN, THAT'S WHY THEY'RE LIKE THAT.
WELL, THEY SAY HAPPY WOMEN MAKE A HAPPY VILLAGE.
WOMEN LIKE THAT, IT'S A DISGRACE! THEY DEFILE THE IRON.
HA! THOSE KINDA WOMEN? WORKING HERE?!
HAPPY ?!

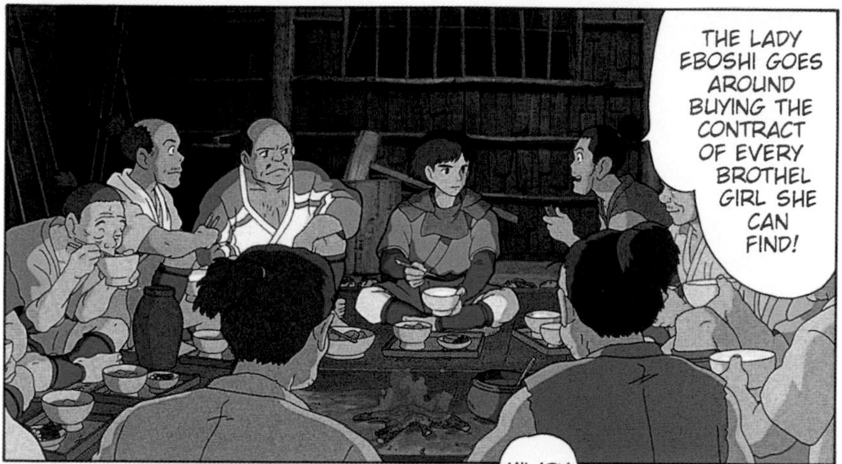
THE LADY EBOSHI GOES AROUND BUYING THE CONTRACT OF EVERY BROTHEL GIRL SHE CAN FIND!
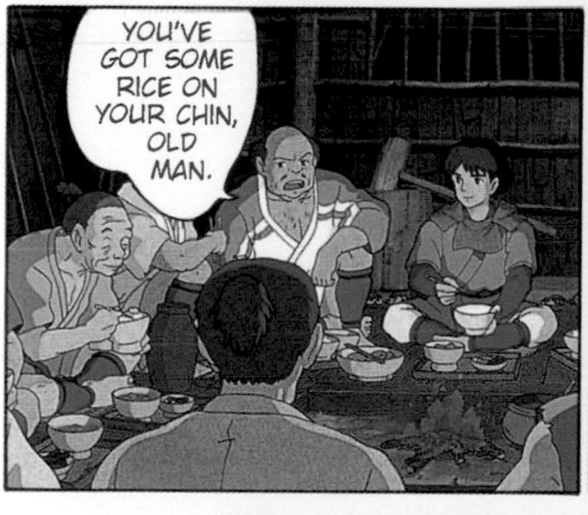
YOU'VE GOT SOME RICE ON YOUR CHIN, OLD MAN.
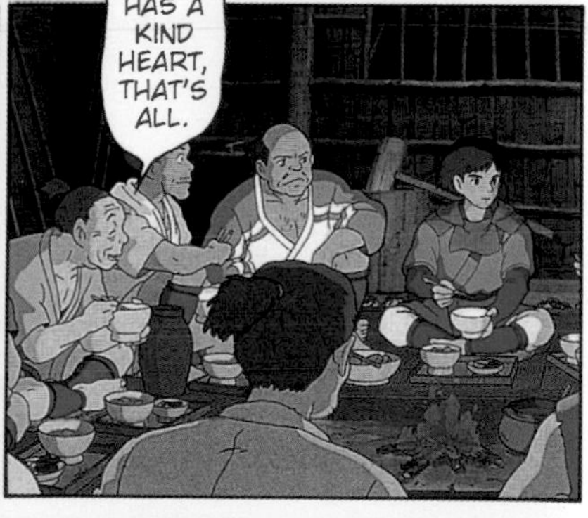
MILADY HAS A KIND HEART, THAT'S ALL.
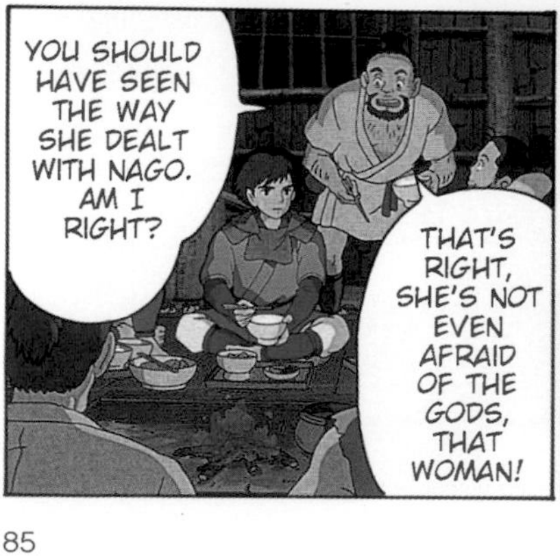
YOU SHOULD HAVE SEEN THE WAY SHE DEALT WITH NAGO. AM I RIGHT?
THAT'S RIGHT, SHE'S NOT EVEN AFRAID OF THE GODS, THAT WOMAN!
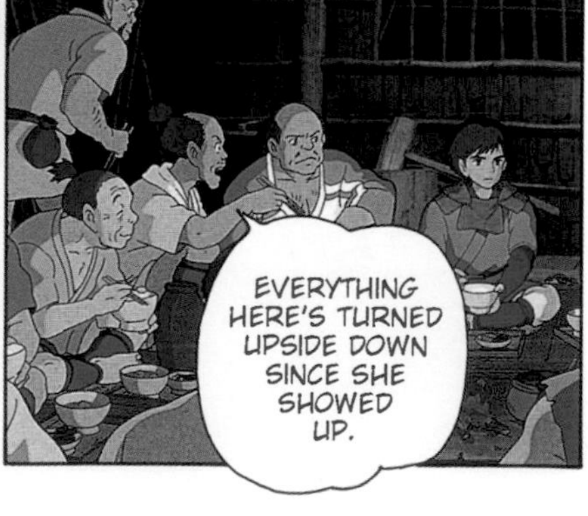
EVERYTHING HERE'S TURNED UPSIDE DOWN SINCE SHE SHOWED UP.

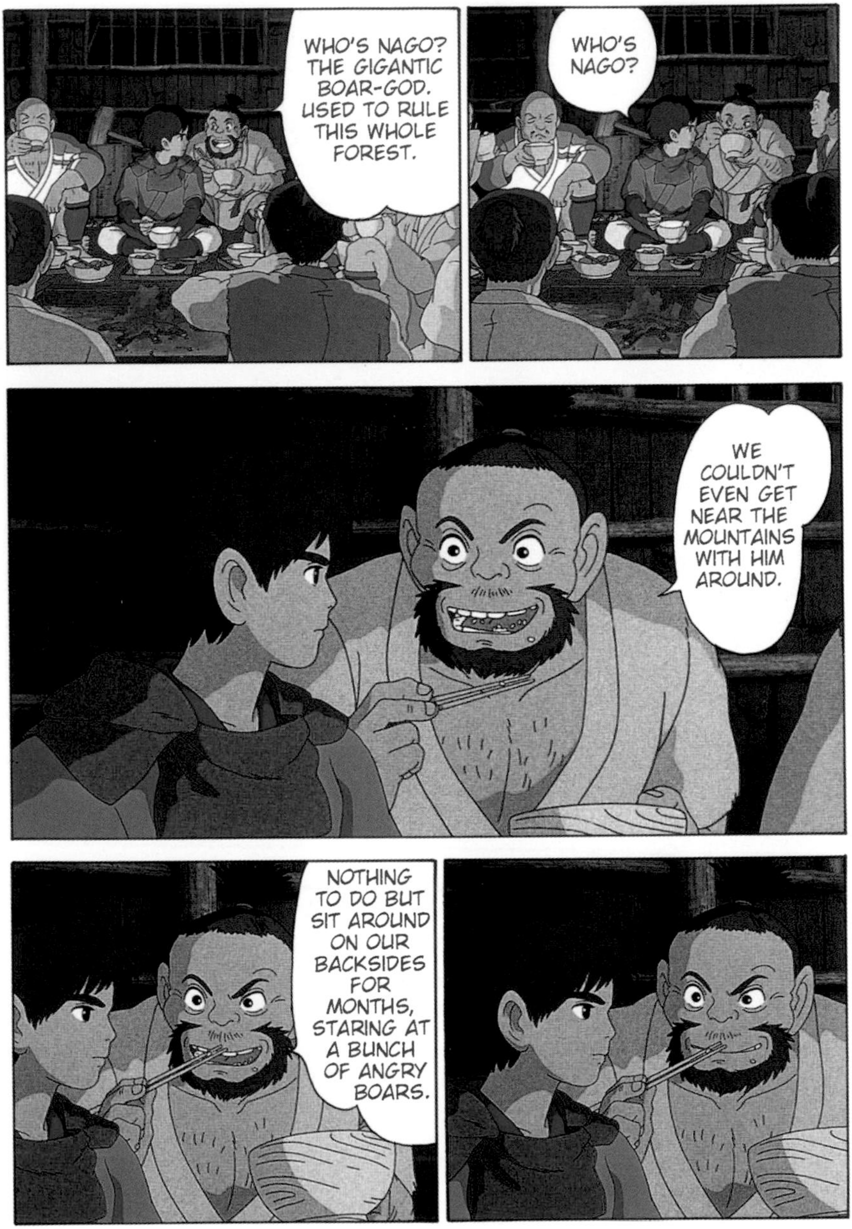
WHO'S NAGO?
WHO'S NAGO? THE GIGANTIC BOAR-GOD. USED TO RULE THIS WHOLE FOREST.
WE COULDN'T EVEN GET NEAR THE MOUNTAINS WITH HIM AROUND.
NOTHING TO DO BUT SIT AROUND ON OUR BACKSIDES FOR MONTHS, STARING AT A BUNCH OF ANGRY BOARS.

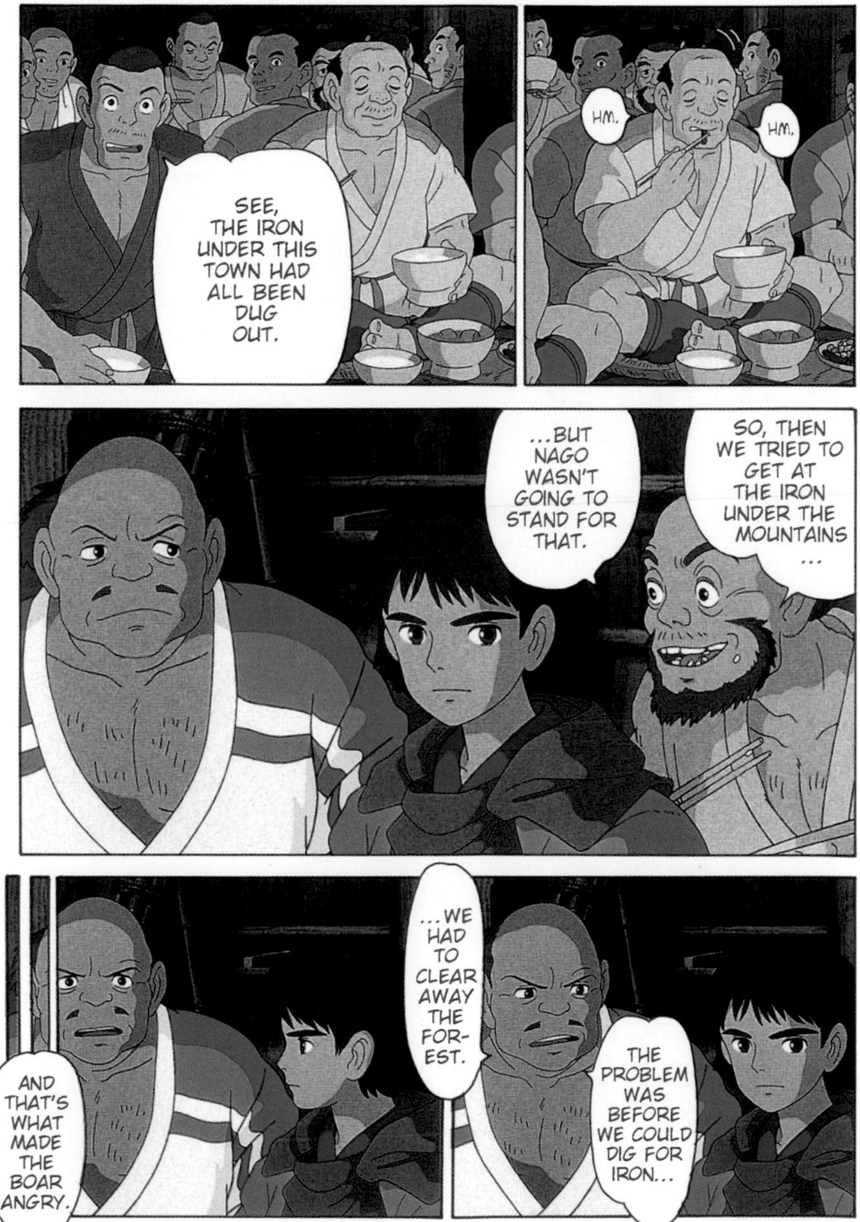
HM.
HM.
SEE, THE IRON UNDER THIS TOWN HAD ALL BEEN DUG OUT.
SO, THEN WE TRIED TO GET AT THE IRON UNDER THE MOUNTAINS...
...BUT NAGO WASN'T GOING TO STAND FOR THAT.
THE PROBLEM WAS BEFORE WE COULD DIG FOR IRON...
...WE HAD TO CLEAR AWAY THE FOR-EST.
AND THAT'S WHAT MADE THE BOAR ANGRY.

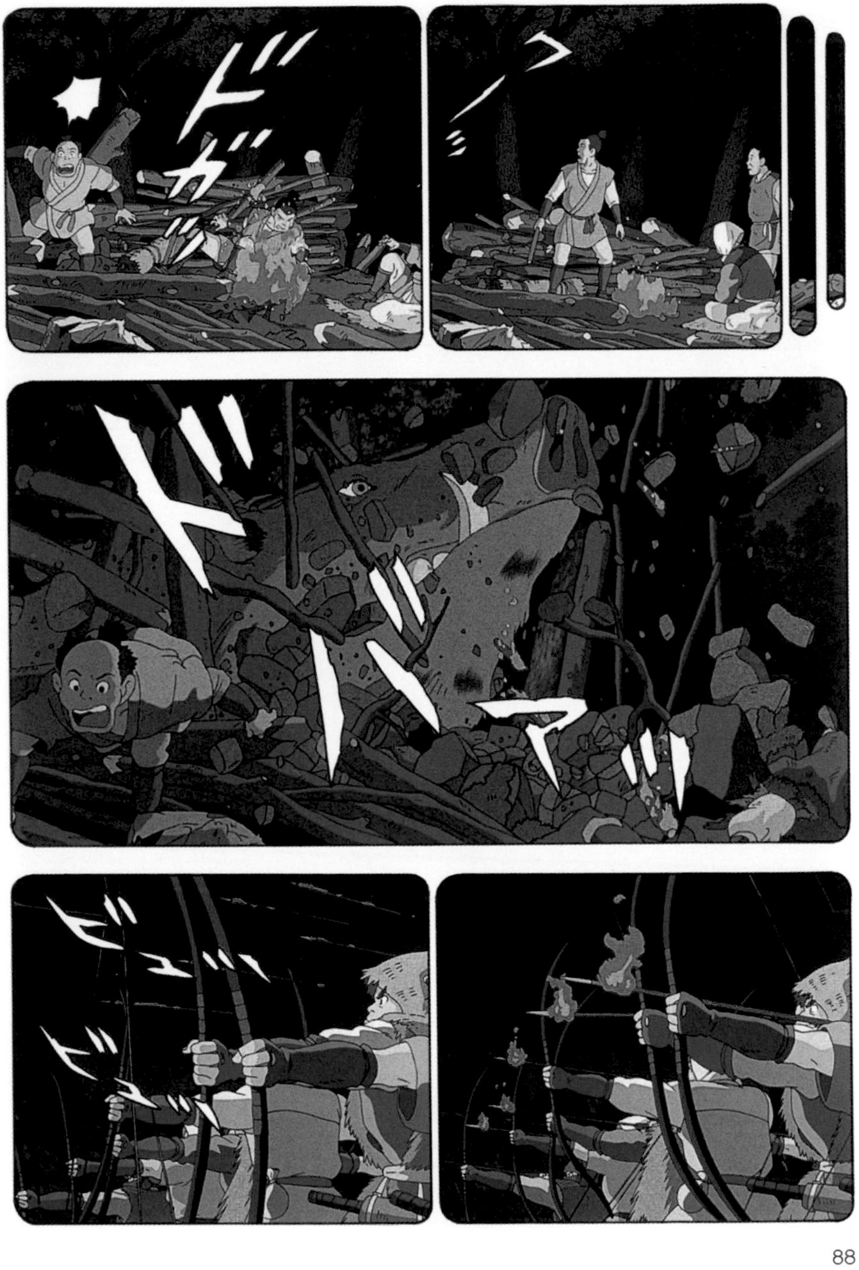
ドガッ
ドバアッ
ビュッ
ビュッ

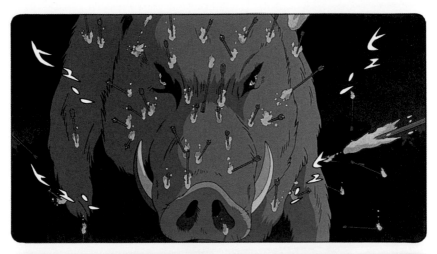

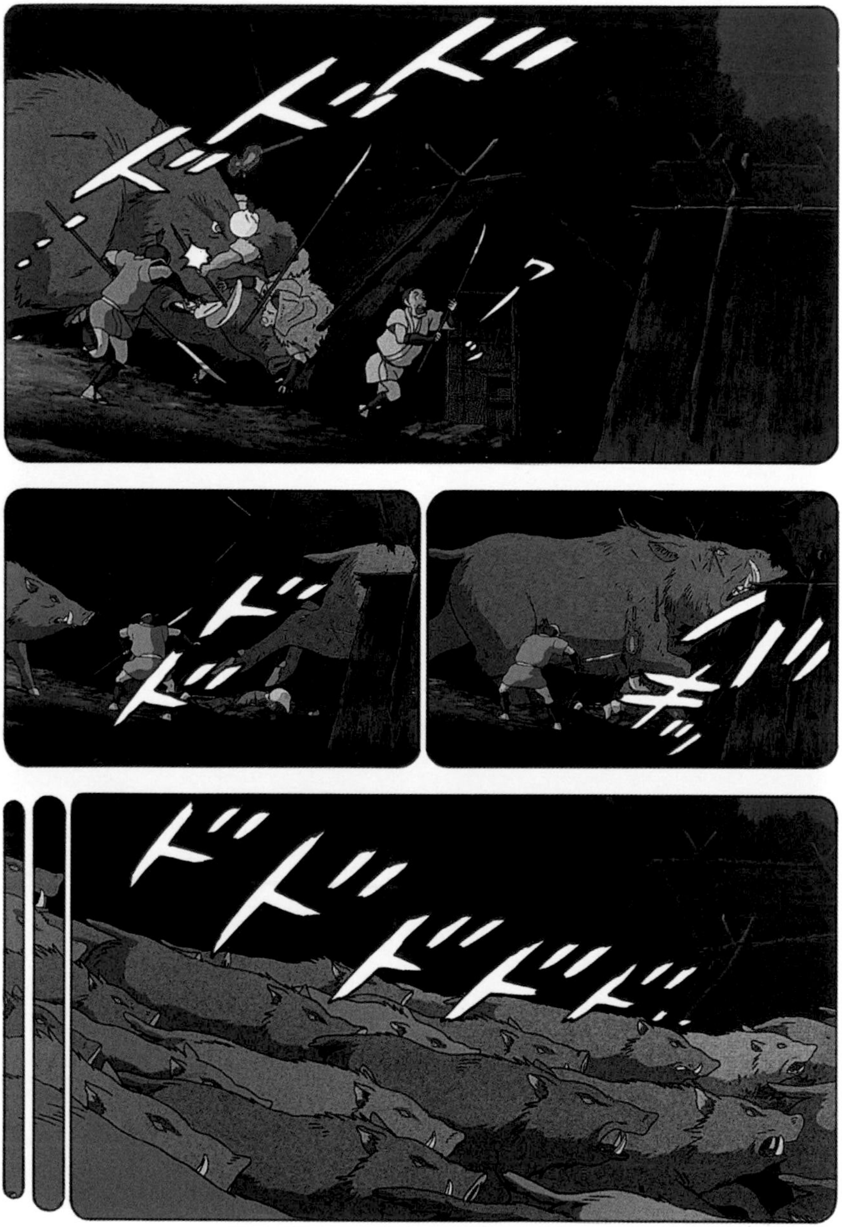

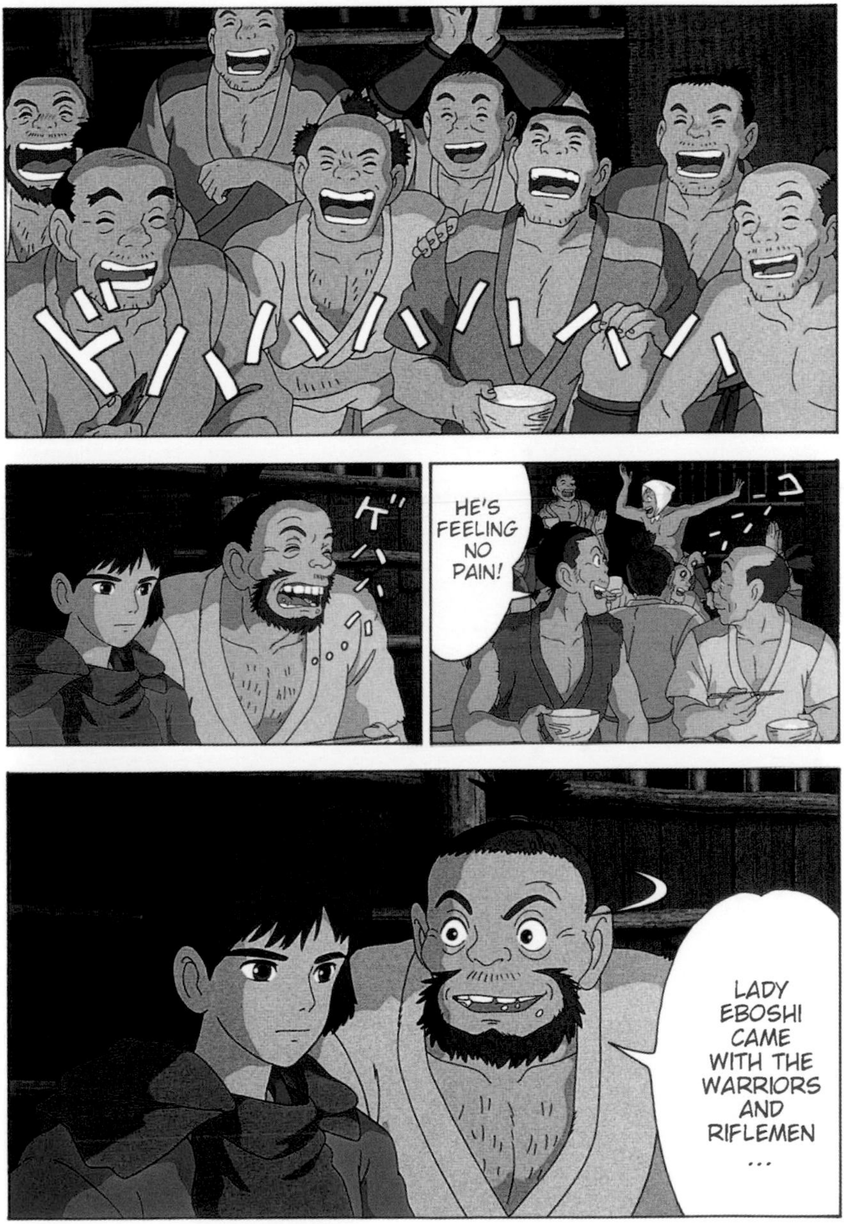
HE'S FEELING NO PAIN!
LADY EBOSHI CAME WITH THE WARRIORS AND RIFLEMEN ...

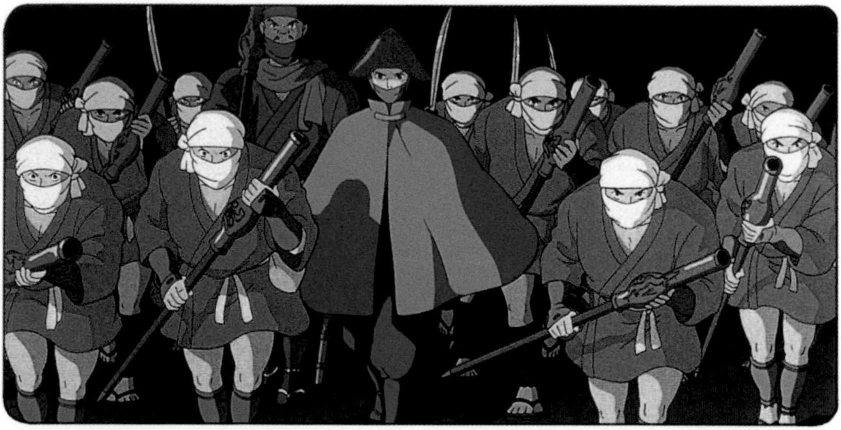

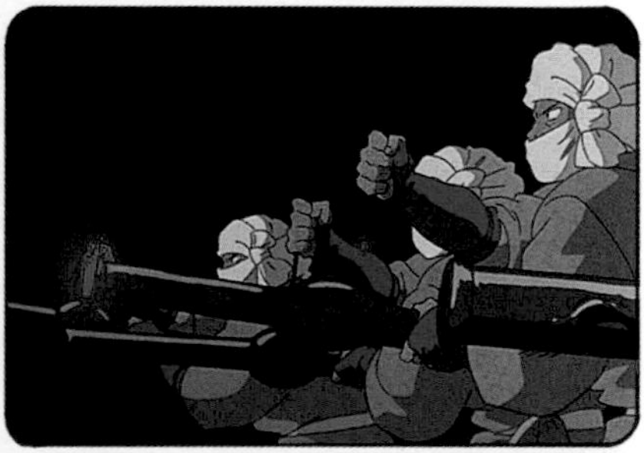

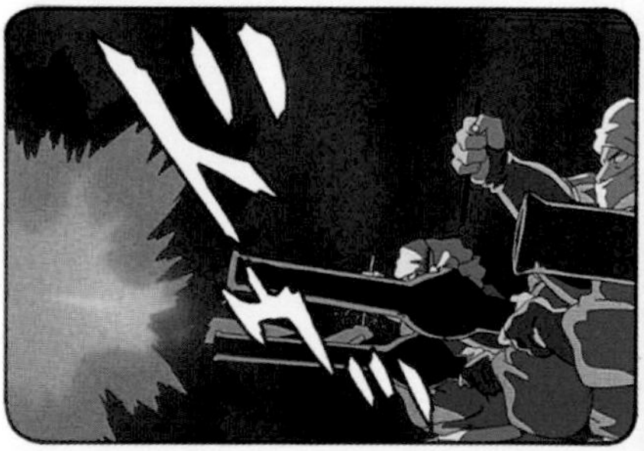

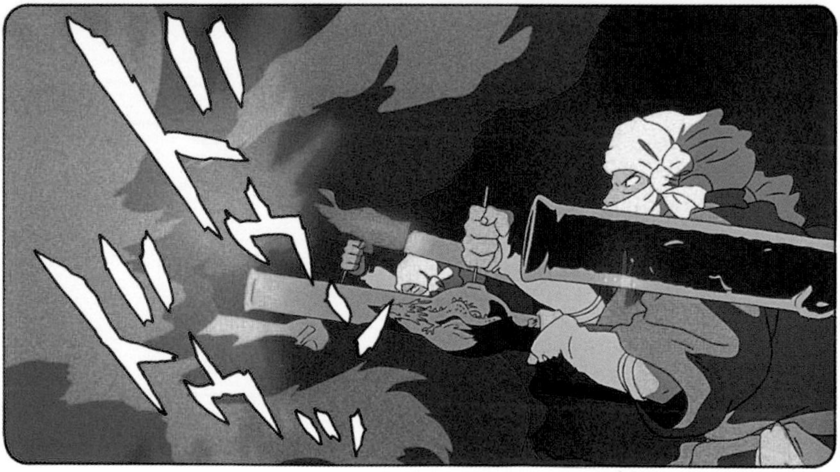

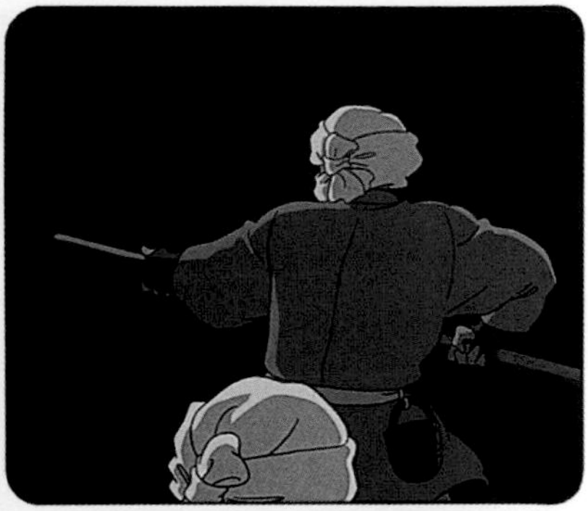
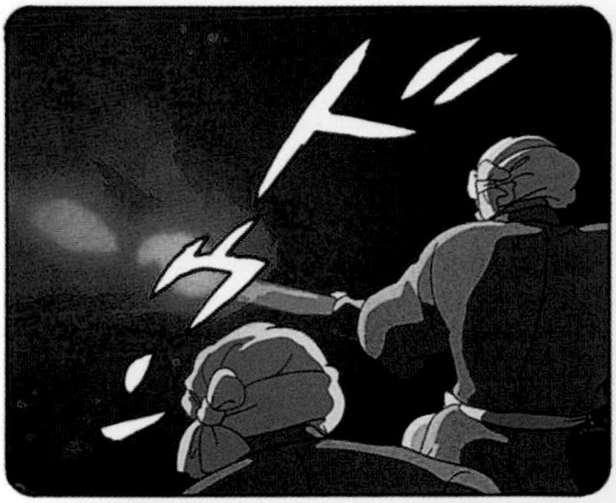
ドゥ…
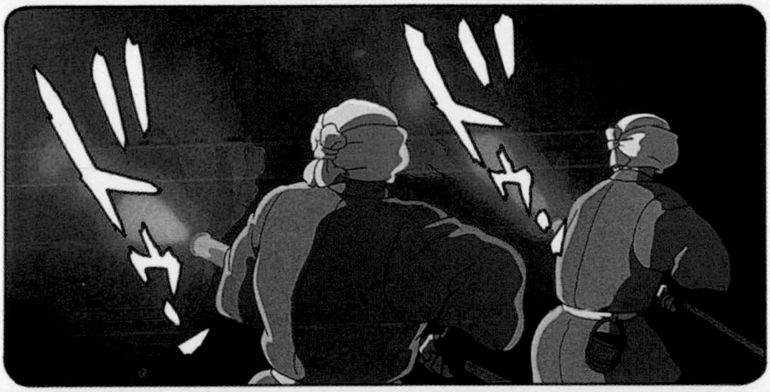
ドゥ…
ドゥ…
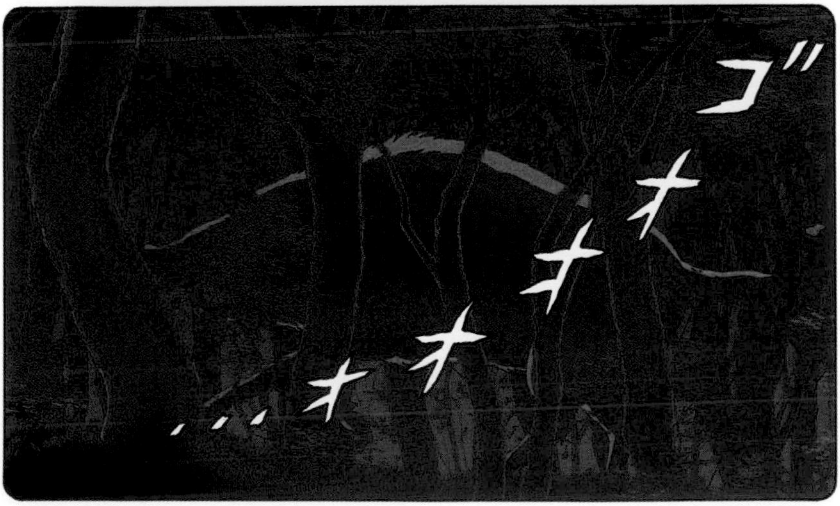
ゴォォォォォ…

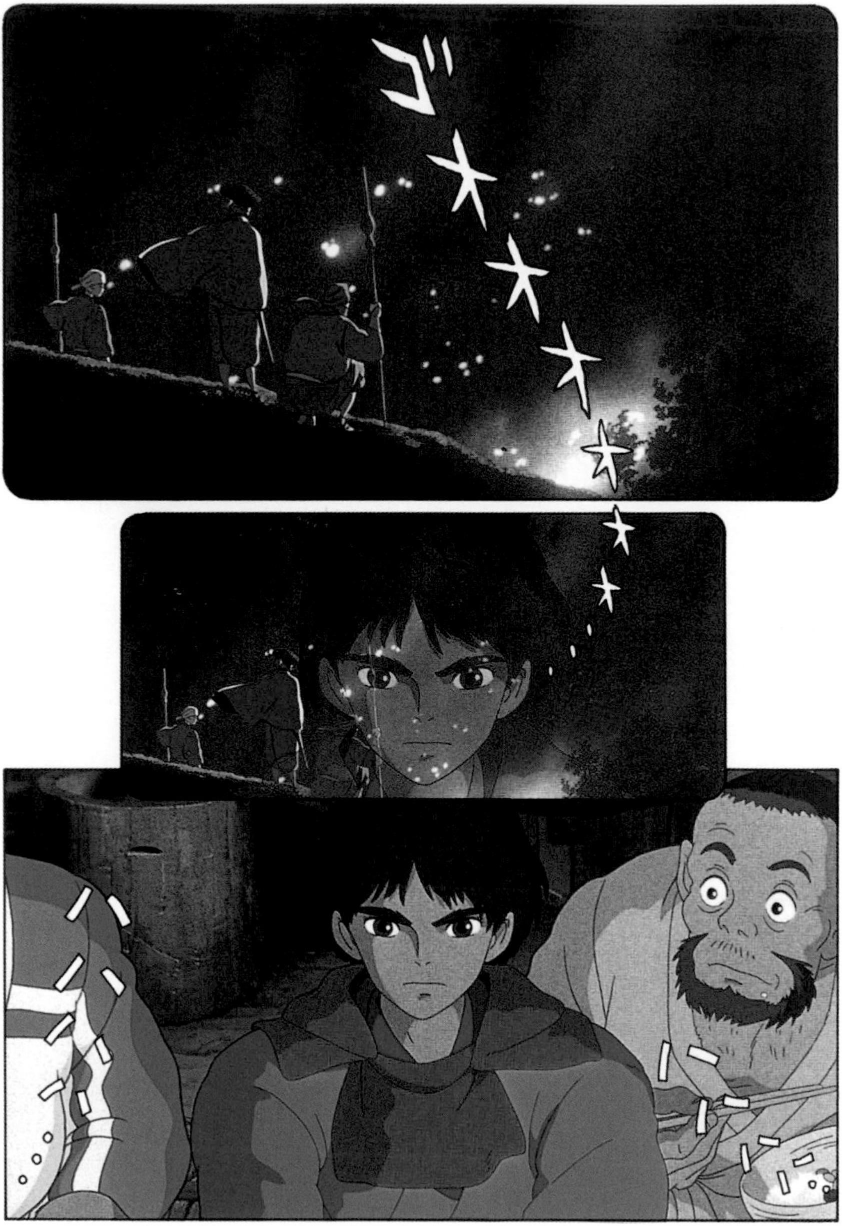
ゴ

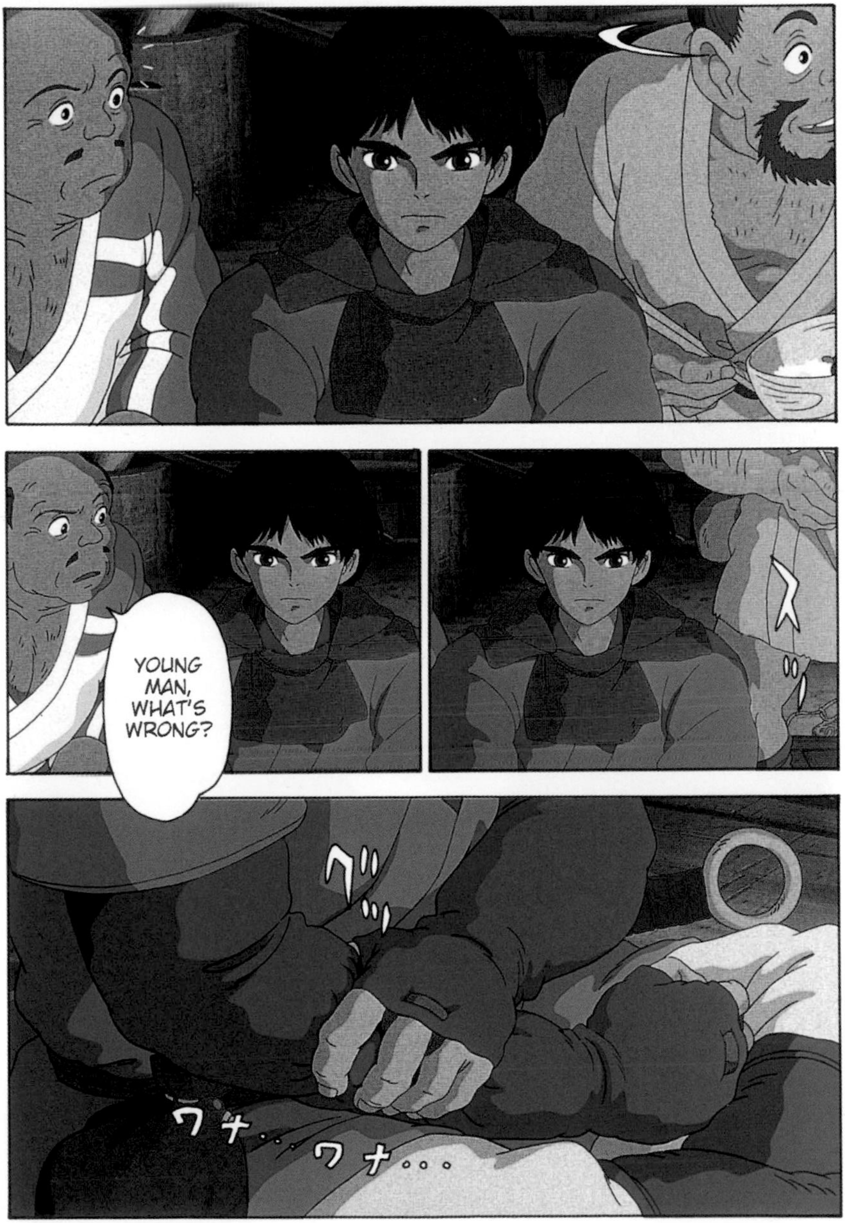
スッ
YOUNG MAN, WHAT'S WRONG?
グッ
ワナ…ワナ…

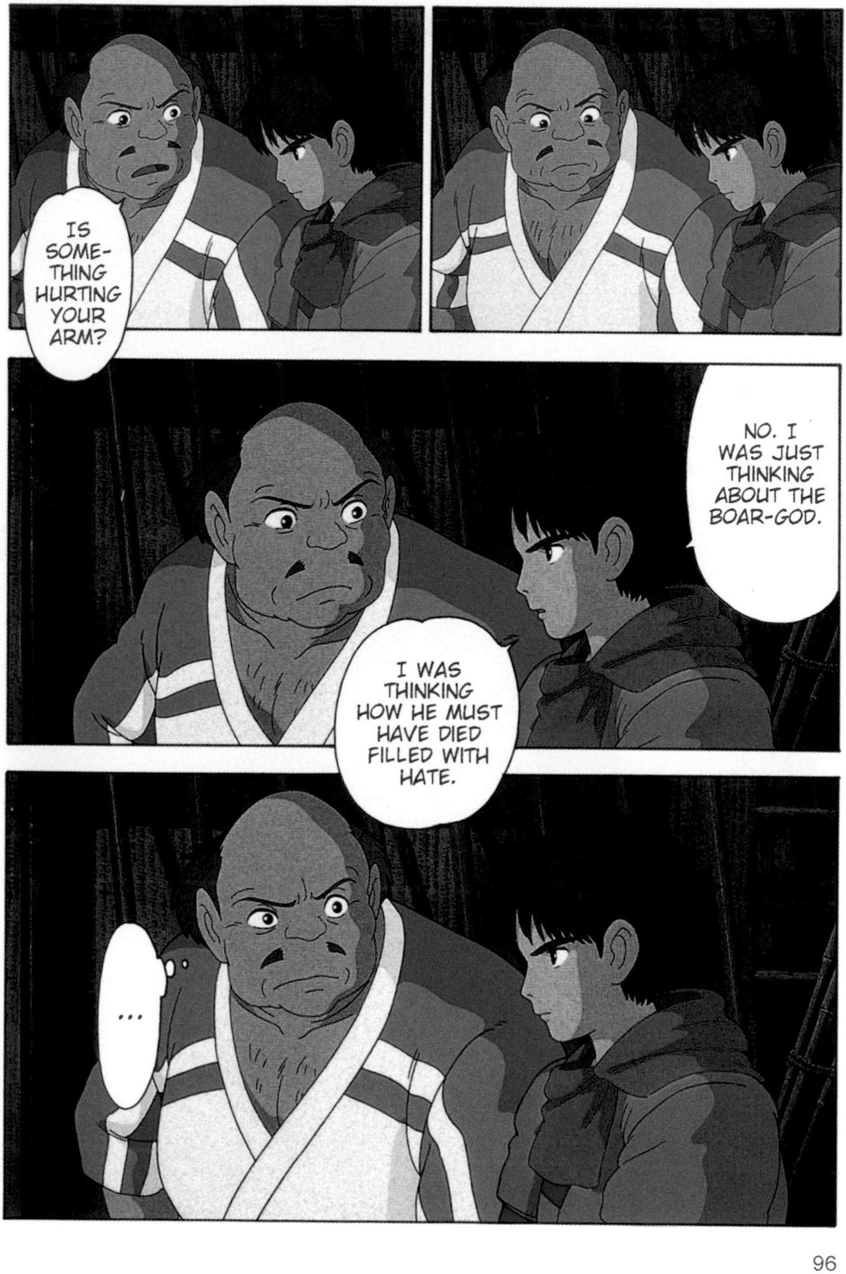
IS SOME-THING HURTING YOUR ARM?
NO. I WAS JUST THINKING ABOUT THE BOAR-GOD.
I WAS THINKING HOW HE MUST HAVE DIED FILLED WITH HATE.
...

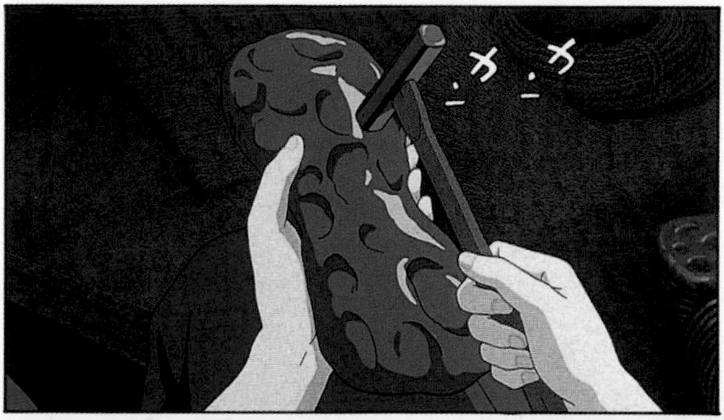
カッカッ
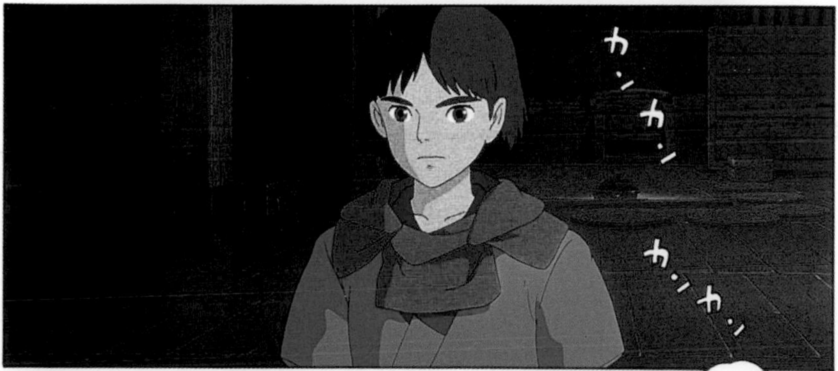
カッカッ
カッカッ
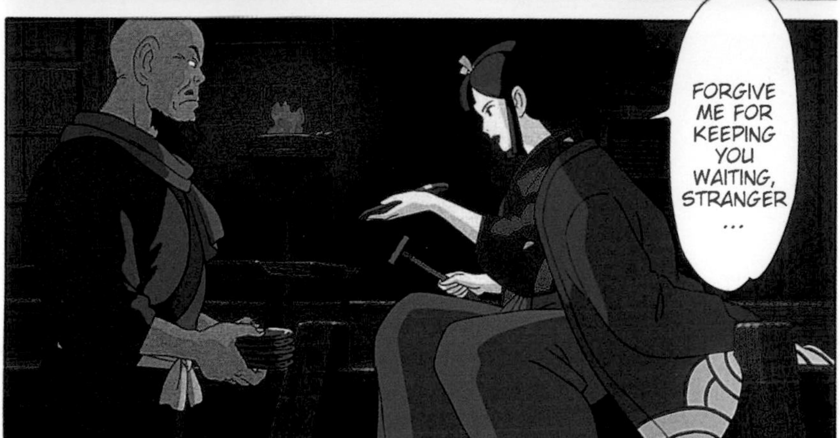
FORGIVE ME FOR KEEPING YOU WAITING, STRANGER ...

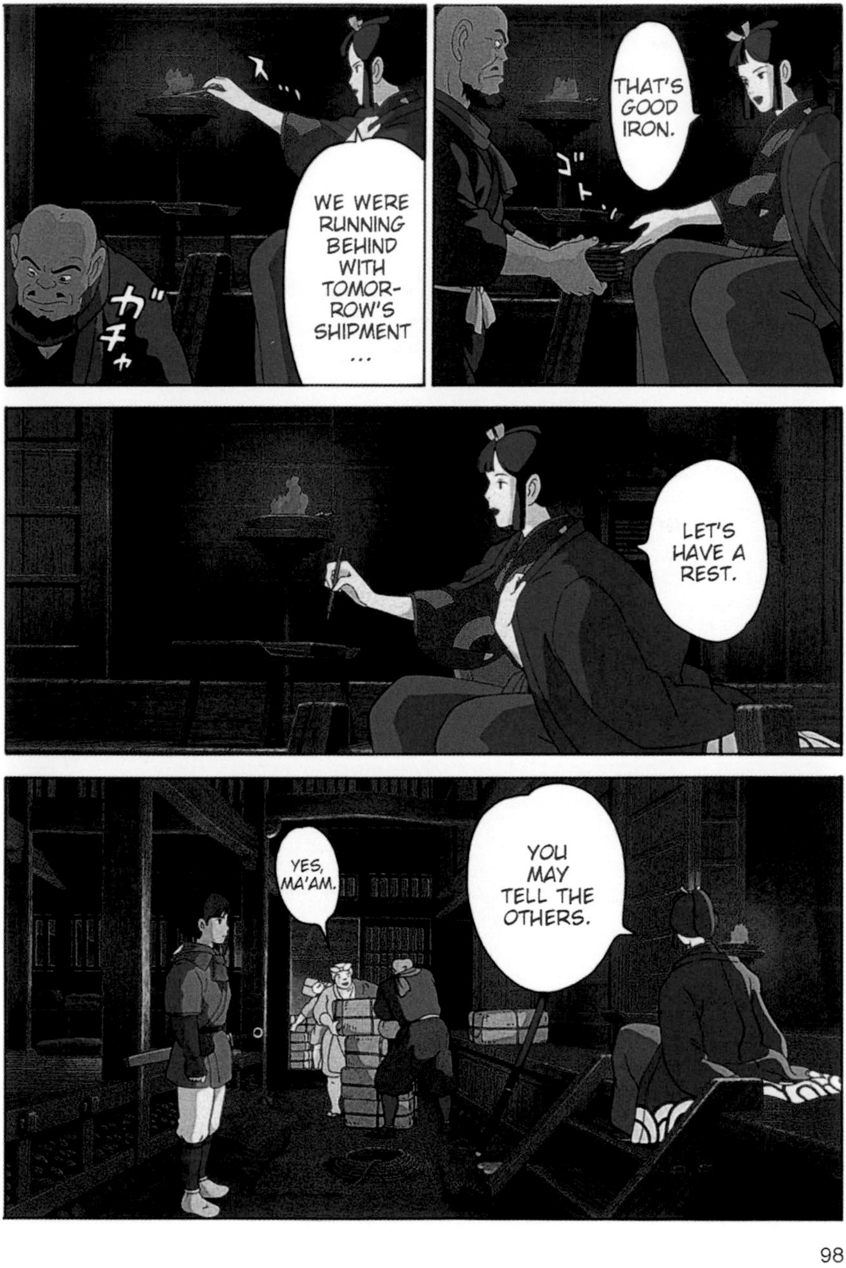
THAT'S GOOD IRON.
ゴトッ
WE WERE RUNNING BEHIND WITH TOMORROW'S SHIPMENT...
ガチャ
LET'S HAVE A REST.
YOU MAY TELL THE OTHERS.
YES, MA'AM.

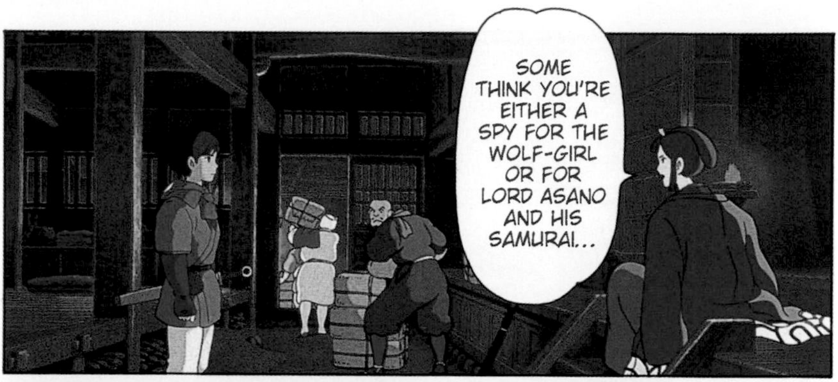
SOME THINK YOU'RE EITHER A SPY FOR THE WOLF-GIRL OR FOR LORD ASANO AND HIS SAMURAI...
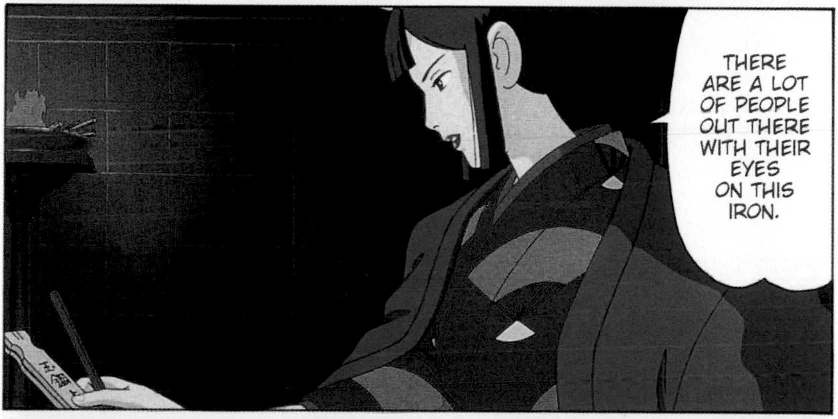
THERE ARE A LOT OF PEOPLE OUT THERE WITH THEIR EYES ON THIS IRON.
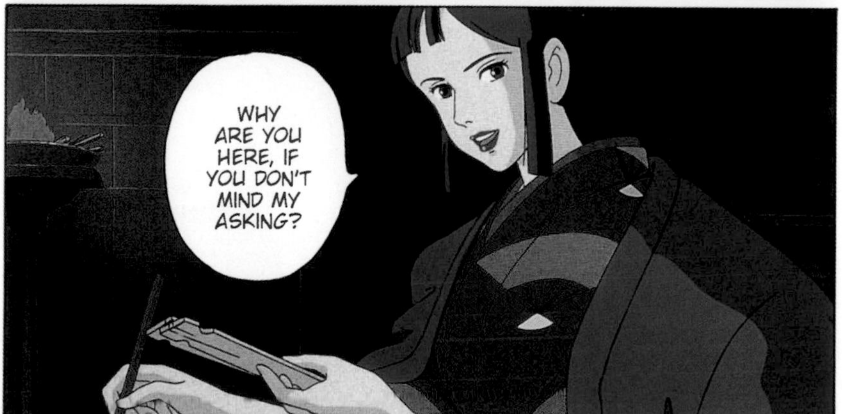
WHY ARE YOU HERE, IF YOU DON'T MIND MY ASKING?

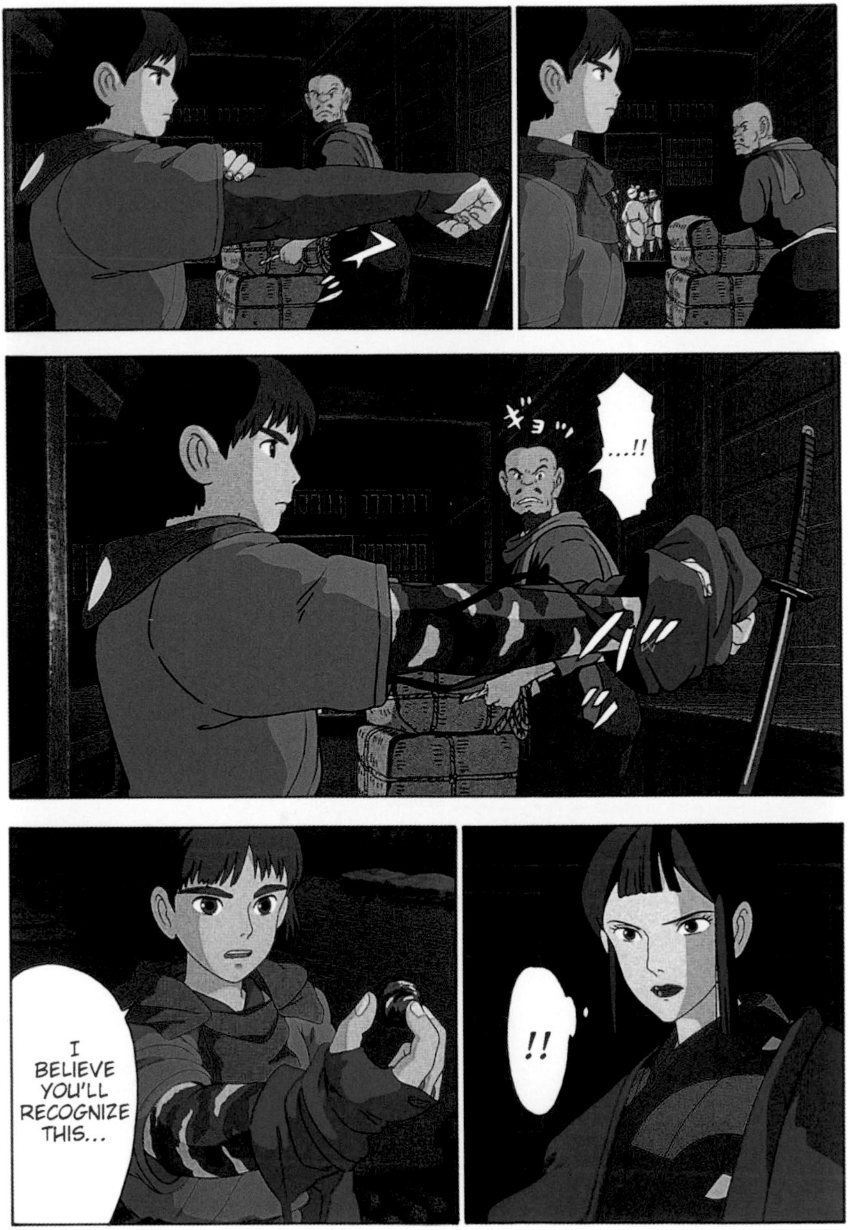
ギョッ
...!!
!!
I BELIEVE YOU'LL RECOGNIZE THIS...

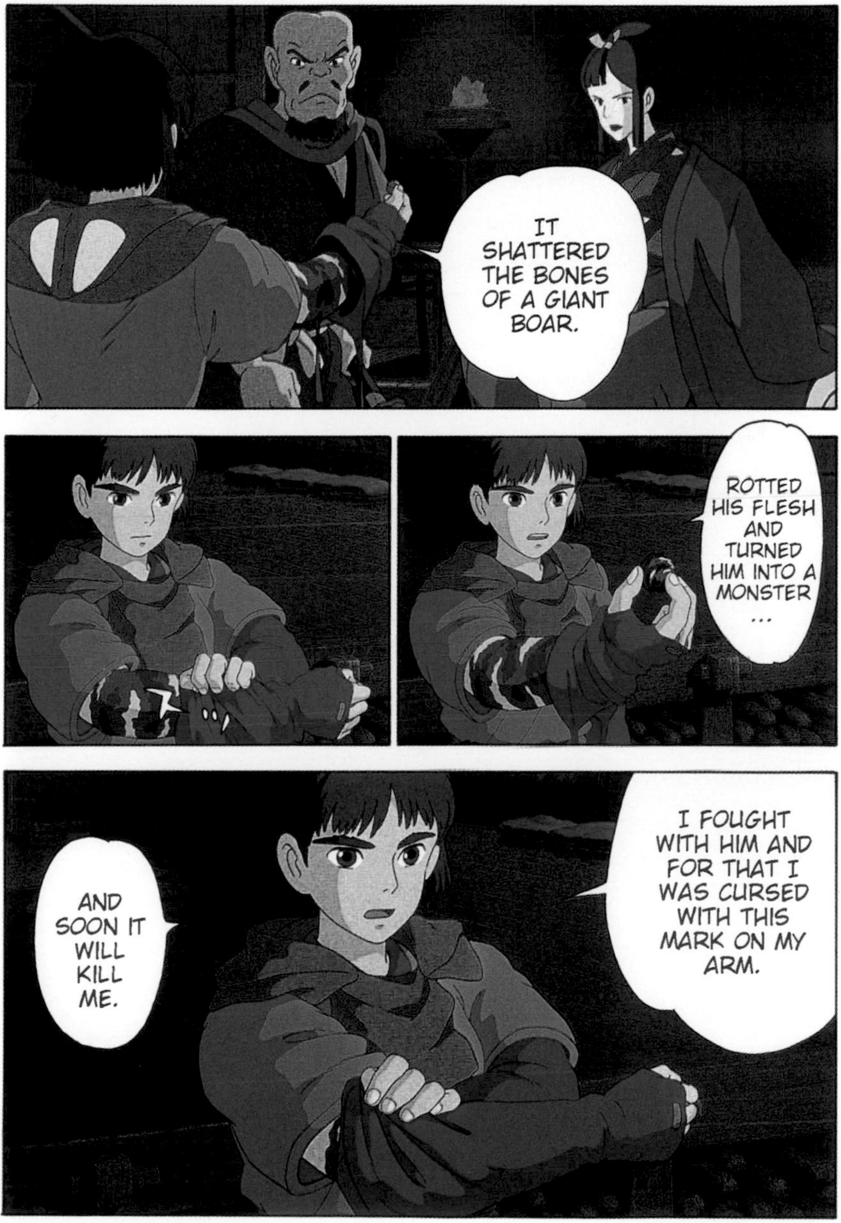
IT SHATTERED THE BONES OF A GIANT BOAR.
ROTTED HIS FLESH AND TURNED HIM INTO A MONSTER ...
I FOUGHT WITH HIM AND FOR THAT I WAS CURSED WITH THIS MARK ON MY ARM.
AND SOON IT WILL KILL ME.

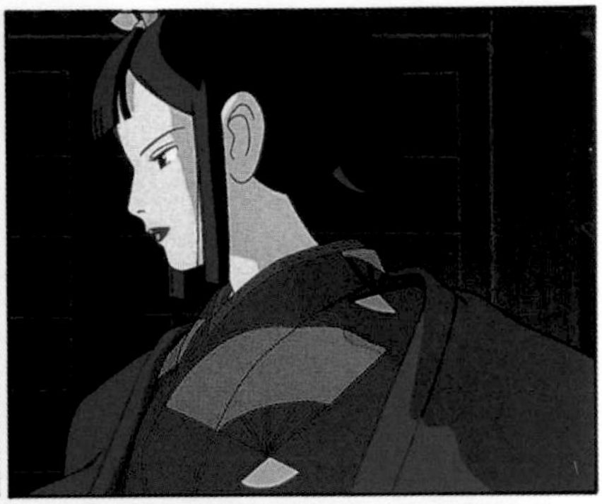
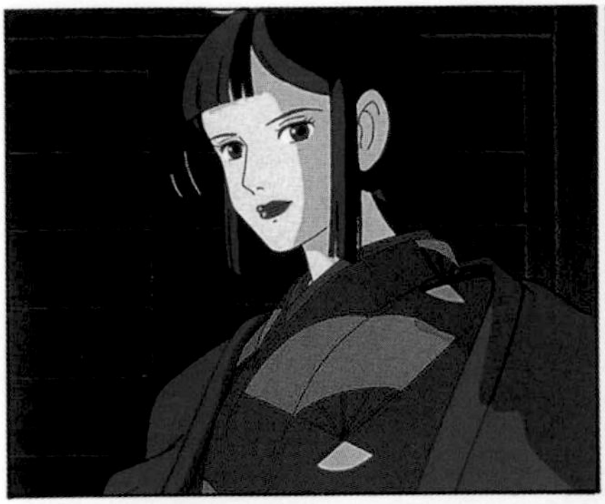
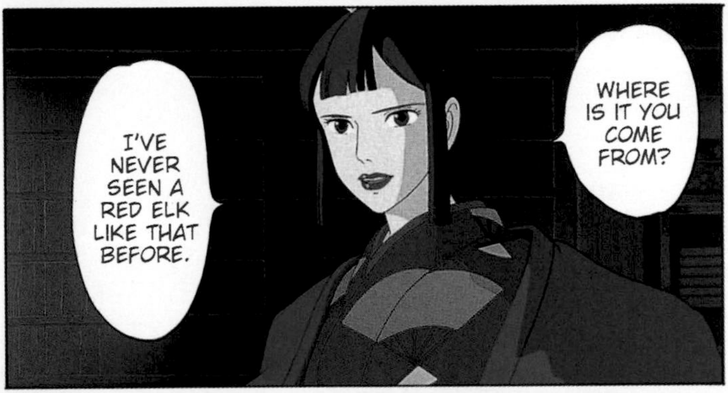
WHERE IS IT YOU COME FROM?
I'VE NEVER SEEN A RED ELK LIKE THAT BEFORE.
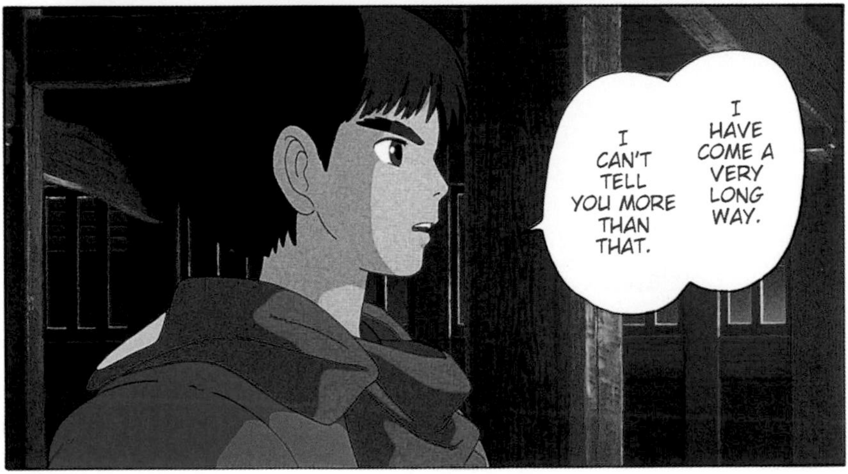
I HAVE COME A VERY LONG WAY.
I CAN'T TELL YOU MORE THAN THAT.

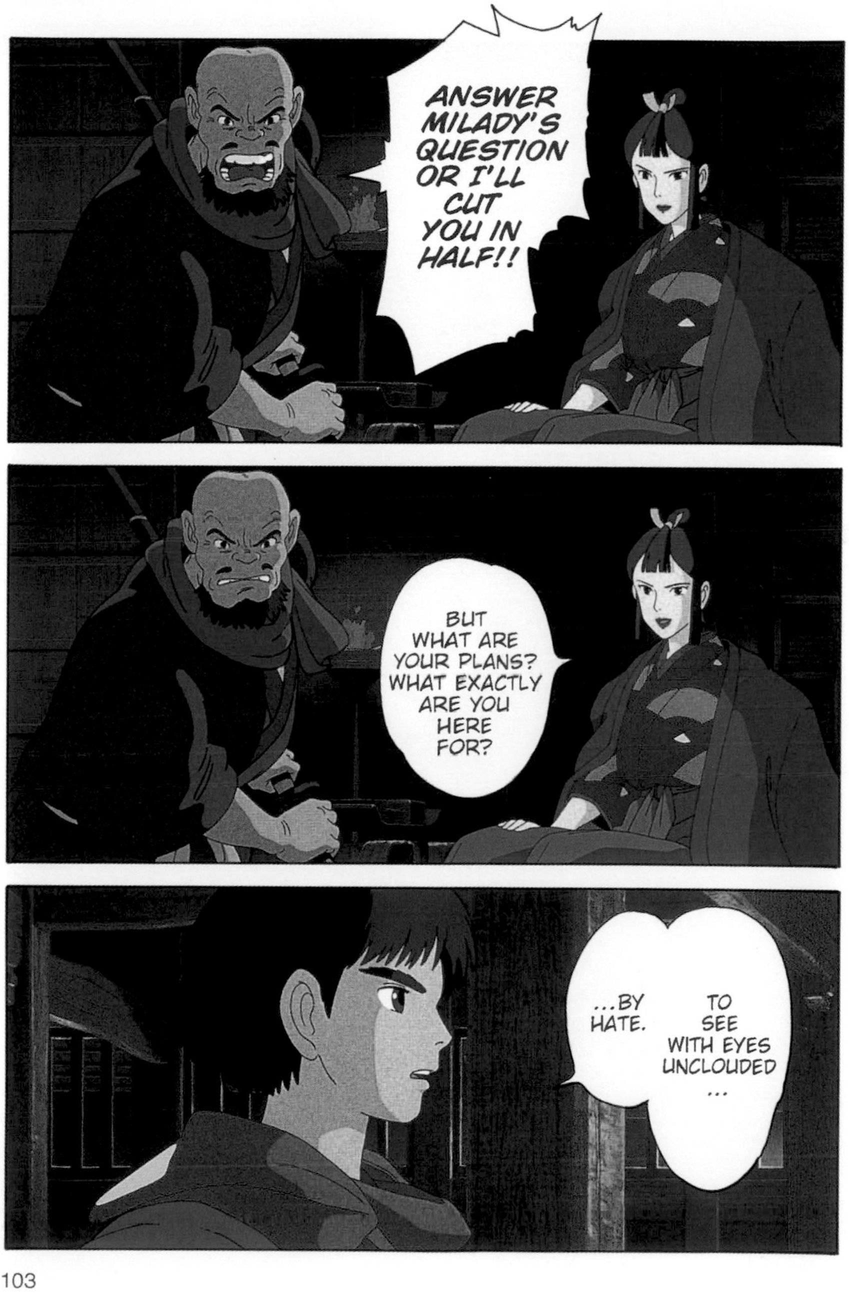
ANSWER MILADY'S QUESTION OR I'LL CUT YOU IN HALF!!
BUT WHAT ARE YOUR PLANS? WHAT EXACTLY ARE YOU HERE FOR?
TO SEE WITH EYES UNCLOUDED ...
...BY HATE.

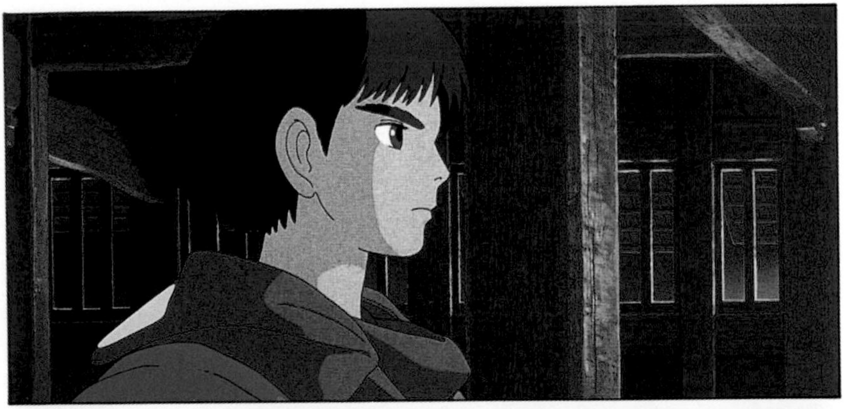

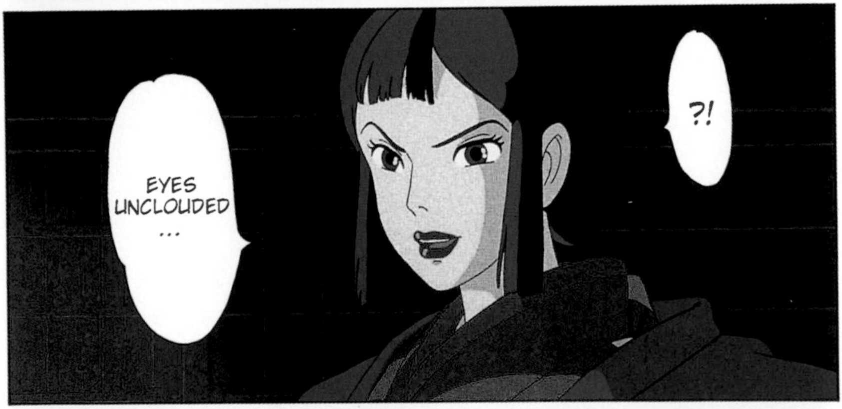
?!
EYES UNCLOUDED ...

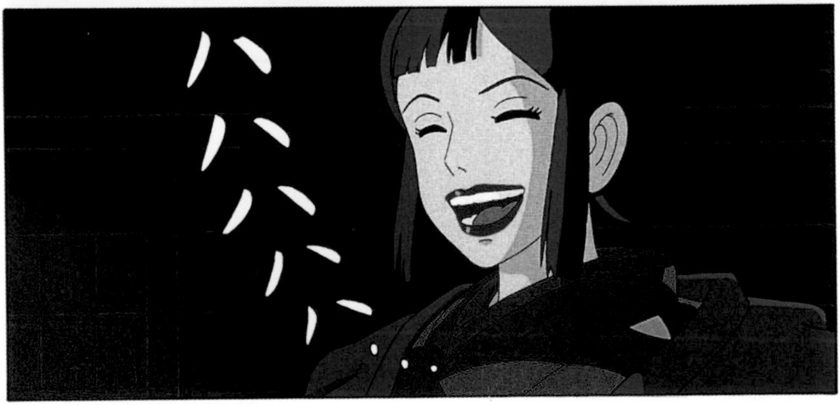

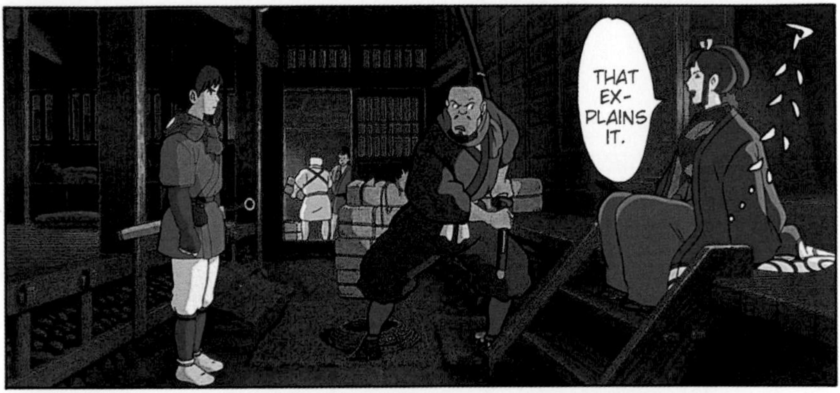
THAT EX-PLAINS IT.

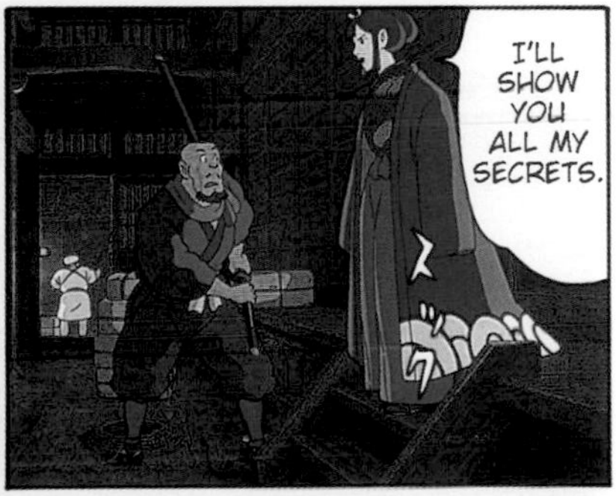
I'LL SHOW YOU ALL MY SECRETS.

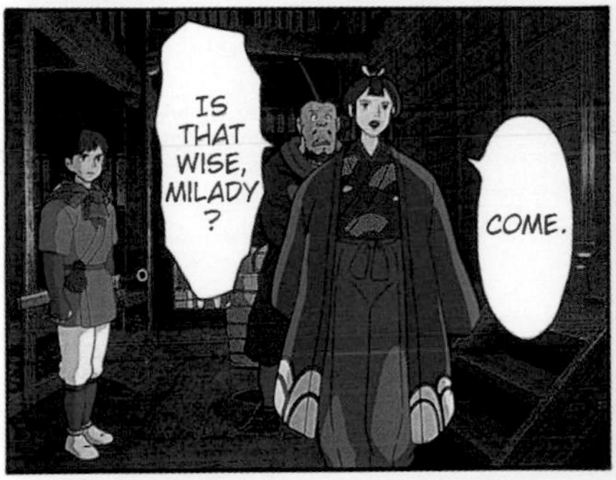
COME.
IS THAT WISE, MILADY?

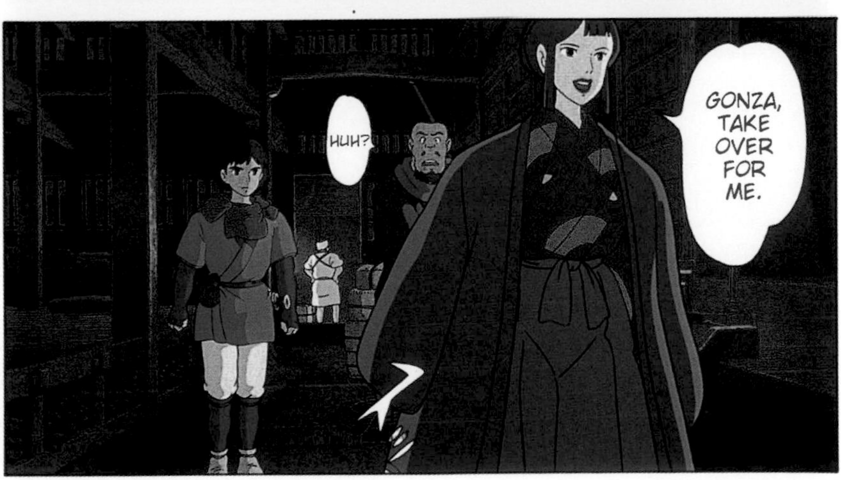
GONZA, TAKE OVER FOR ME.
HUH?

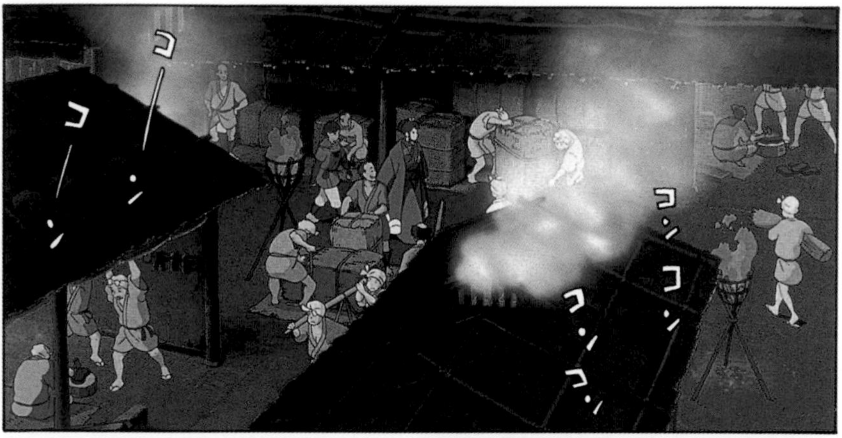
コーン
コーン
コン
コン
コン
コン
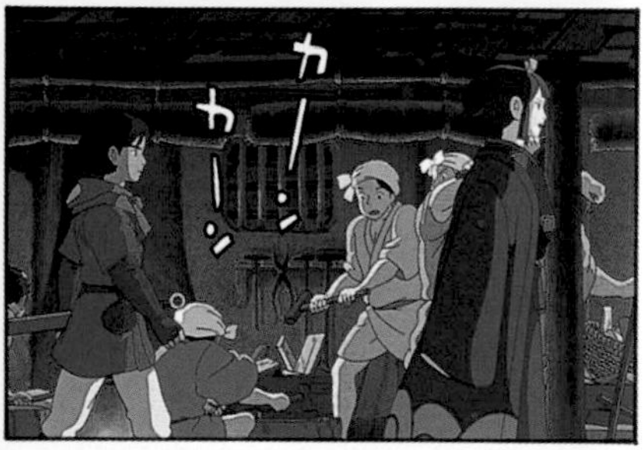
カーン
カーン
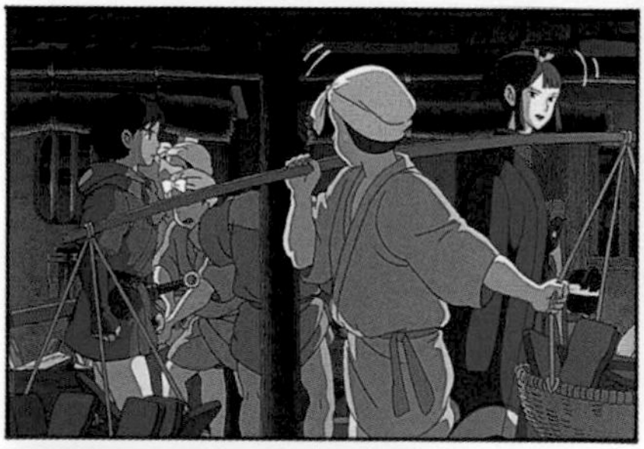
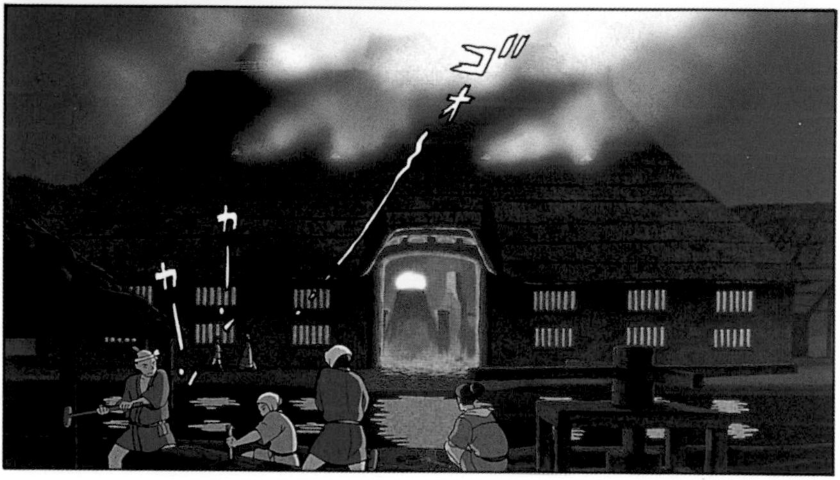
ゴォー
カーン
カーン

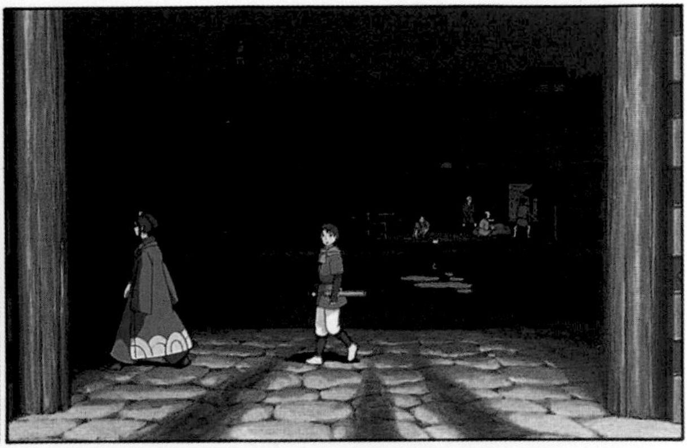

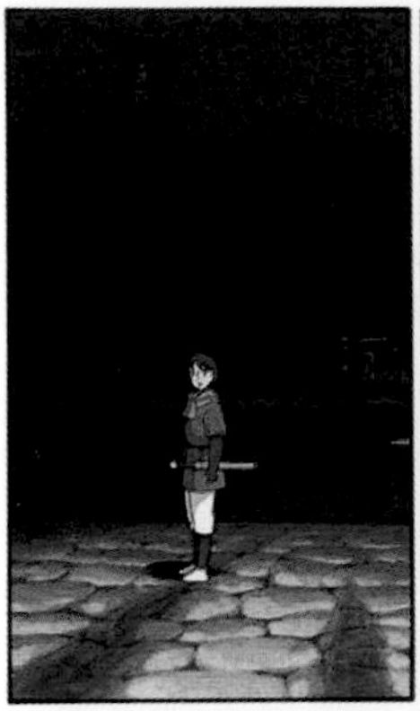

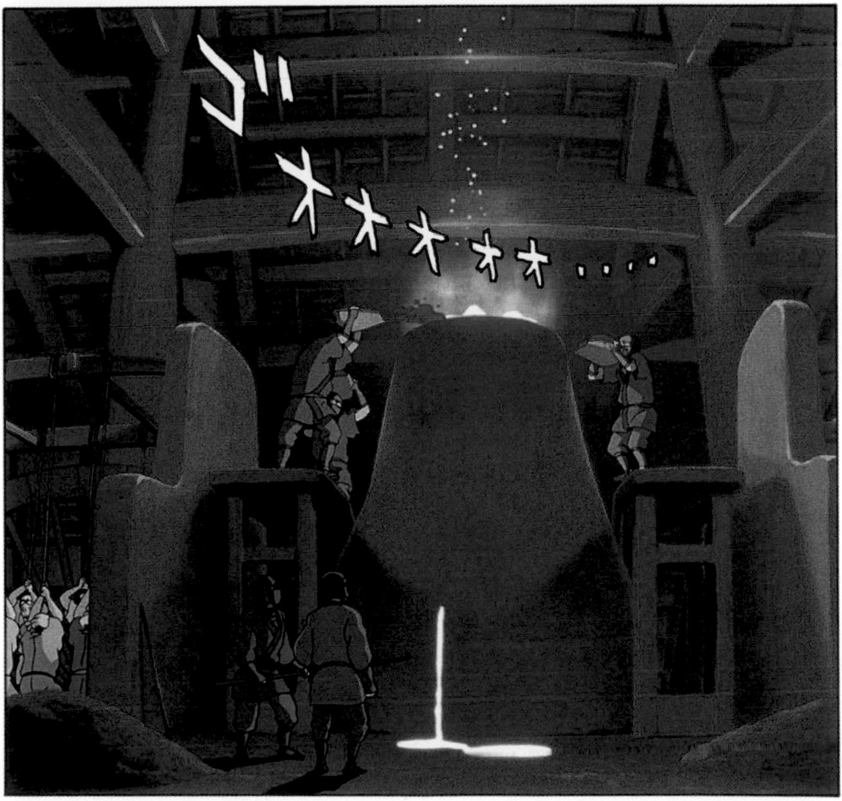
ゴオオオオオ....

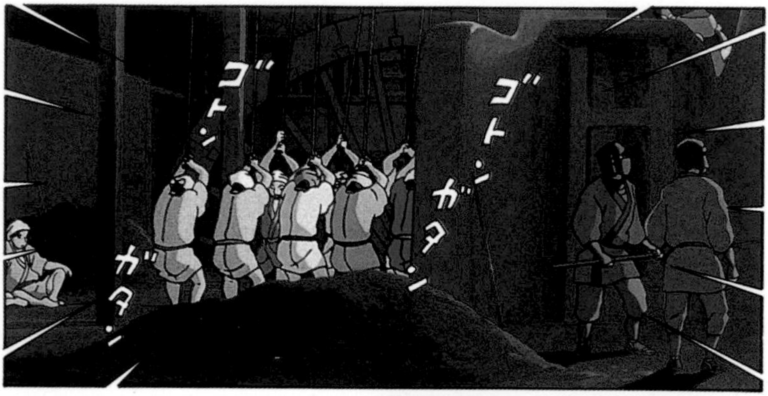
ゴトン
ガタン
ゴトン
ガタン

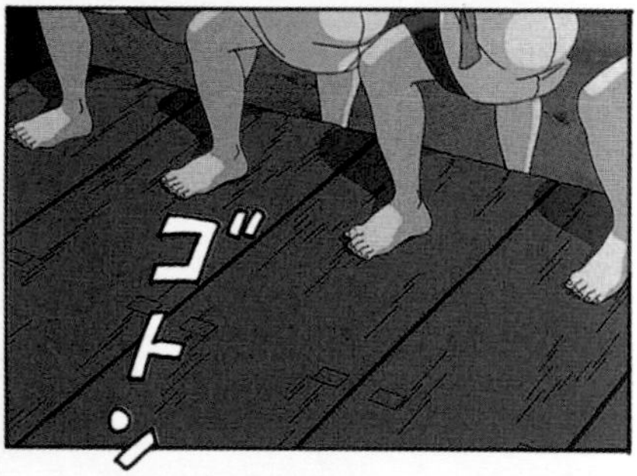
ゴトン

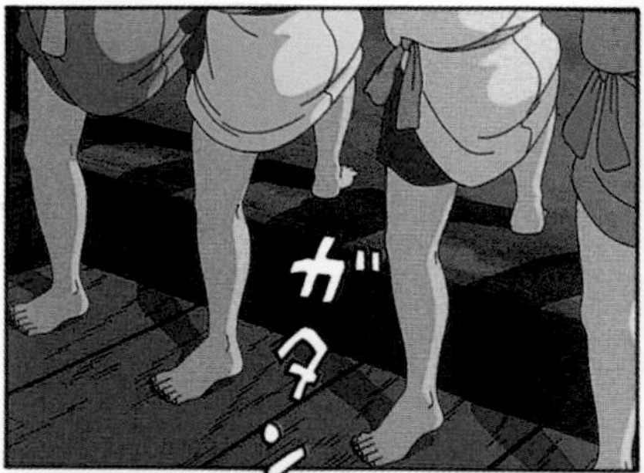
ガタン

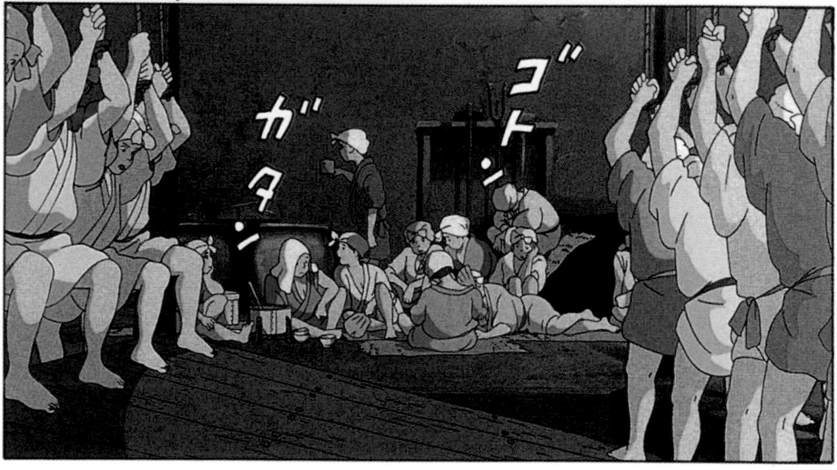
ゴトン
ガタン

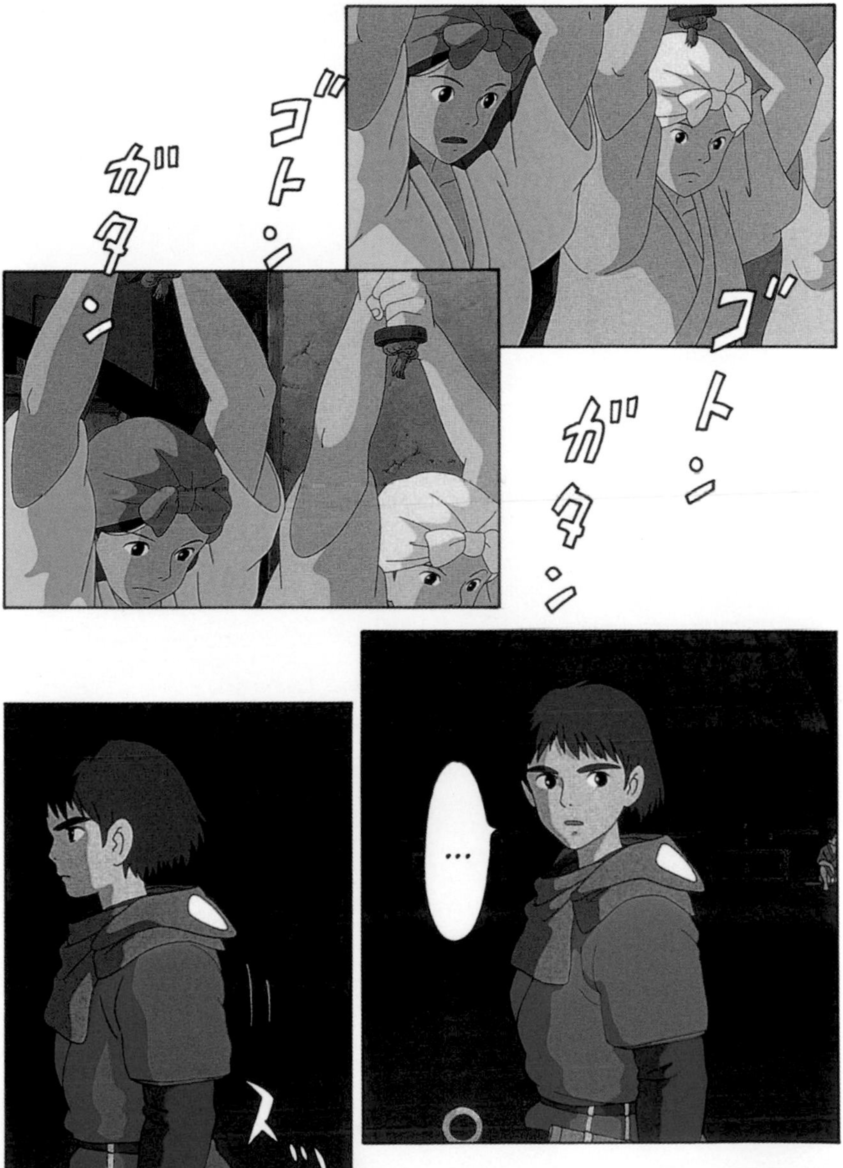
ゴトン
ガタン
ゴトン
ガタン
…
スッ

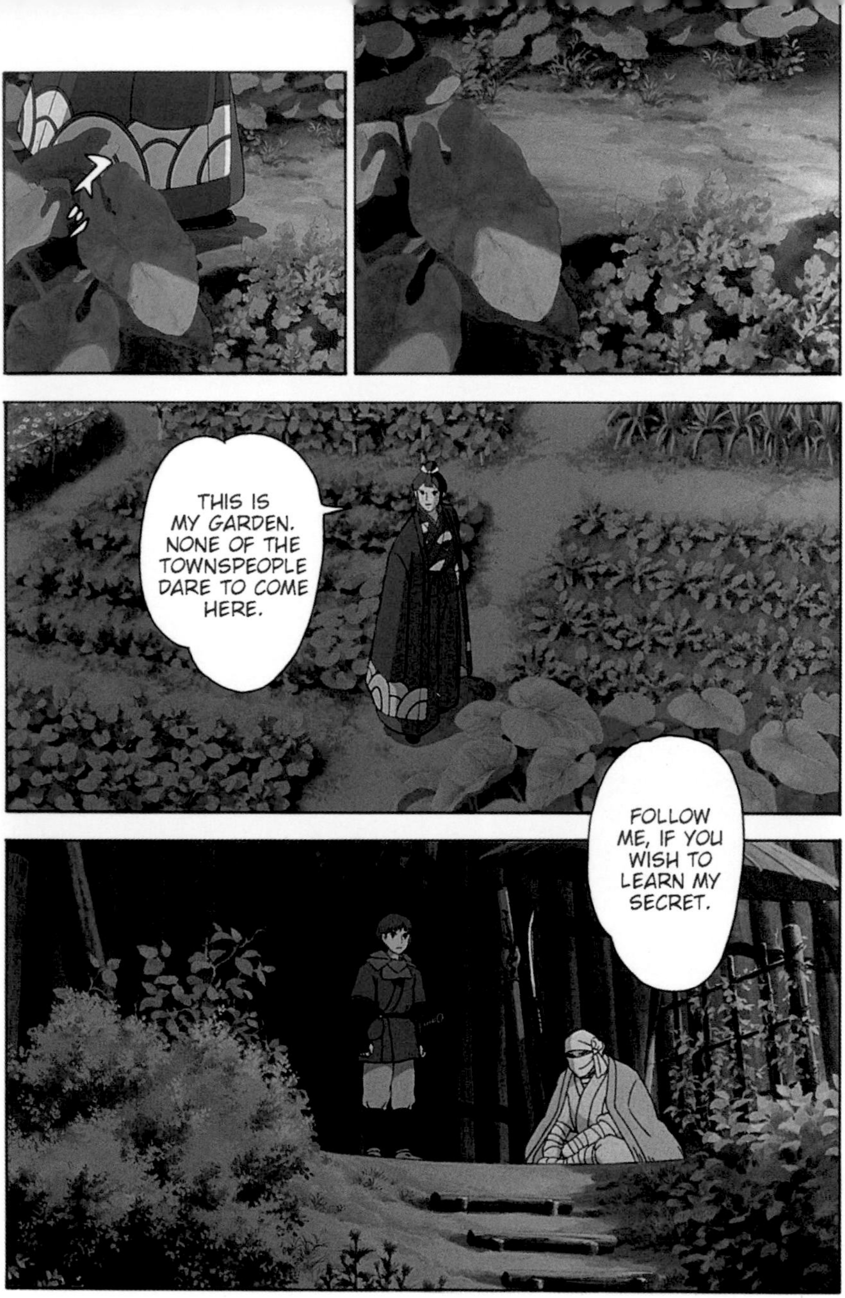
THIS IS MY GARDEN. NONE OF THE TOWNSPEOPLE DARE TO COME HERE.
FOLLOW ME, IF YOU WISH TO LEARN MY SECRET.

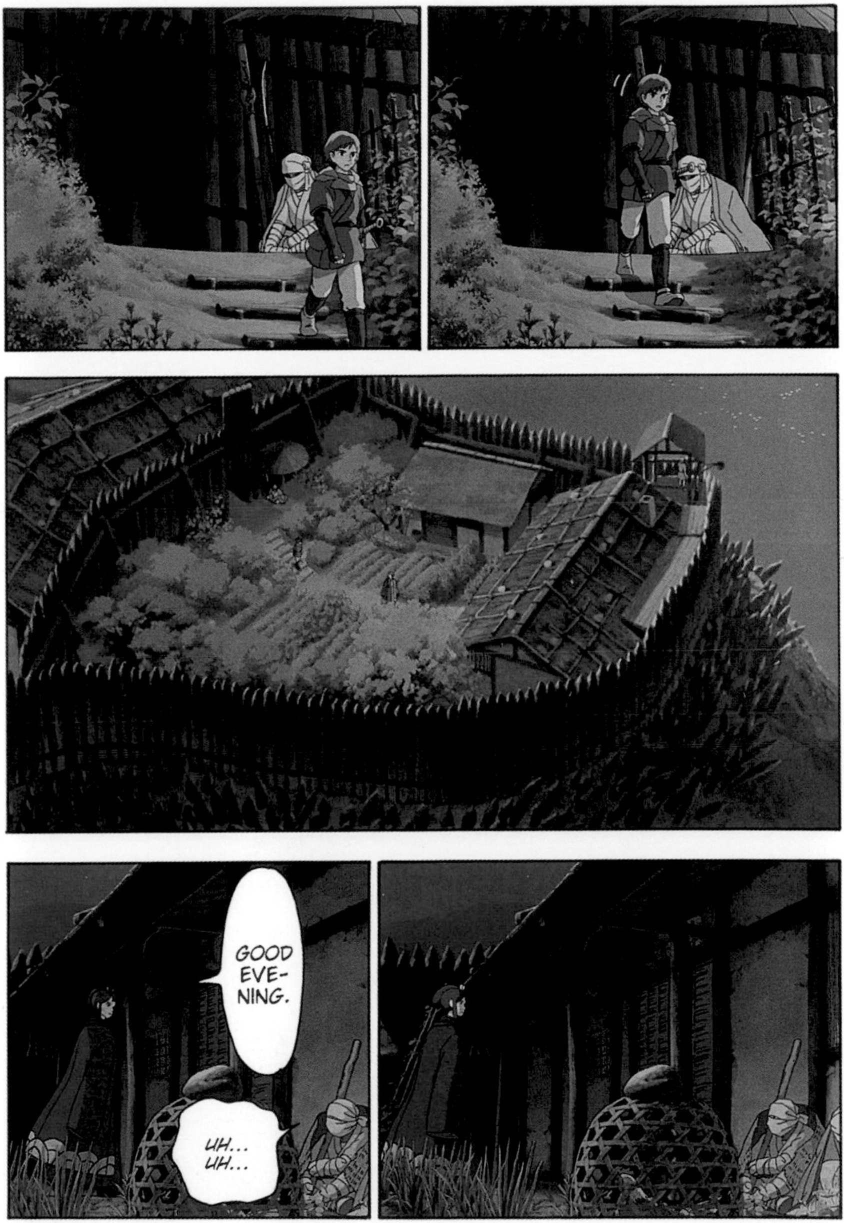
GOOD EVE-NING.
UH... UH...

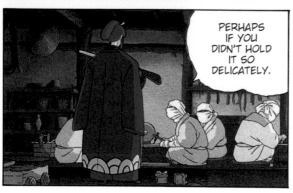

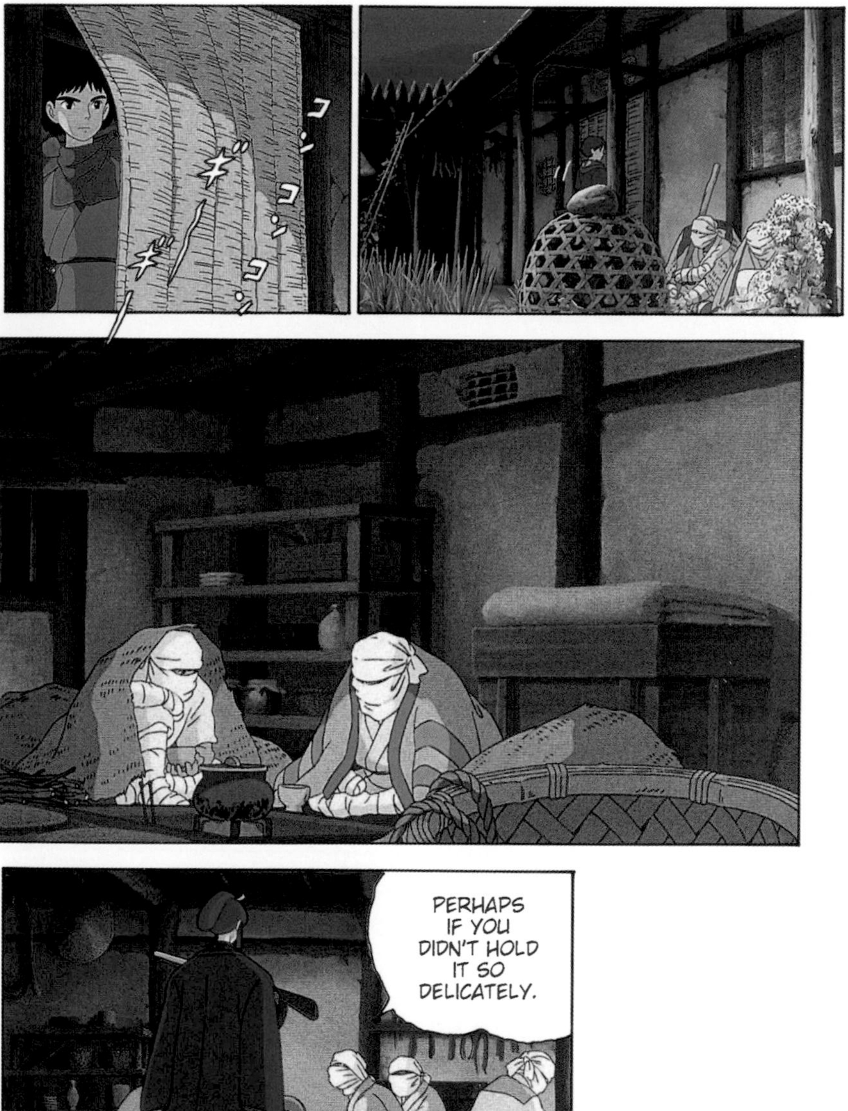
PERHAPS IF YOU DIDN'T HOLD IT SO DELICATELY.

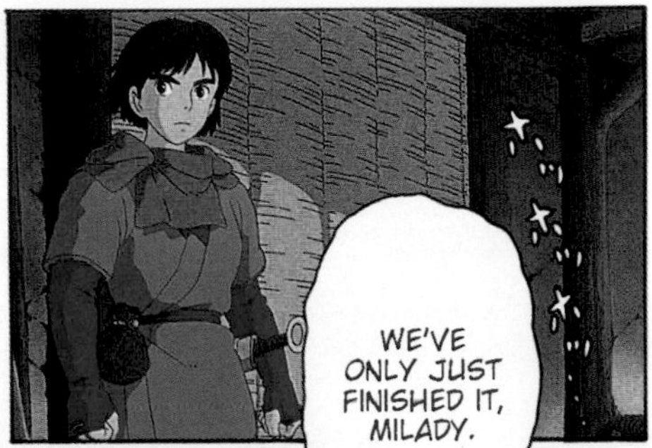
WE'VE ONLY JUST FINISHED IT, MILADY.

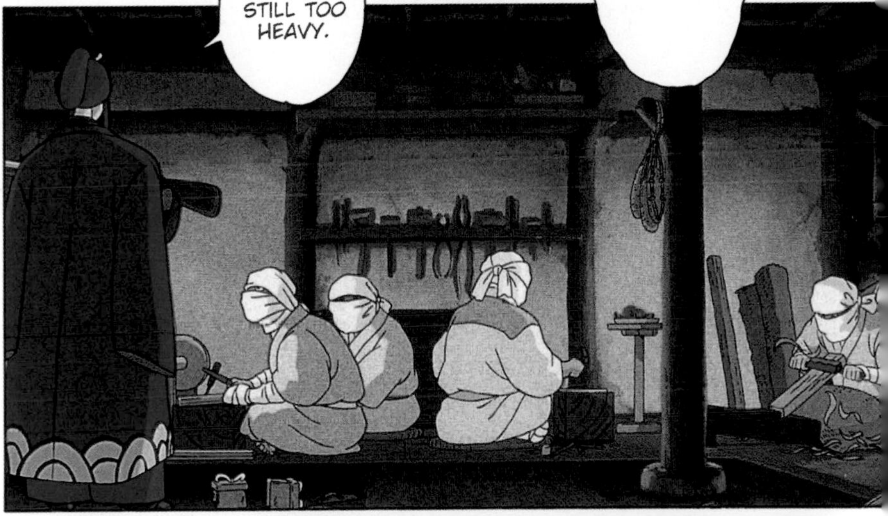
IT'S STILL TOO HEAVY.

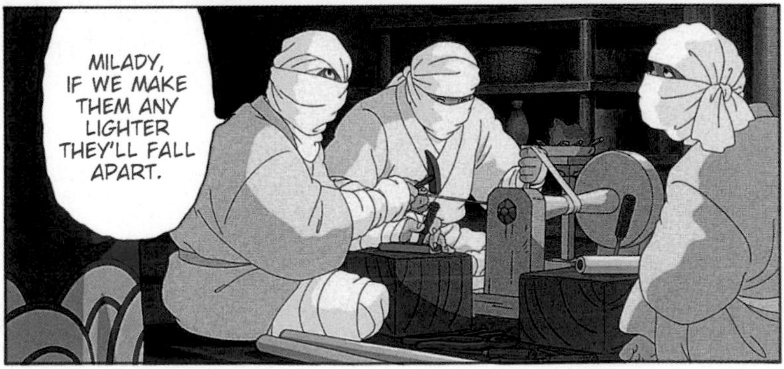
MILADY, IF WE MAKE THEM ANY LIGHTER THEY'LL FALL APART.

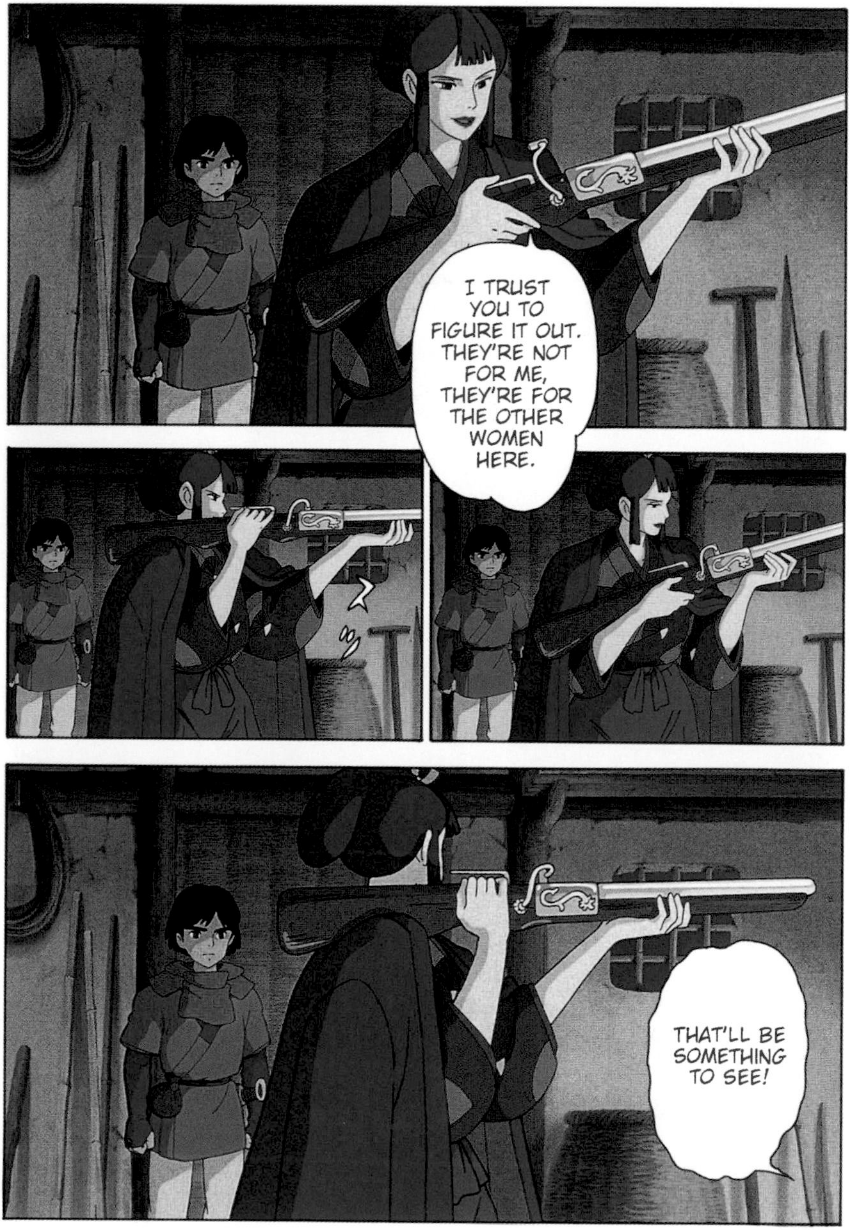
I TRUST YOU TO FIGURE IT OUT. THEY'RE NOT FOR ME, THEY'RE FOR THE OTHER WOMEN HERE.
THAT'LL BE SOMETHING TO SEE!

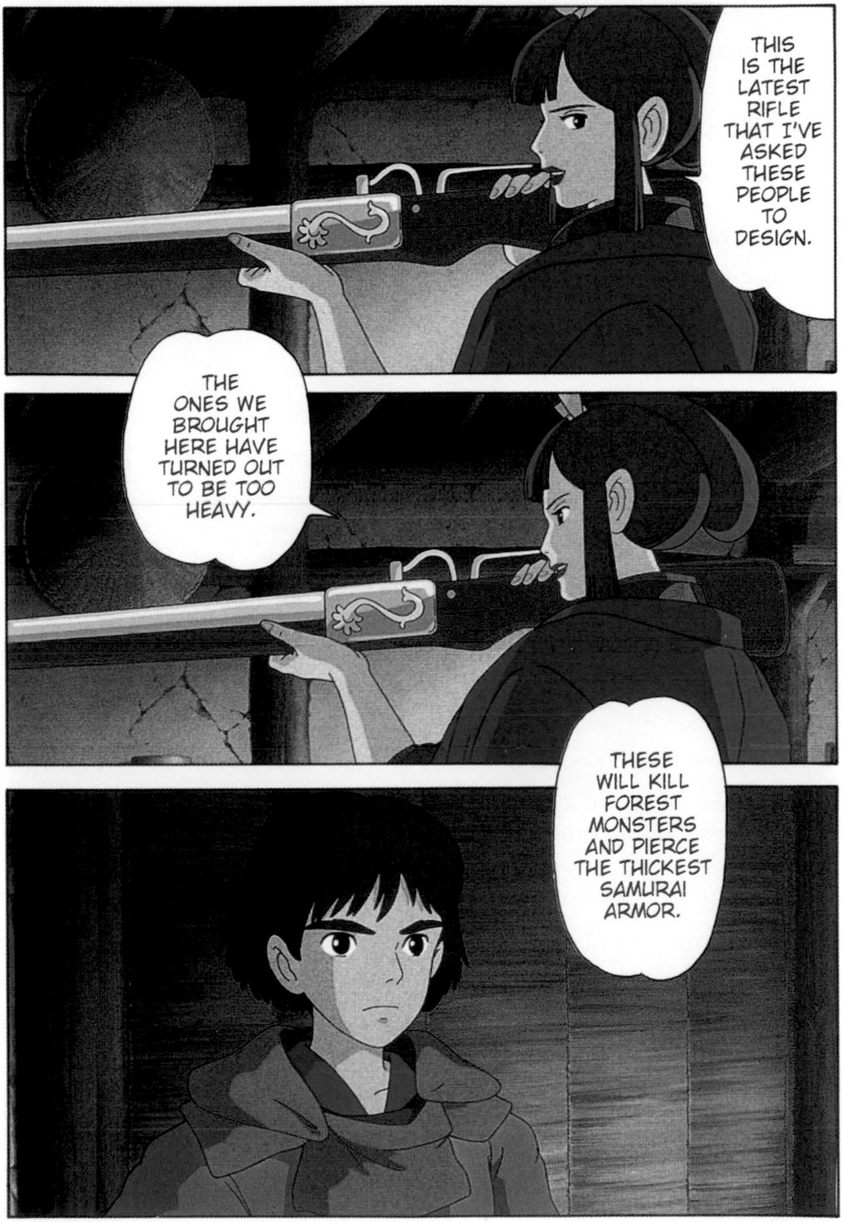
THIS IS THE LATEST RIFLE THAT I'VE ASKED THESE PEOPLE TO DESIGN.
THE ONES WE BROUGHT HERE HAVE TURNED OUT TO BE TOO HEAVY.
THESE WILL KILL FOREST MONSTERS AND PIERCE THE THICKEST SAMURAI ARMOR.

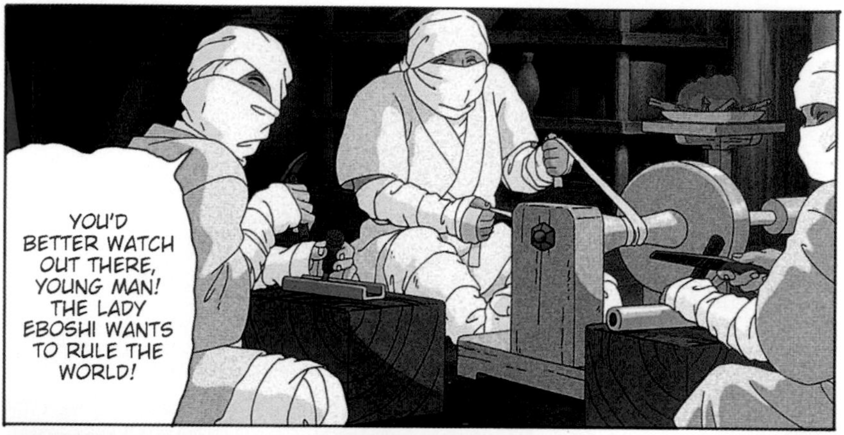
YOU'D BETTER WATCH OUT THERE, YOUNG MAN! THE LADY EBOSHI WANTS TO RULE THE WORLD!

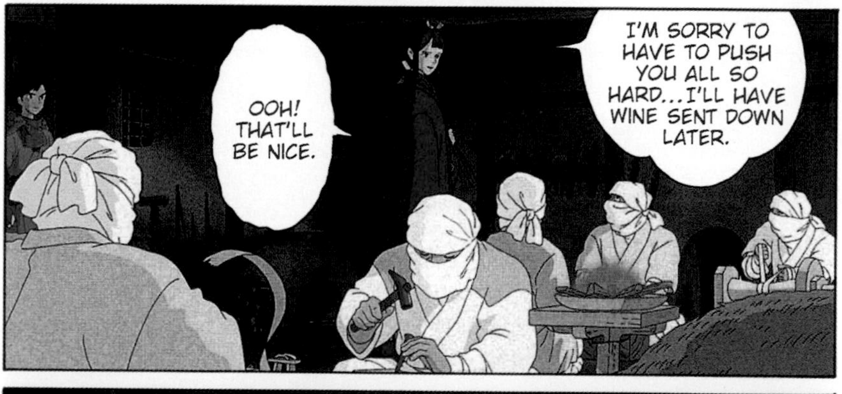
I'M SORRY TO HAVE TO PUSH YOU ALL SO HARD...I'LL HAVE WINE SENT DOWN LATER.
OOH! THAT'LL BE NICE.

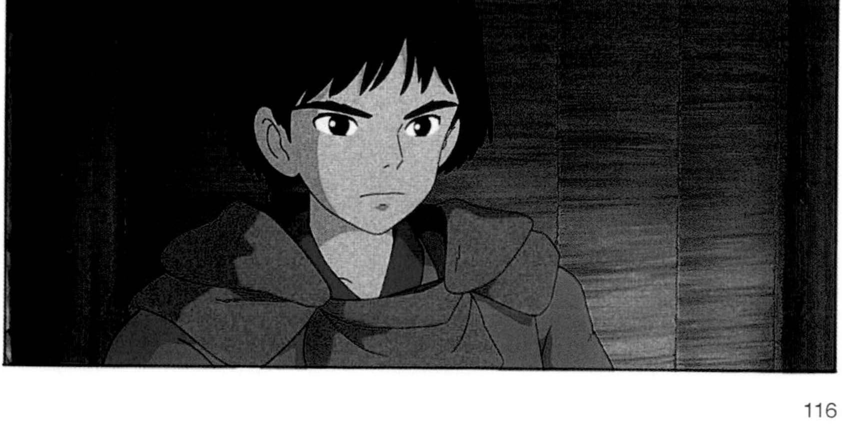

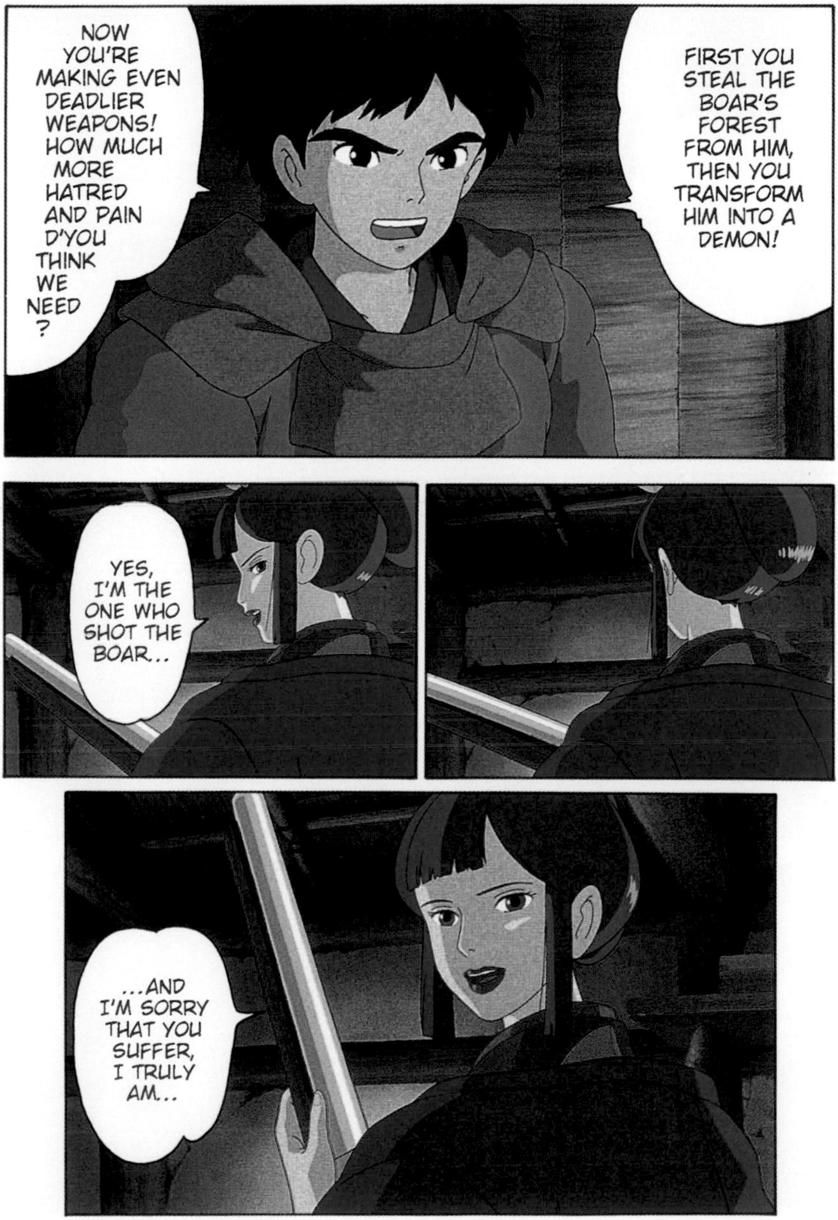
FIRST YOU STEAL THE BOAR'S FOREST FROM HIM, THEN YOU TRANSFORM HIM INTO A DEMON!
NOW YOU'RE MAKING EVEN DEADLIER WEAPONS! HOW MUCH MORE HATRED AND PAIN D'YOU THINK WE NEED?
YES, I'M THE ONE WHO SHOT THE BOAR...
...AND I'M SORRY THAT YOU SUFFER, I TRULY AM...

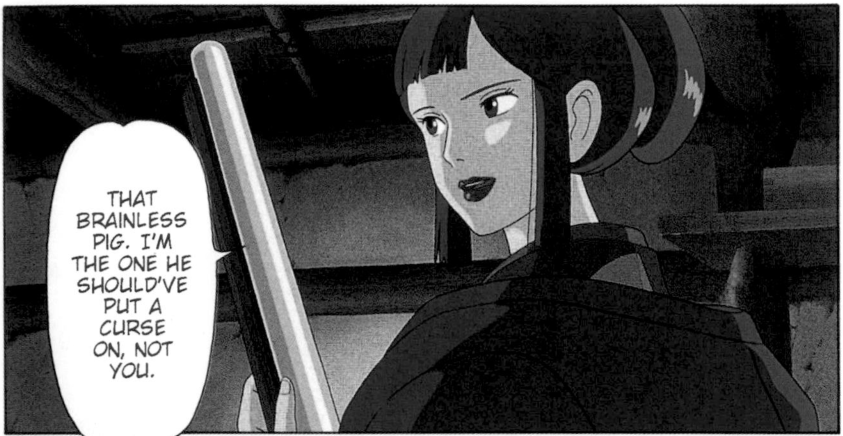
THAT BRAINLESS PIG. I'M THE ONE HE SHOULD'VE PUT A CURSE ON, NOT YOU.
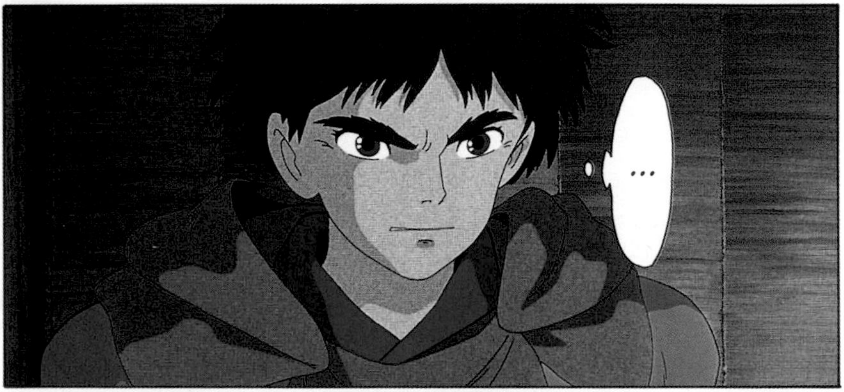
...
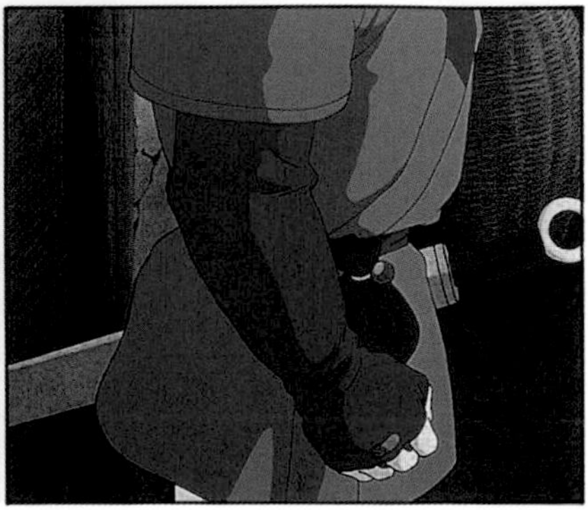
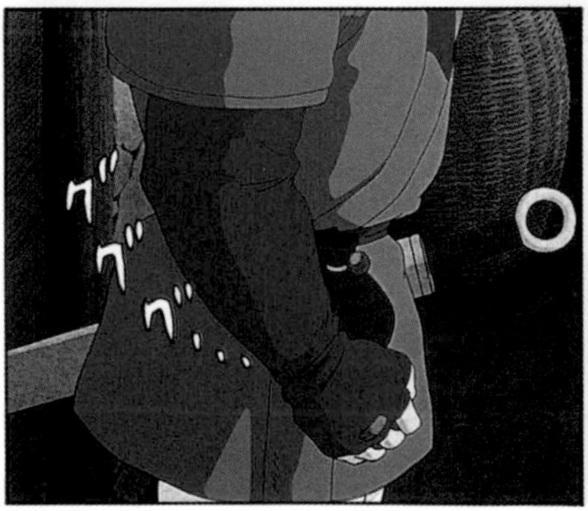

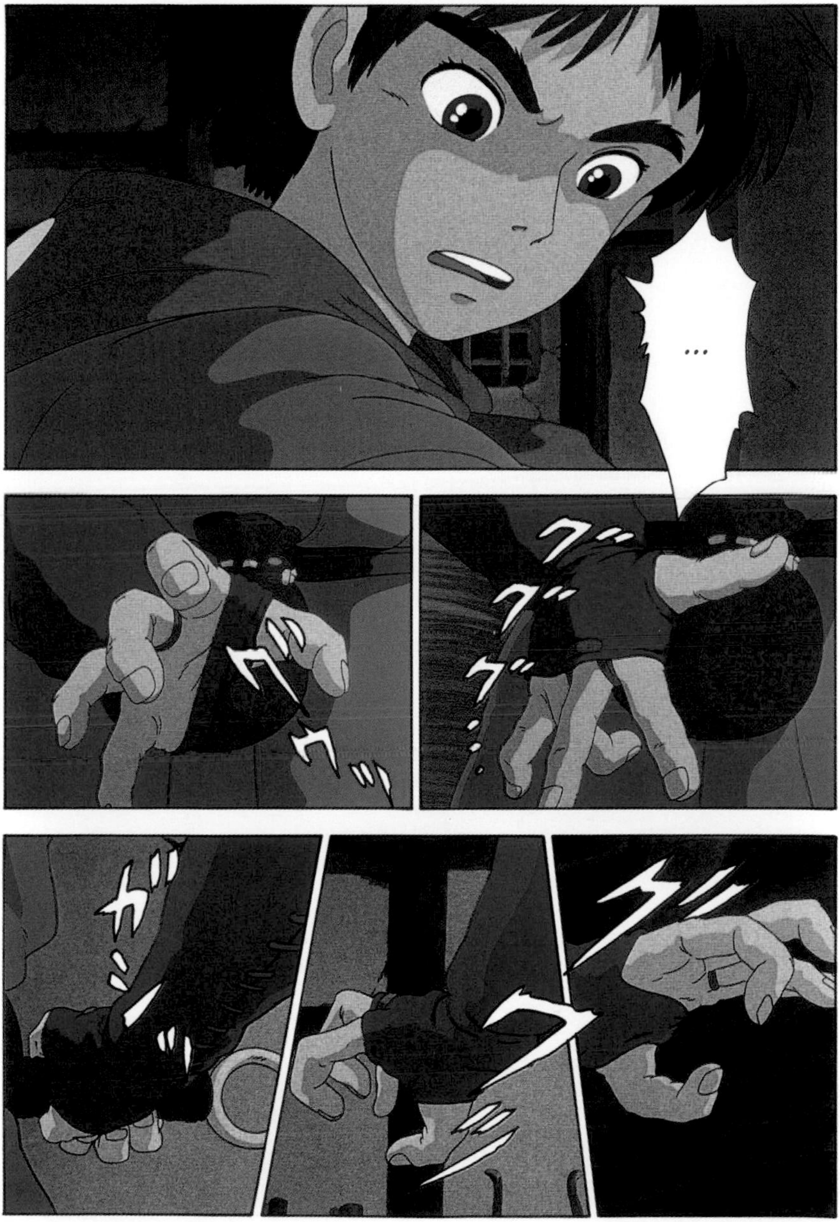
...

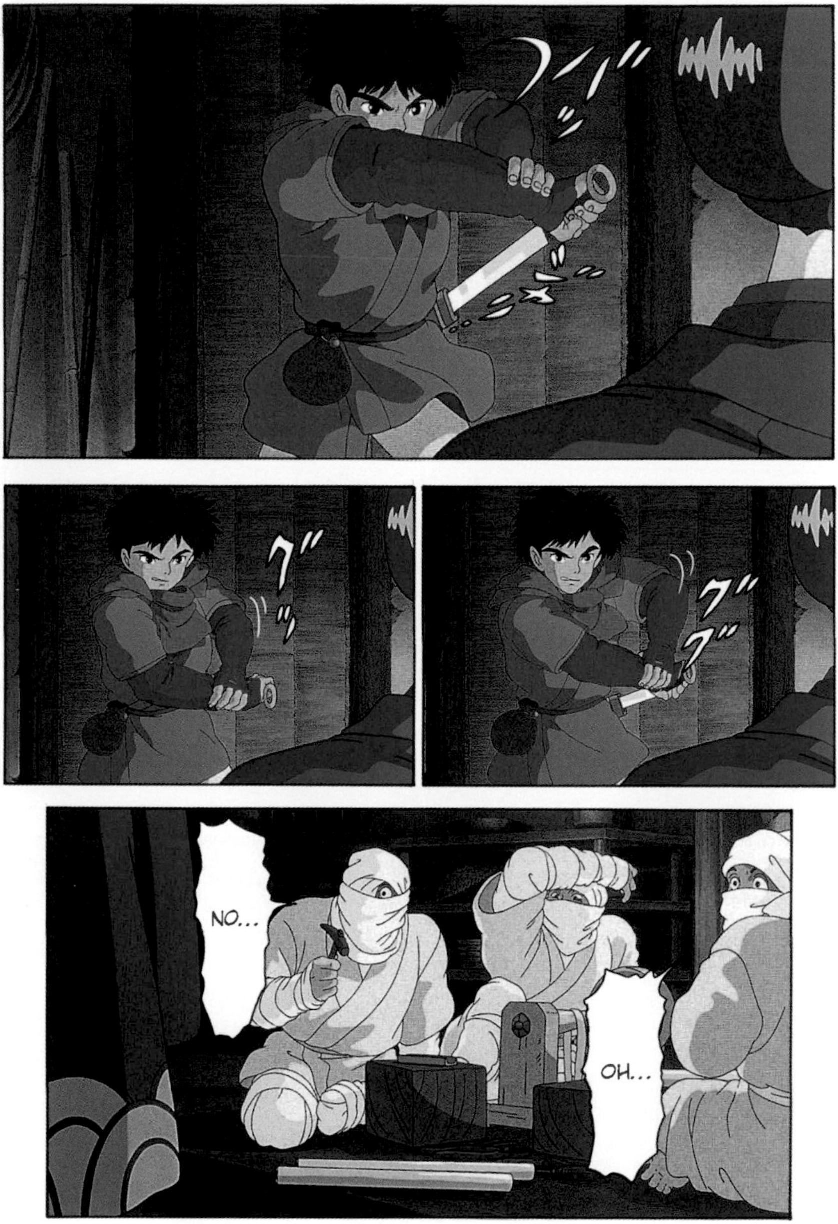
NO...
OH...

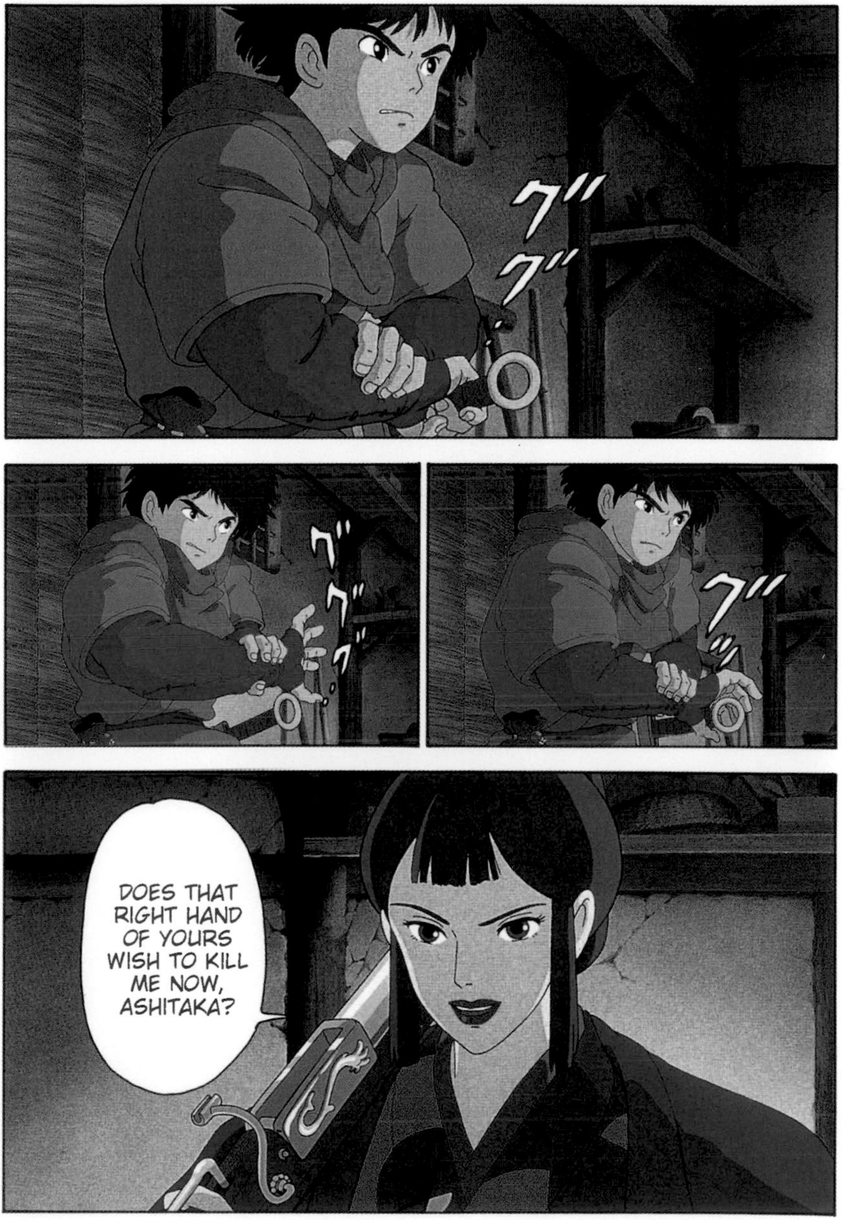
ググ
グッ
グググ
DOES THAT RIGHT HAND OF YOURS WISH TO KILL ME NOW, ASHITAKA?

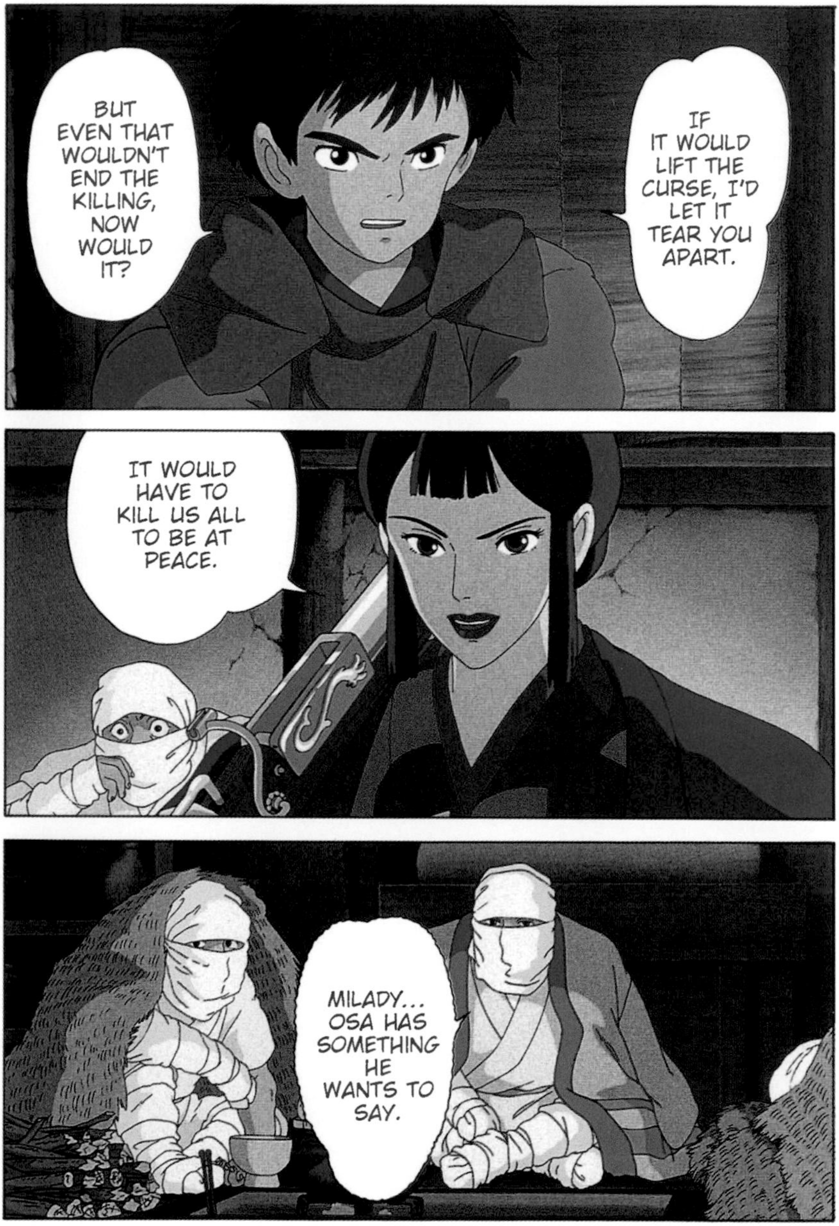
IF IT WOULD LIFT THE CURSE, I'D LET IT TEAR YOU APART.
BUT EVEN THAT WOULDN'T END THE KILLING, NOW WOULD IT?
IT WOULD HAVE TO KILL US ALL TO BE AT PEACE.
MILADY... OSA HAS SOMETHING HE WANTS TO SAY.

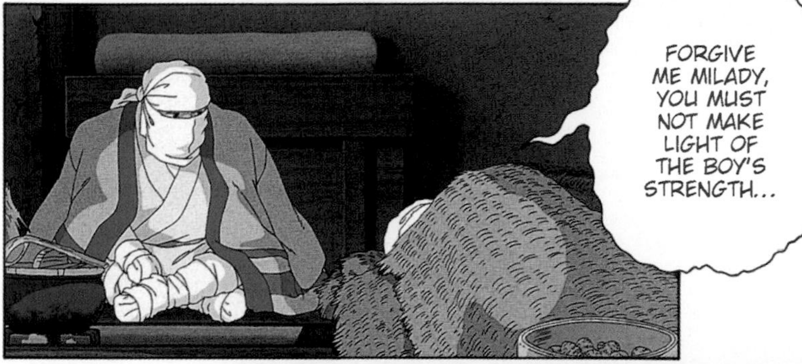
FORGIVE ME MILADY, YOU MUST NOT MAKE LIGHT OF THE BOY'S STRENGTH...

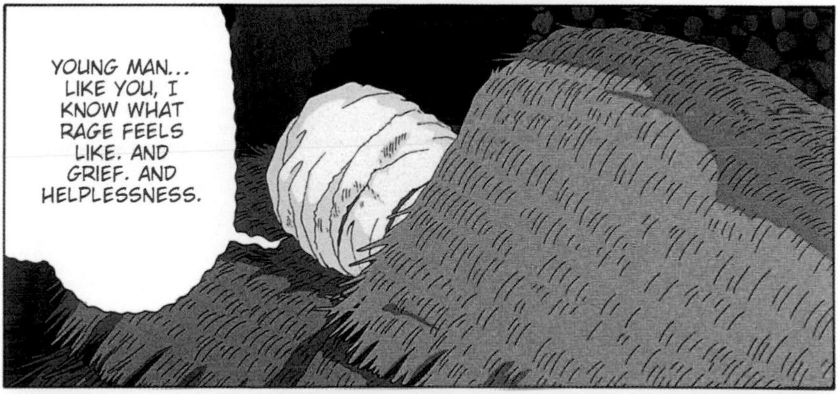
YOUNG MAN... LIKE YOU, I KNOW WHAT RAGE FEELS LIKE. AND GRIEF. AND HELPLESSNESS.

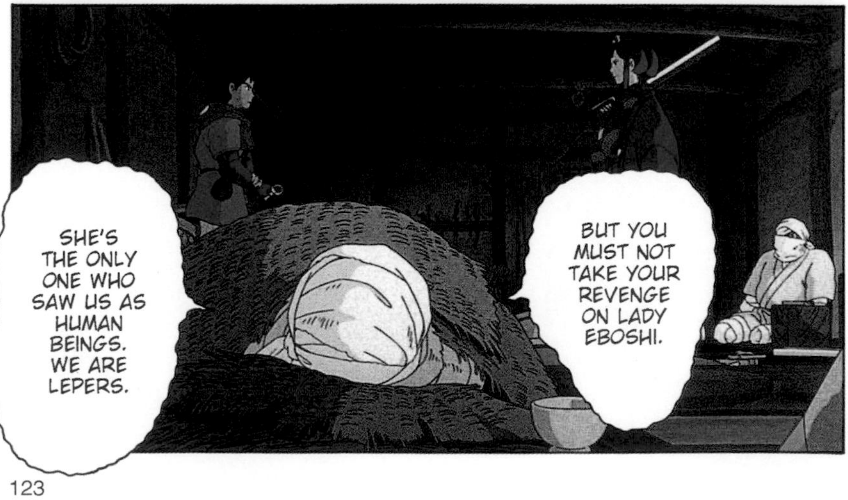
BUT YOU MUST NOT TAKE YOUR REVENGE ON LADY EBOSHI.
SHE'S THE ONLY ONE WHO SAW US AS HUMAN BEINGS. WE ARE LEPERS.

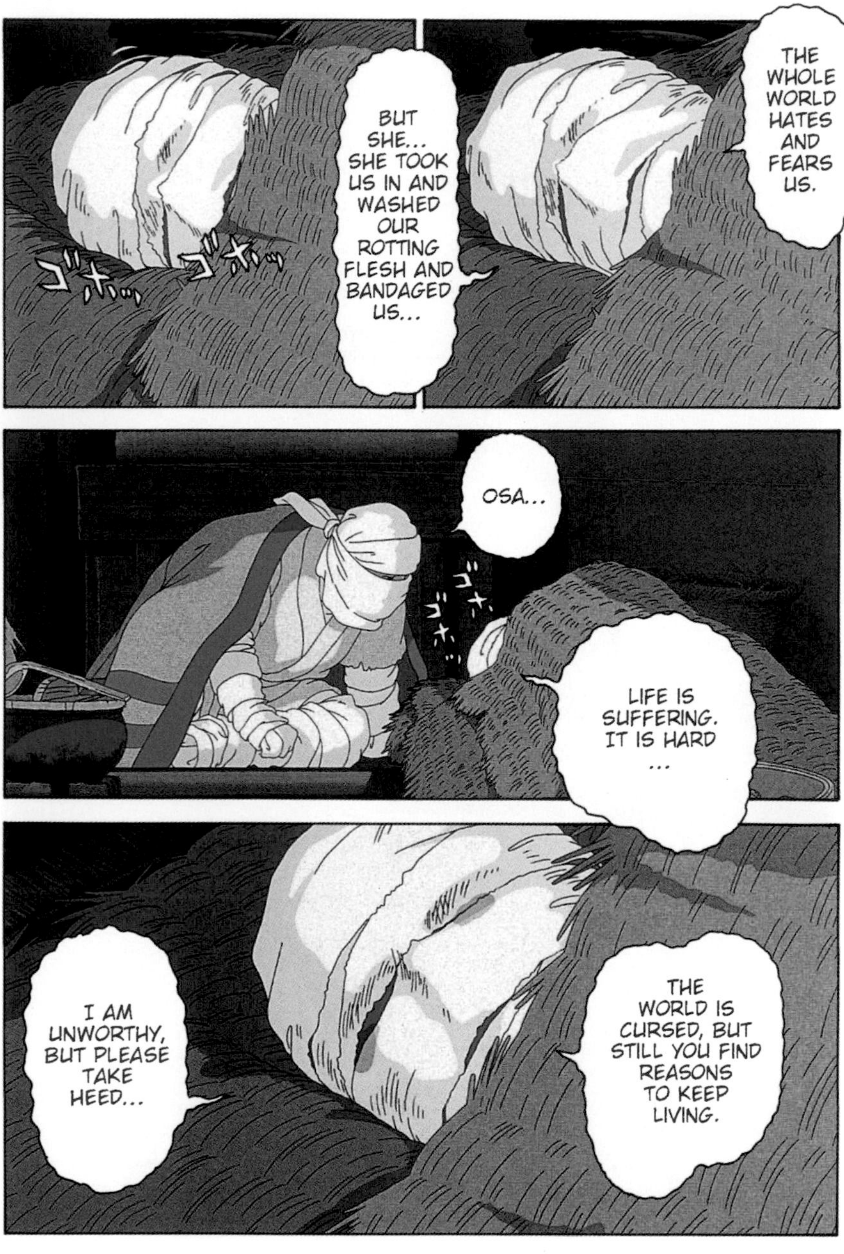
THE WHOLE WORLD HATES AND FEARS US.
BUT SHE... SHE TOOK US IN AND WASHED OUR ROTTING FLESH AND BANDAGED US...
OSA...
LIFE IS SUFFERING. IT IS HARD ...
THE WORLD IS CURSED, BUT STILL YOU FIND REASONS TO KEEP LIVING.
I AM UNWORTHY, BUT PLEASE TAKE HEED...

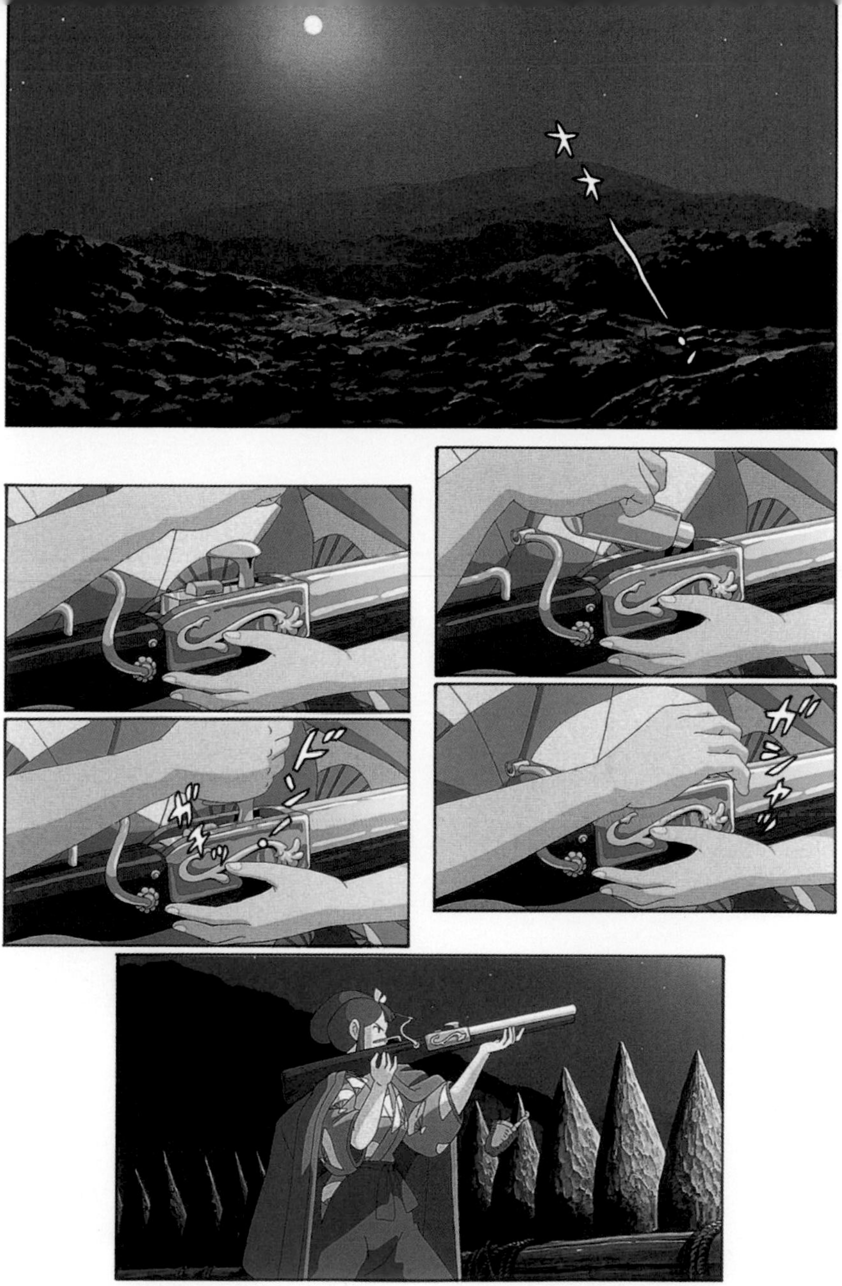
ガシャッ
ドーン
ガチッ

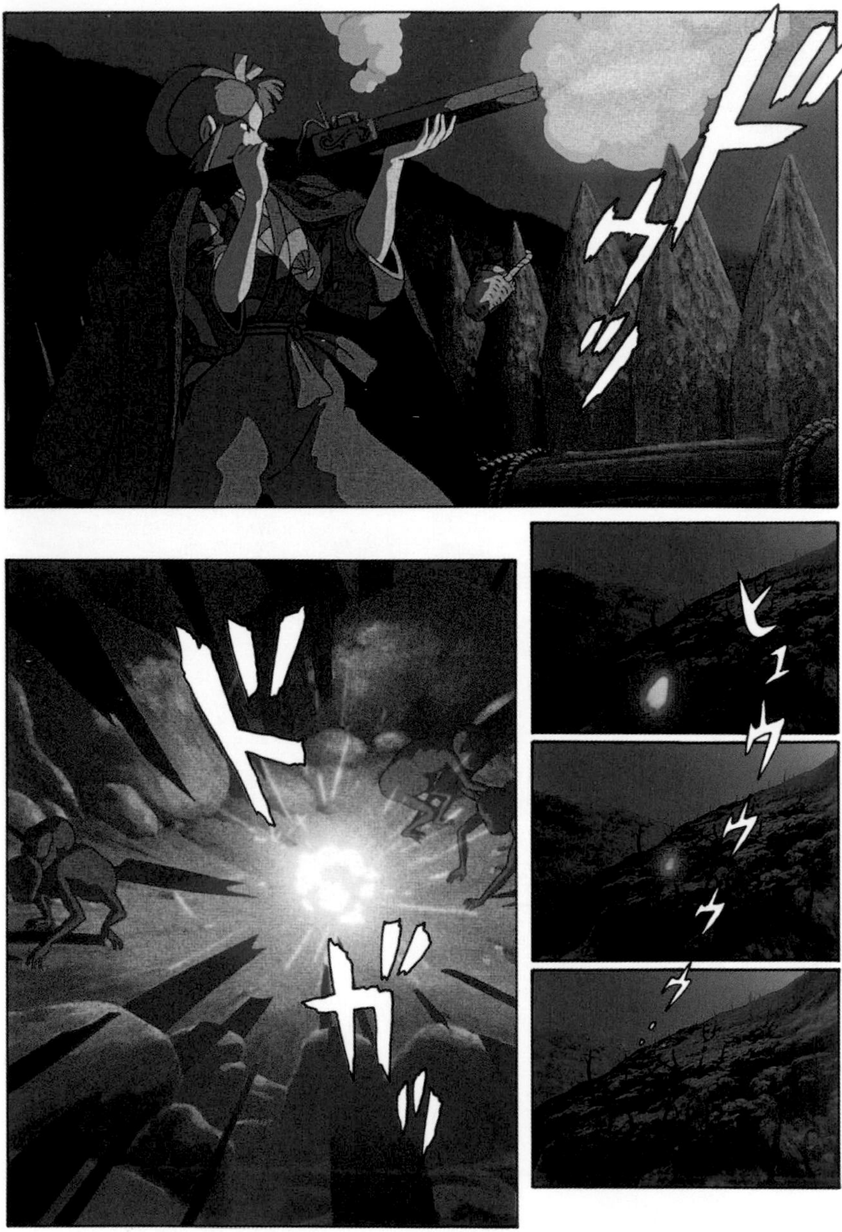
ドドウッ
ヒュウゥゥゥ…
ドガッ

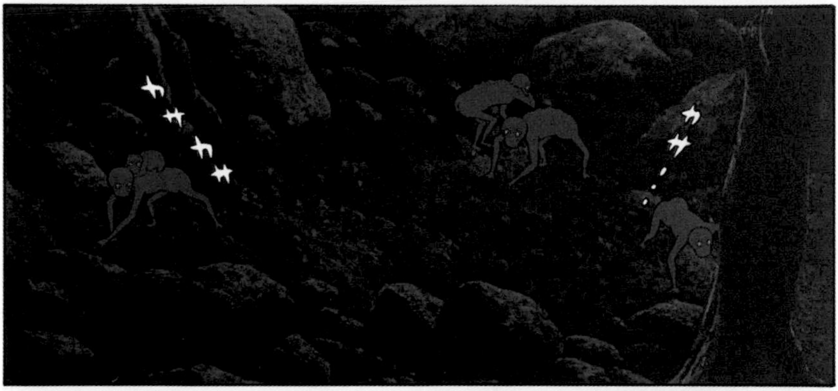

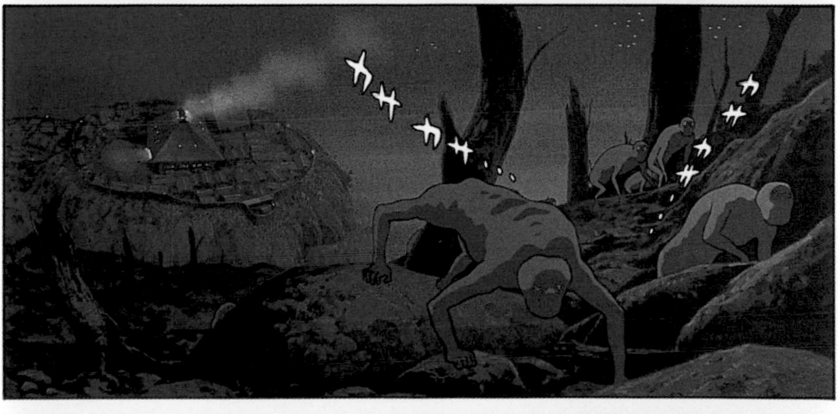

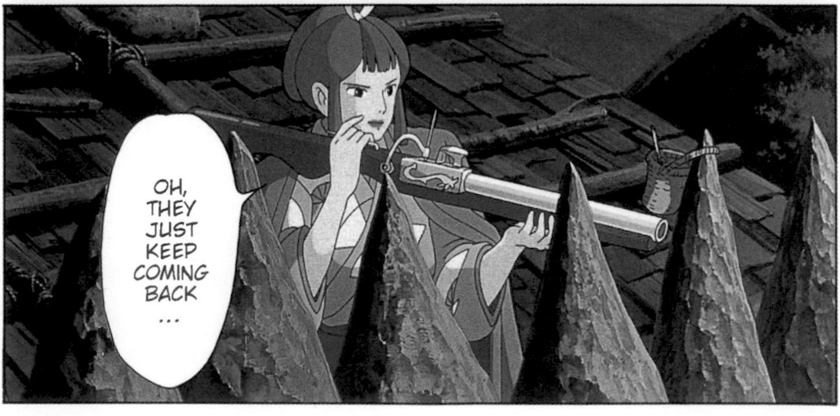
OH, THEY JUST KEEP COMING BACK ...

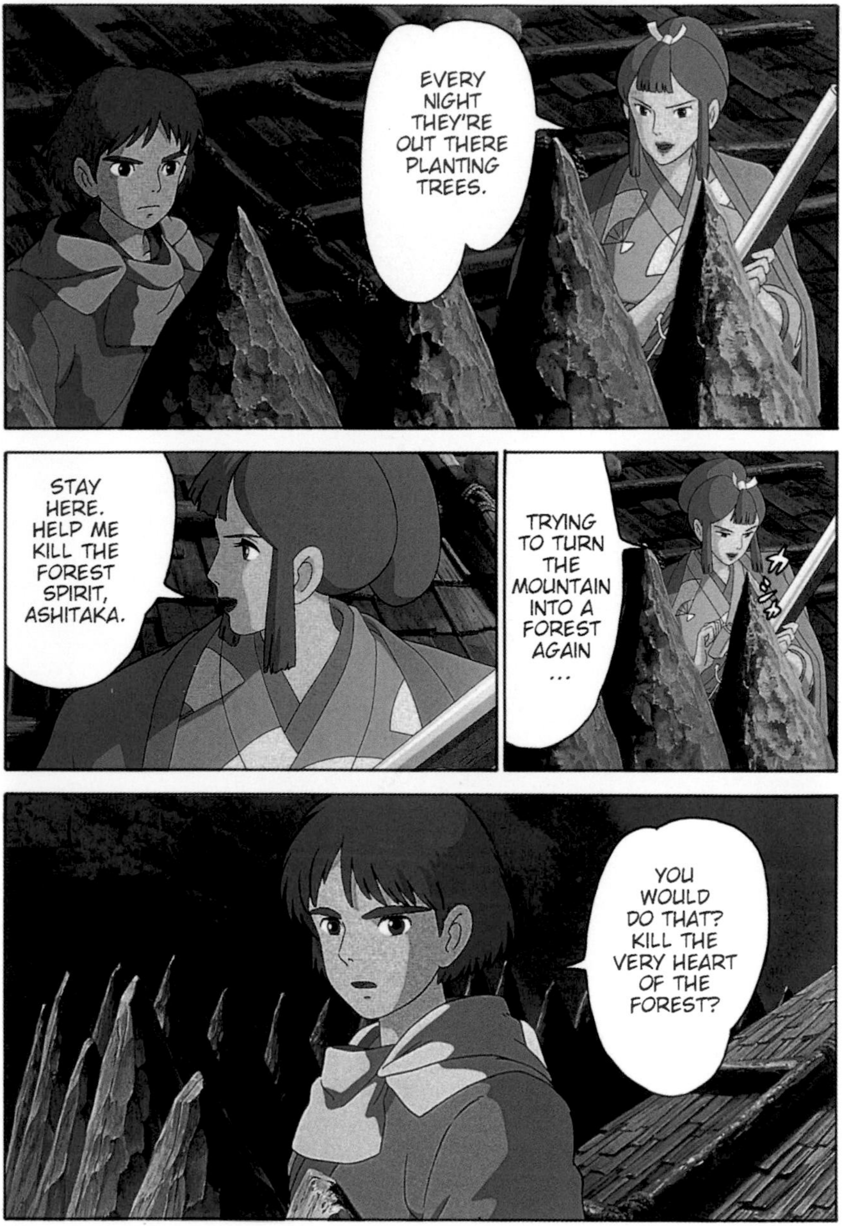
EVERY NIGHT THEY'RE OUT THERE PLANTING TREES.
TRYING TO TURN THE MOUNTAIN INTO A FOREST AGAIN ...
STAY HERE. HELP ME KILL THE FOREST SPIRIT, ASHITAKA.
YOU WOULD DO THAT? KILL THE VERY HEART OF THE FOREST?

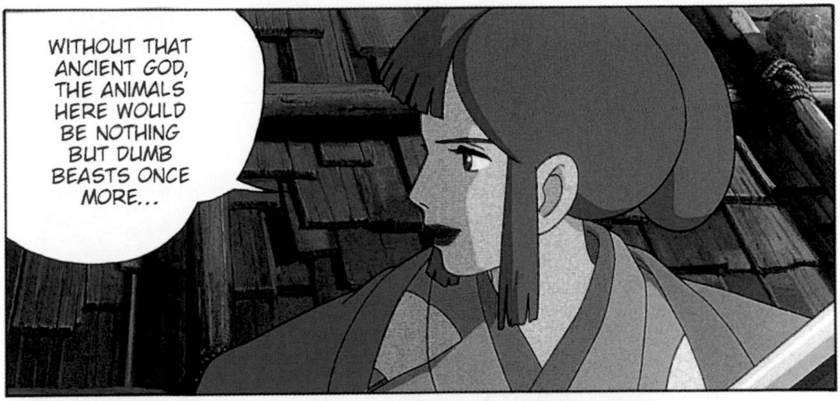
WITHOUT THAT ANCIENT GOD, THE ANIMALS HERE WOULD BE NOTHING BUT DUMB BEASTS ONCE MORE...

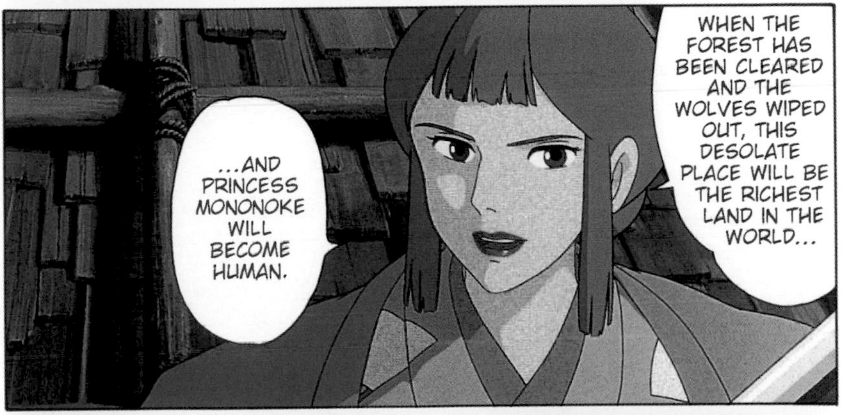
WHEN THE FOREST HAS BEEN CLEARED AND THE WOLVES WIPED OUT, THIS DESOLATE PLACE WILL BE THE RICHEST LAND IN THE WORLD...
...AND PRINCESS MONONOKE WILL BECOME HUMAN.

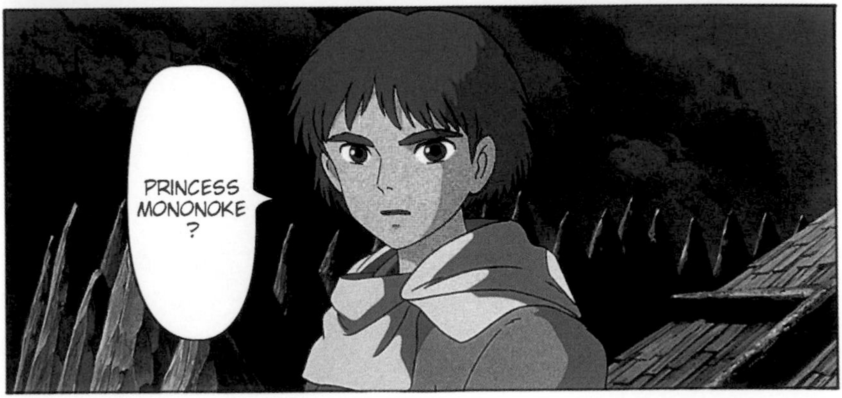
PRINCESS MONONOKE ?

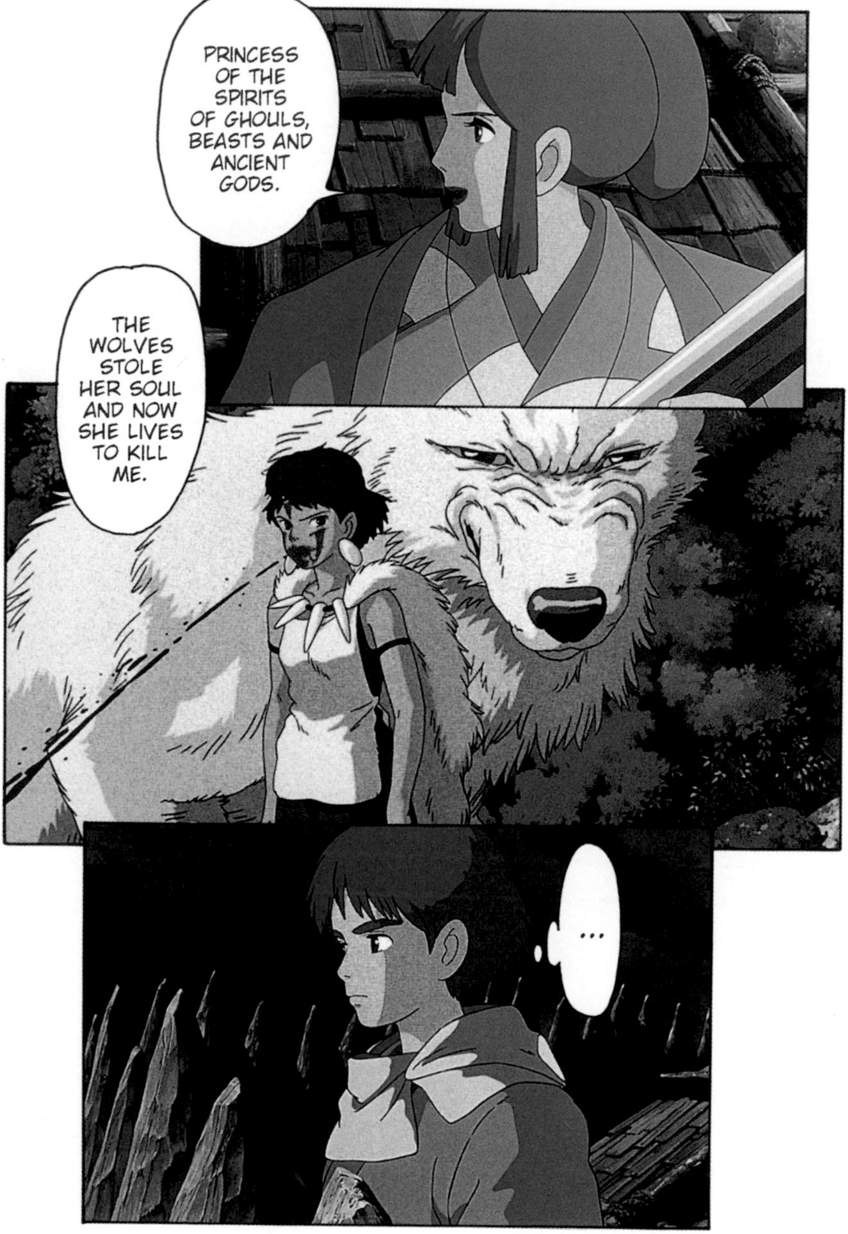
PRINCESS OF THE SPIRITS OF GHOULS, BEASTS AND ANCIENT GODS.
THE WOLVES STOLE HER SOUL AND NOW SHE LIVES TO KILL ME.
...

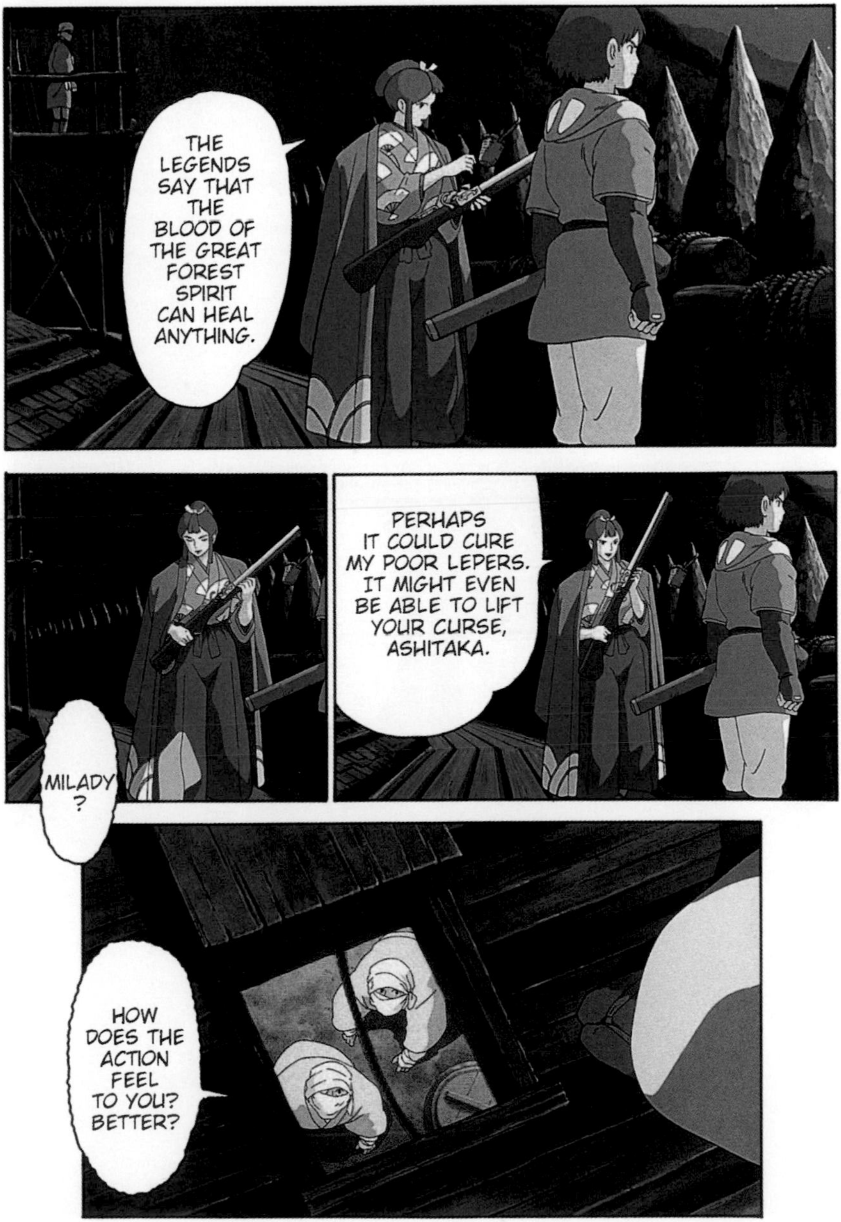
THE LEGENDS SAY THAT THE BLOOD OF THE GREAT FOREST SPIRIT CAN HEAL ANYTHING.
PERHAPS IT COULD CURE MY POOR LEPERS. IT MIGHT EVEN BE ABLE TO LIFT YOUR CURSE, ASHITAKA.
MILADY?
HOW DOES THE ACTION FEEL TO YOU? BETTER?

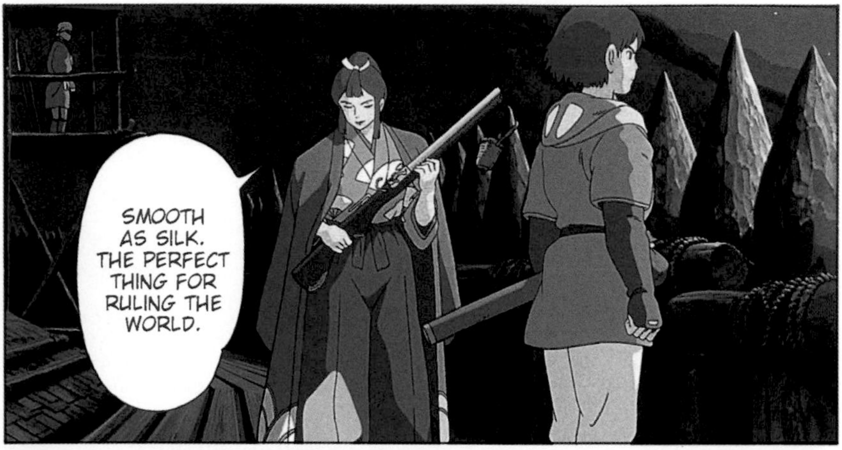
SMOOTH AS SILK. THE PERFECT THING FOR RULING THE WORLD.
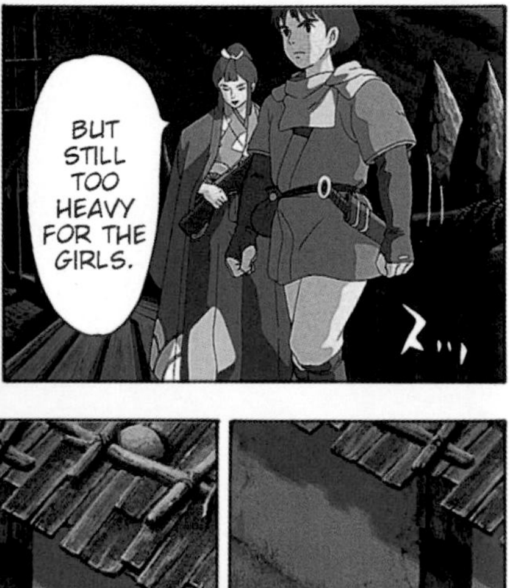
BUT STILL TOO HEAVY FOR THE GIRLS.
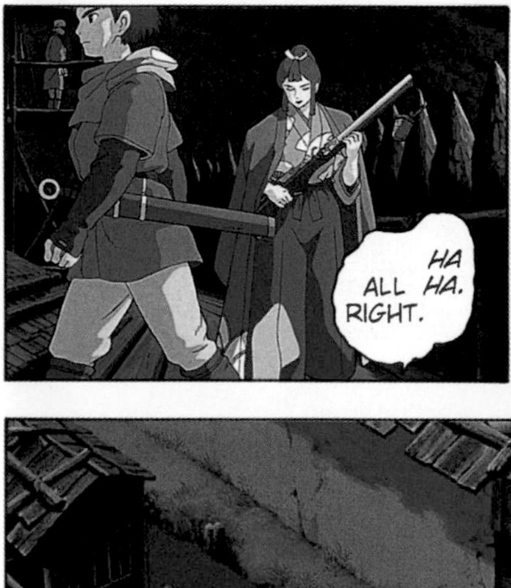
HA HA. ALL RIGHT.
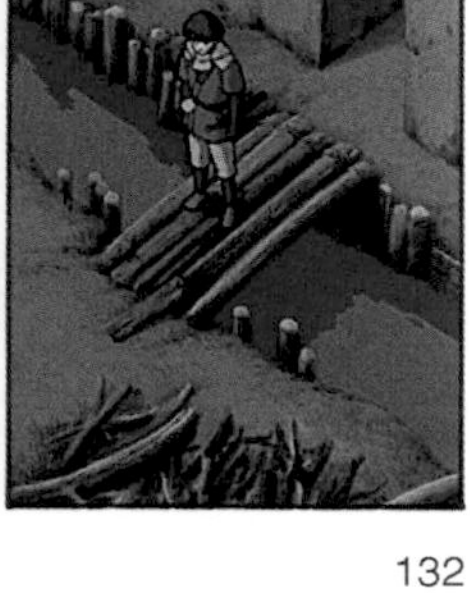
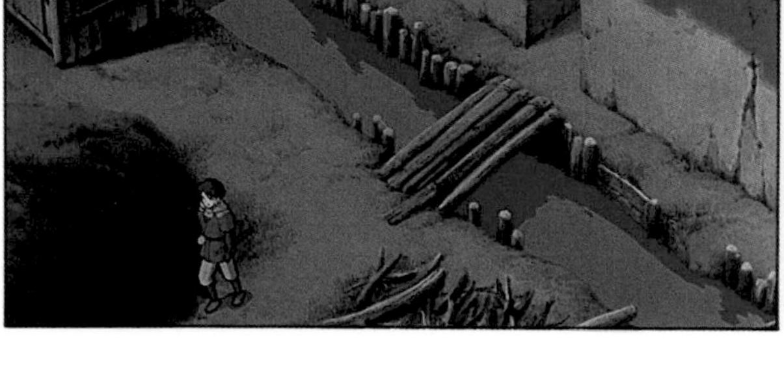

ツカ
ツカ

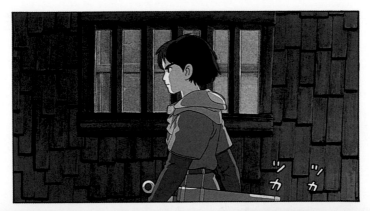

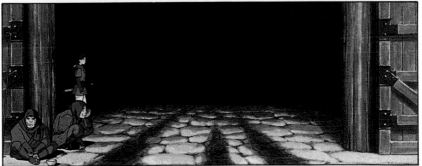

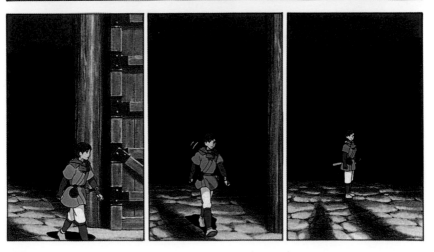

WELL, LOOK WHO'S HERE.

UH?

GOOD EVENING. IS IT ALL RIGHT IF I WORK THE BELLOW FOR A WHILE?

HEY, WAIT.

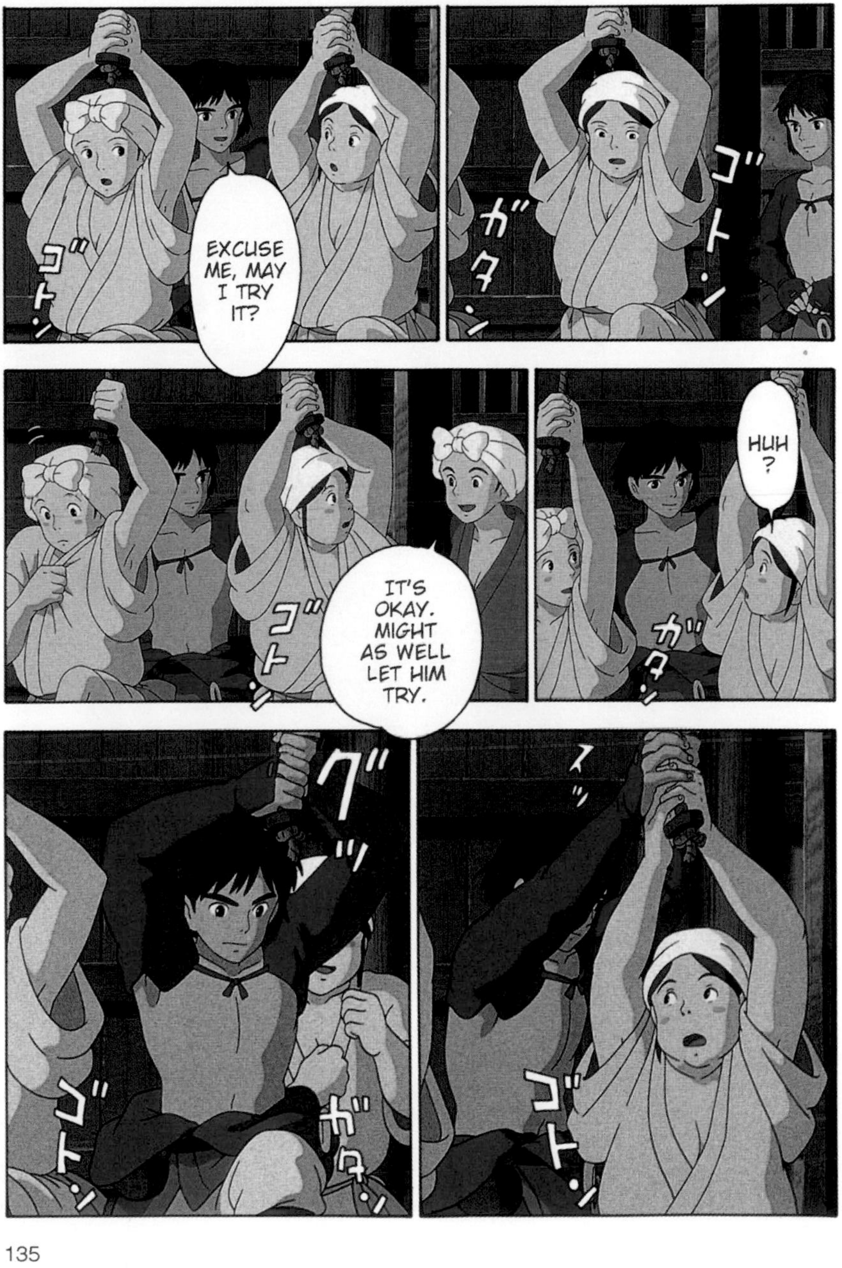
ゴトン
ガタン
ゴトン
EXCUSE ME, MAY I TRY IT?
HUH?
ガタン
ゴトン
IT'S OKAY. MIGHT AS WELL LET HIM TRY.
スッ
ゴトン
グッ
ゴトン
ガタン

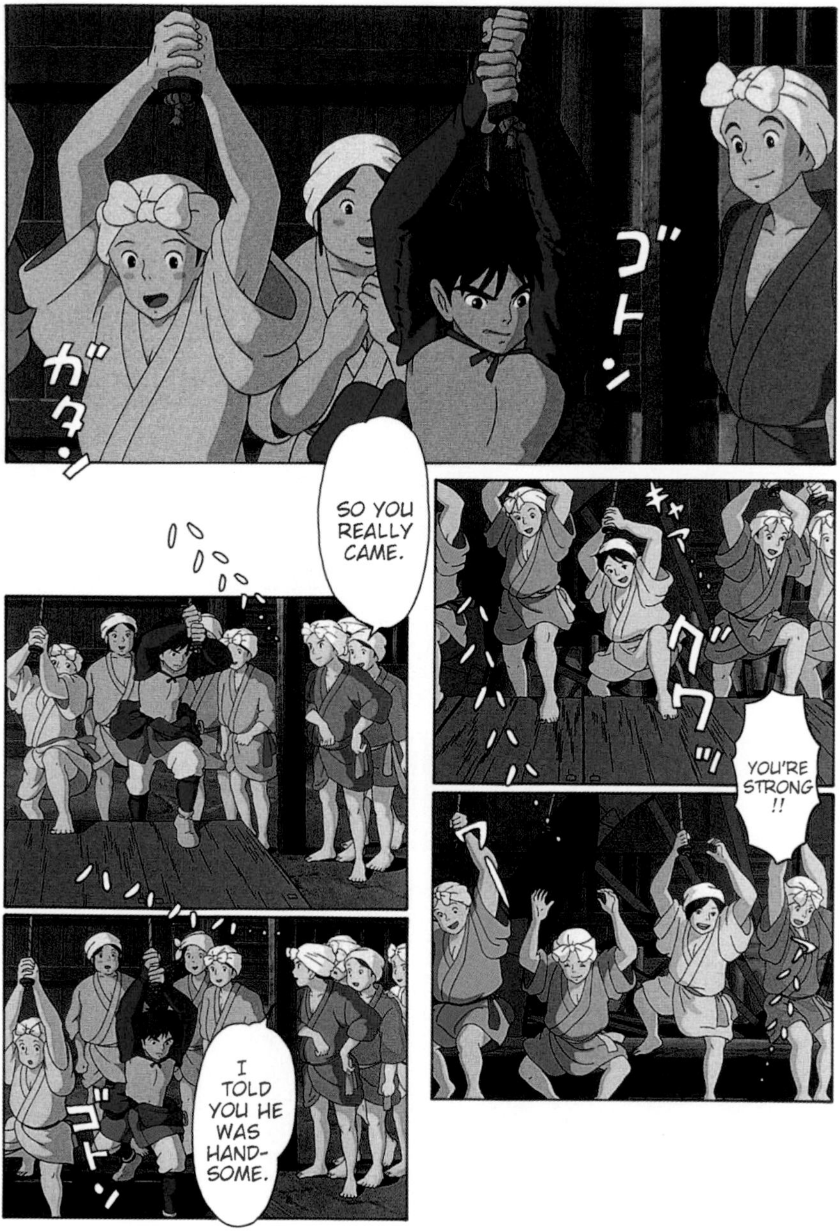
ゴトン
ガタン
キャア
YOU'RE STRONG!!
SO YOU REALLY CAME.
I TOLD YOU HE WAS HAND-SOME.
ゴトン

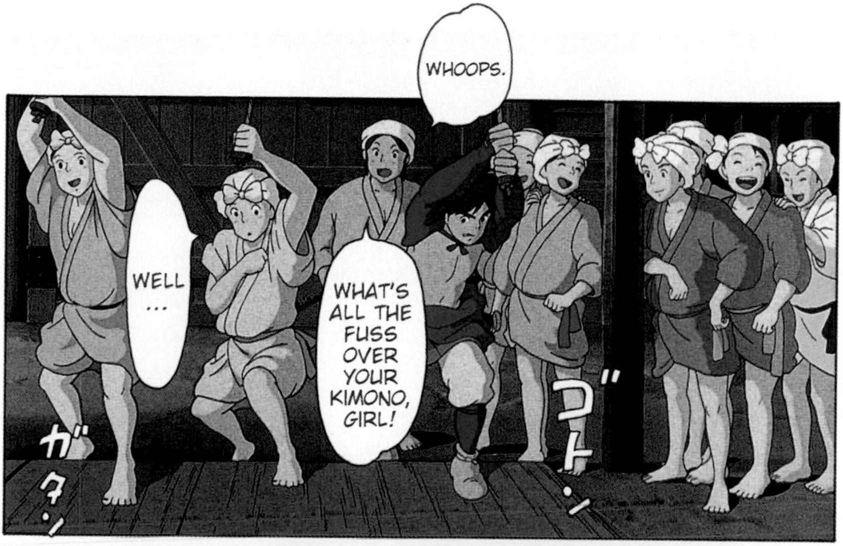
WHOOPS.
ゴトッ
WHAT'S ALL THE FUSS OVER YOUR KIMONO, GIRL!
WELL ...
ガタッ

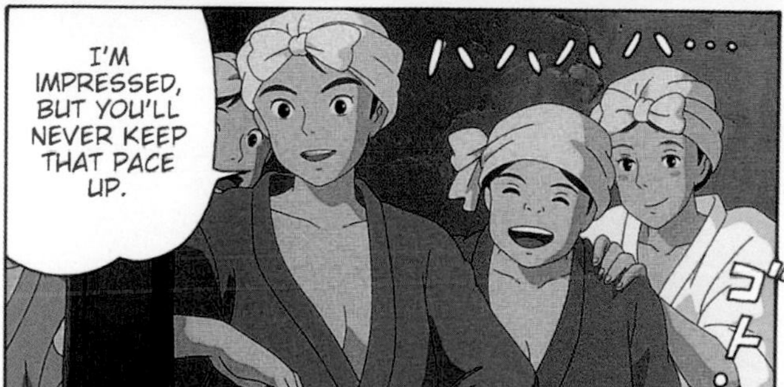
ハハハハ...
ゴトッ
I'M IMPRESSED, BUT YOU'LL NEVER KEEP THAT PACE UP.

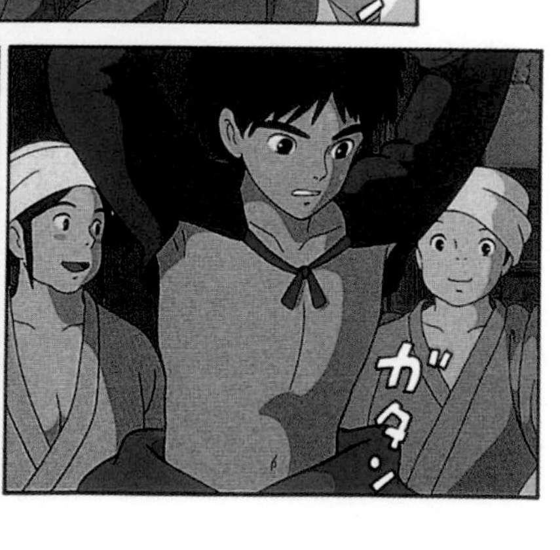
ガタッ

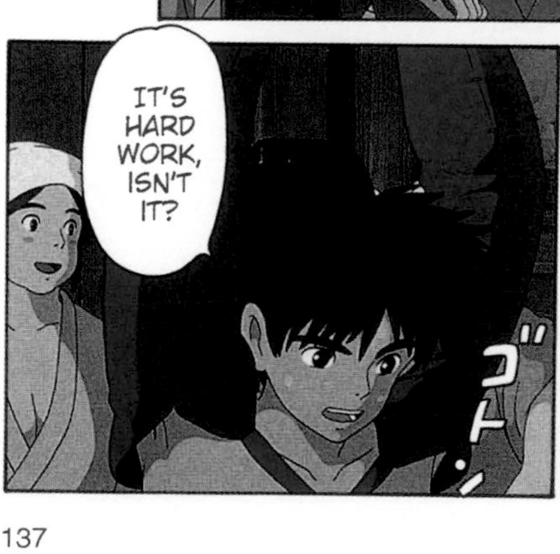
IT'S HARD WORK, ISN'T IT?
ゴトッ

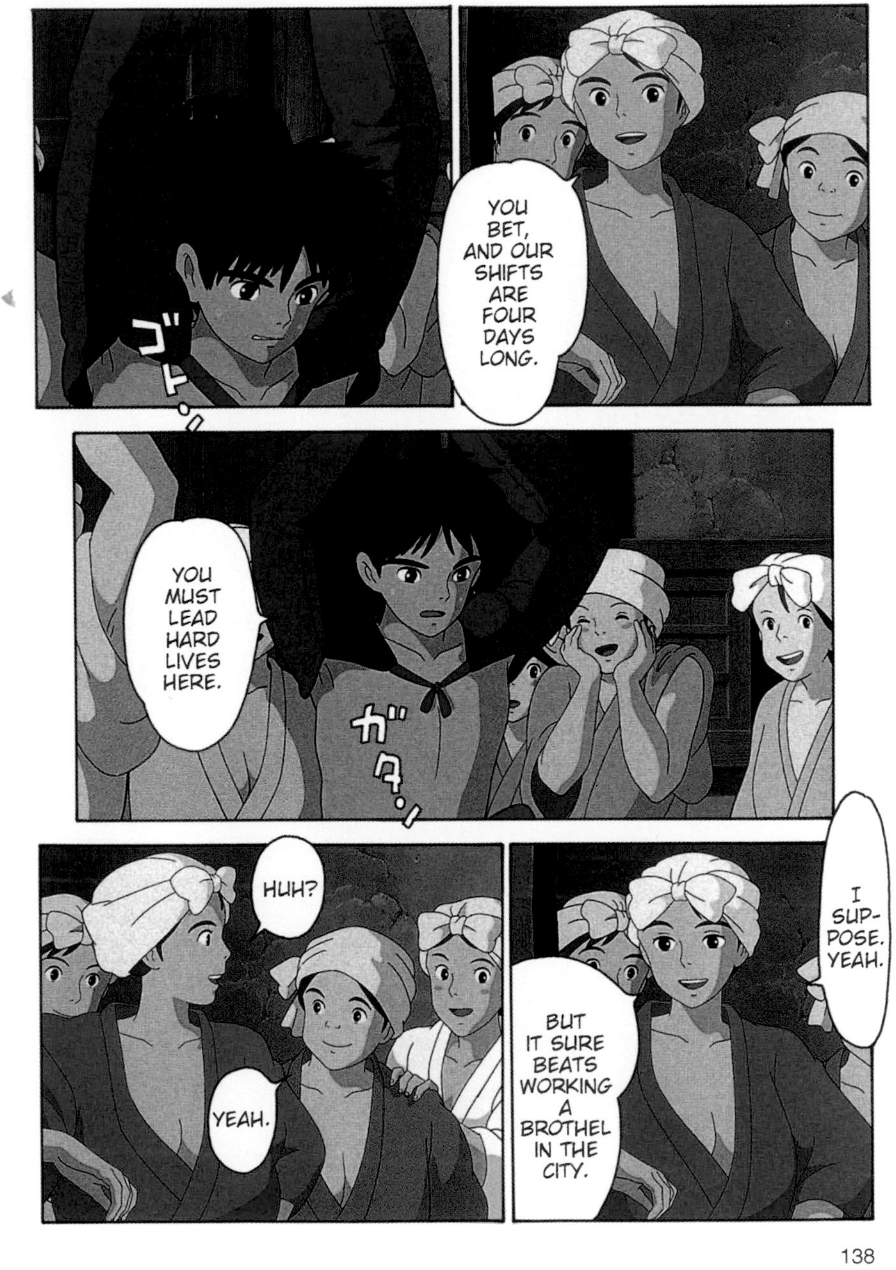
YOU BET, AND OUR SHIFTS ARE FOUR DAYS LONG.
ゴト
YOU MUST LEAD HARD LIVES HERE.
ガタ
I SUP-POSE. YEAH.
BUT IT SURE BEATS WORKING A BROTHEL IN THE CITY.
HUH?
YEAH.

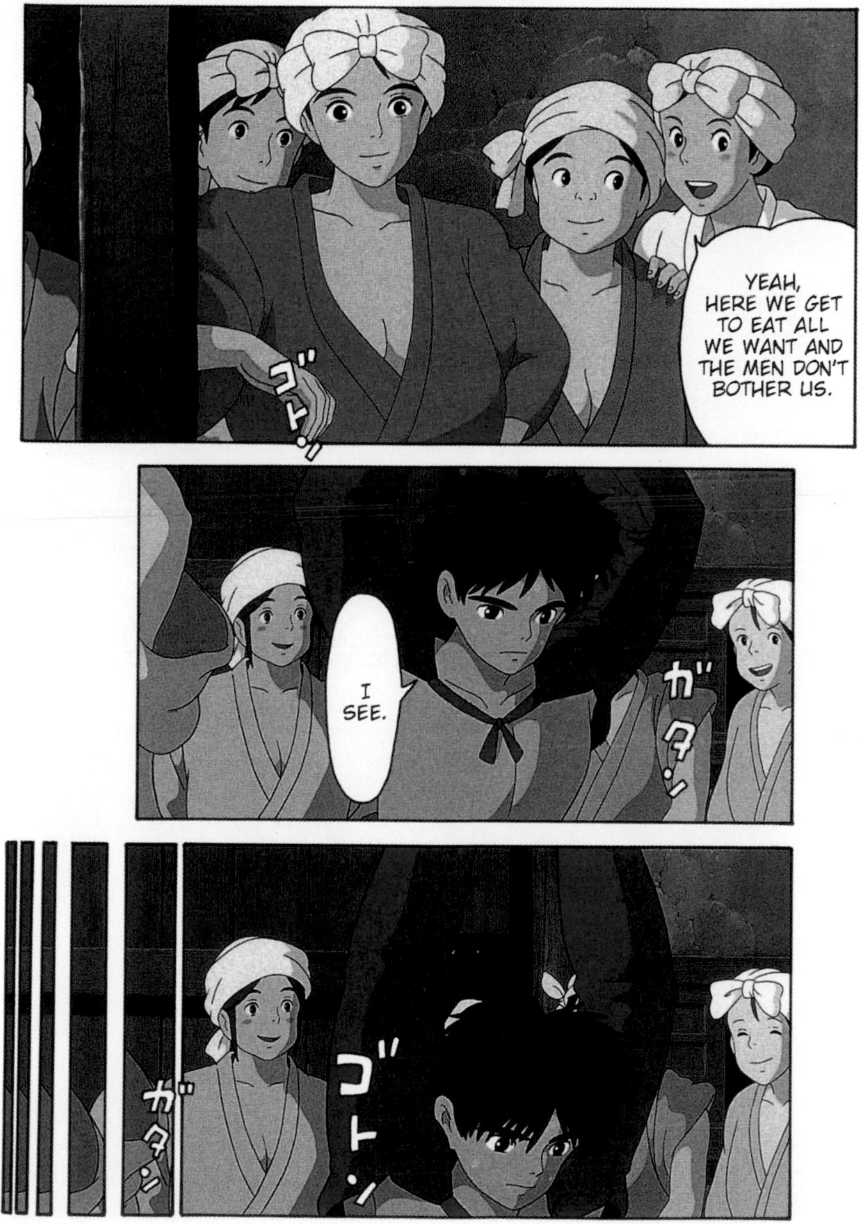
YEAH, HERE WE GET TO EAT ALL WE WANT AND THE MEN DON'T BOTHER US.
ゴトッ
ガタン
I SEE.
ゴトッ
ガタン

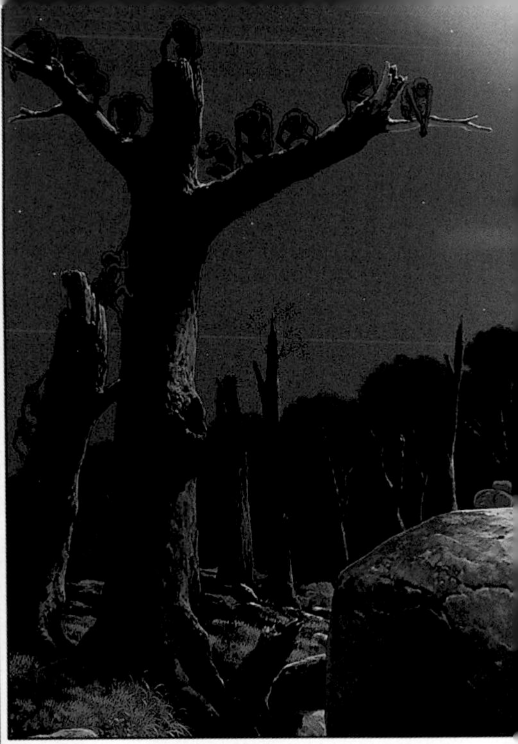

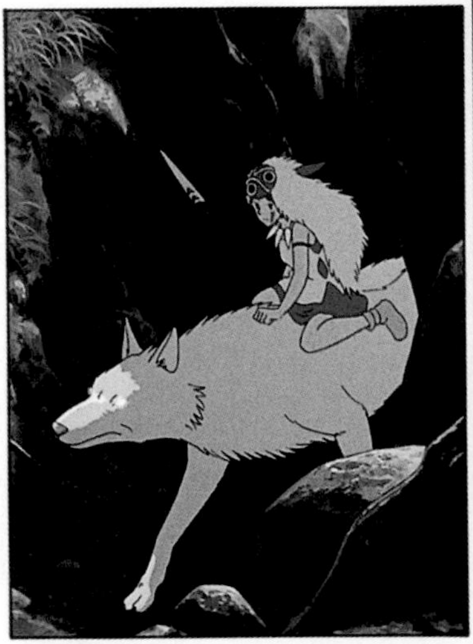

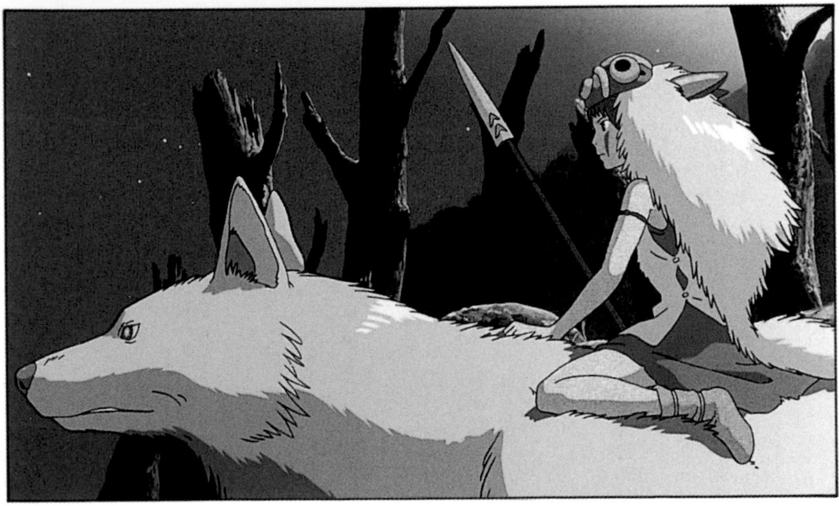

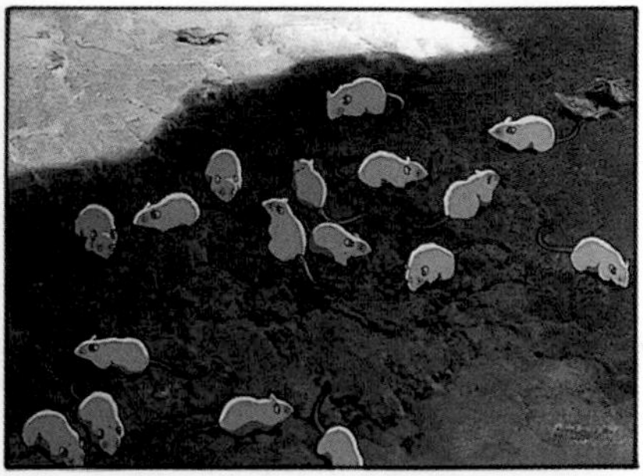
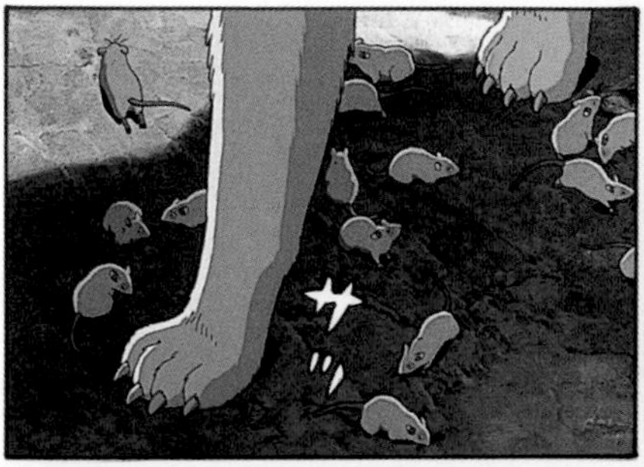
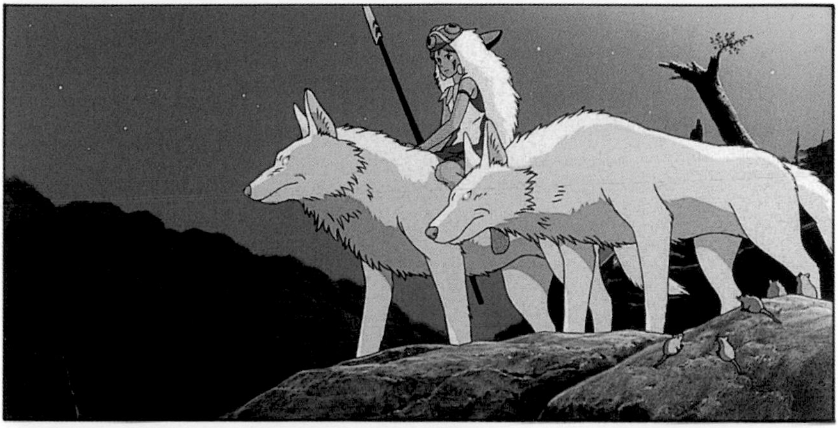
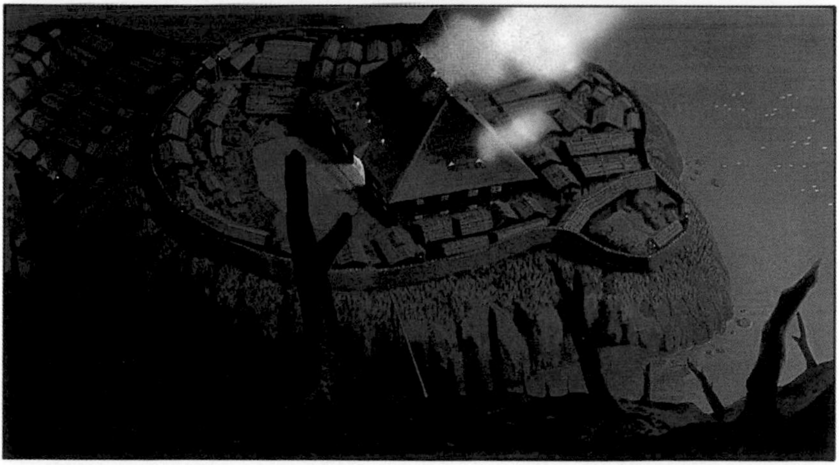

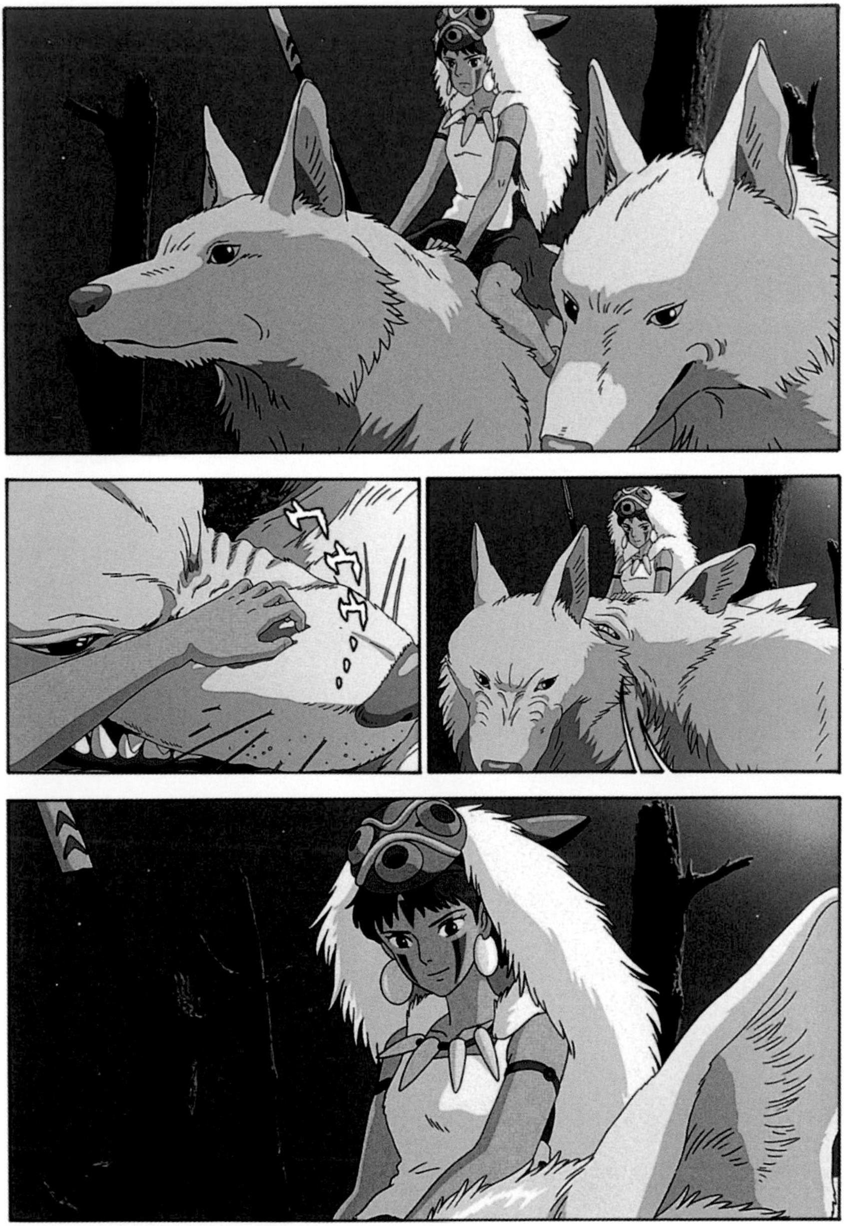

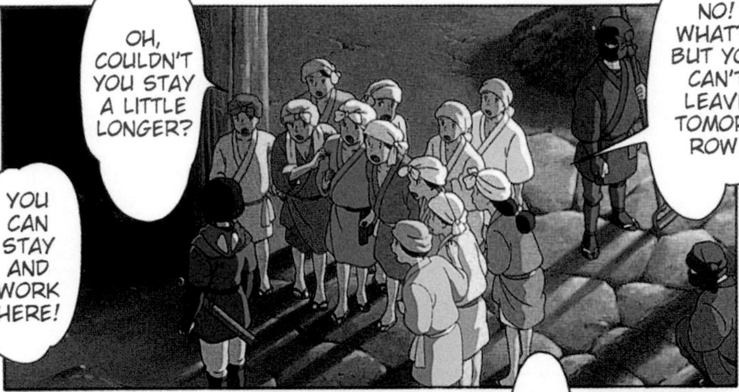
NO! WHAT?! BUT YOU CAN'T LEAVE TOMORROW.
OH, COULDN'T YOU STAY A LITTLE LONGER?
YOU CAN STAY AND WORK HERE!
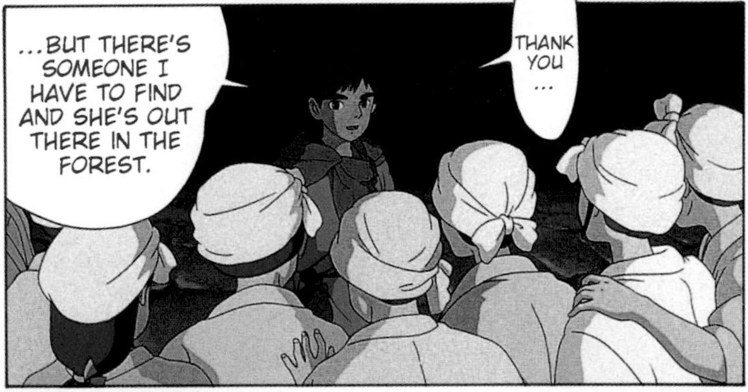
THANK YOU ...
...BUT THERE'S SOMEONE I HAVE TO FIND AND SHE'S OUT THERE IN THE FOREST.
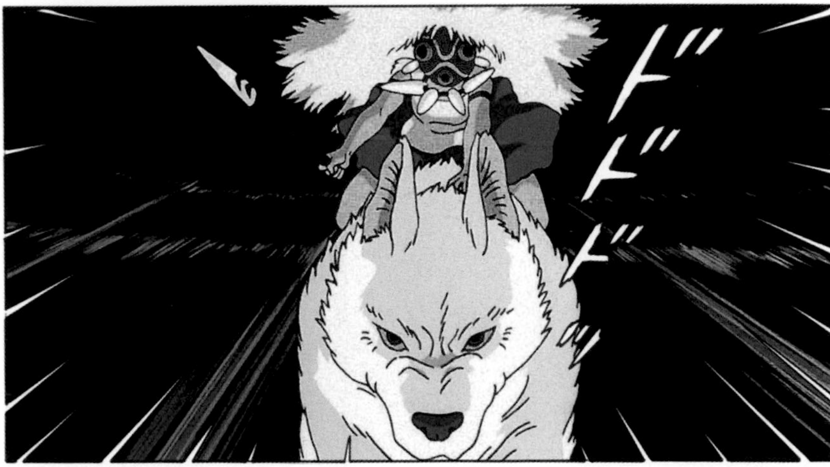
ドドドド

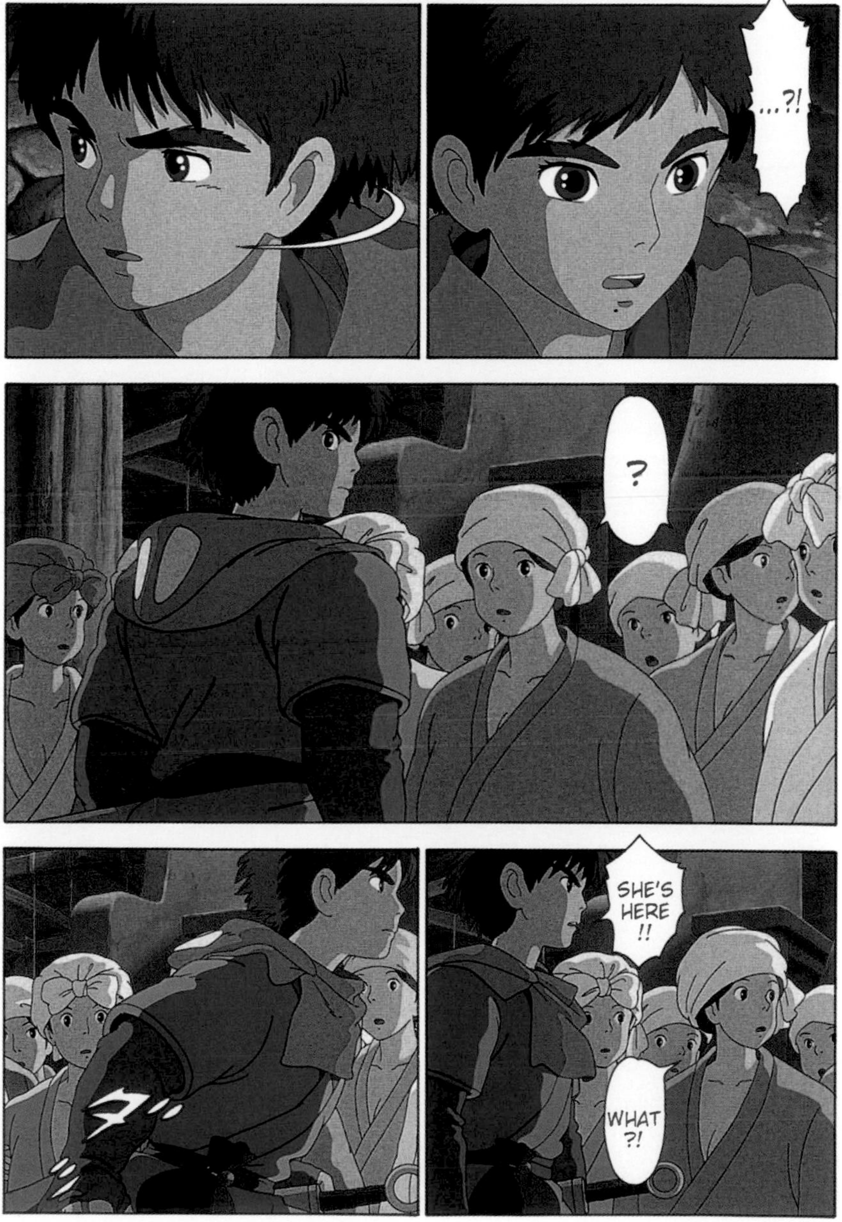
...?!
?
SHE'S HERE !!
WHAT ?!

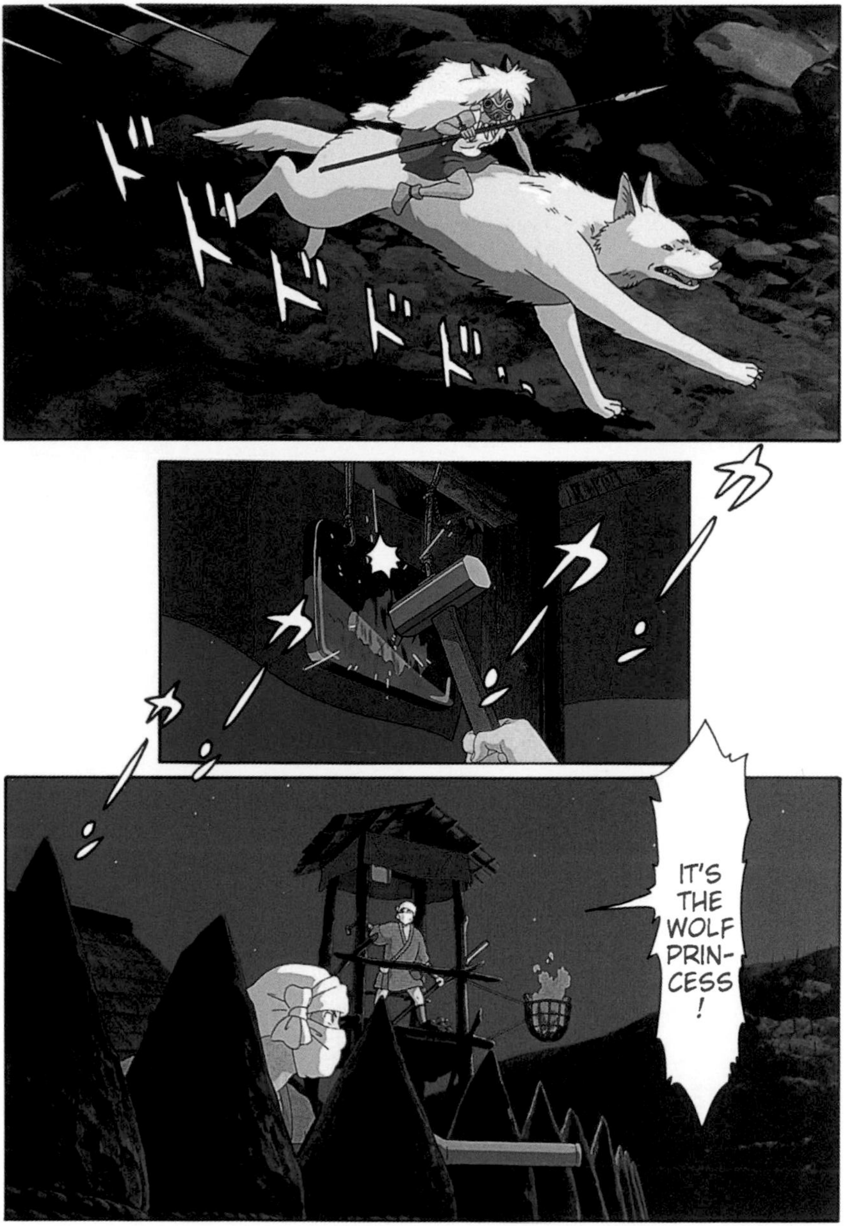
IT'S THE WOLF PRIN-CESS!

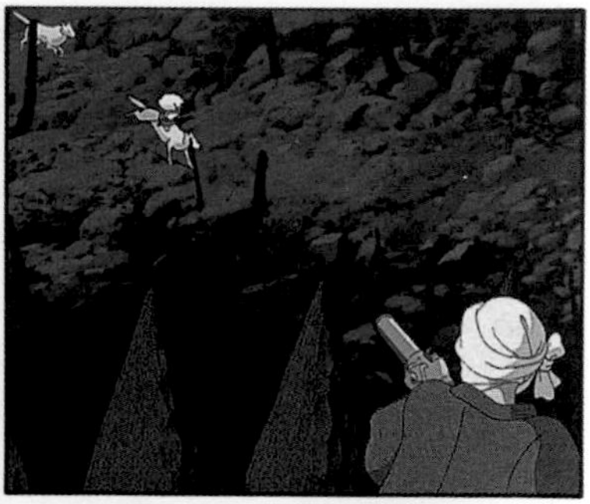
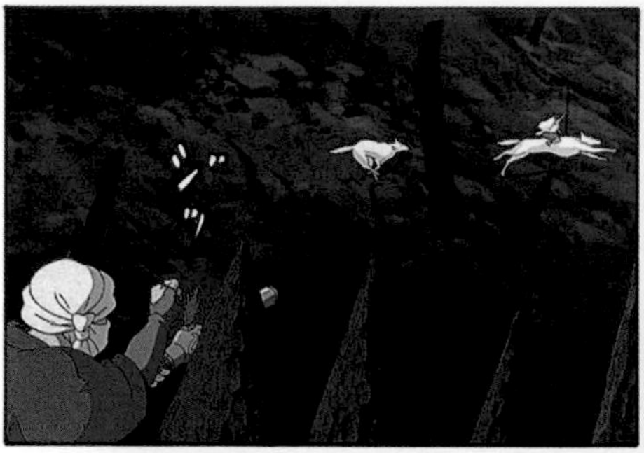
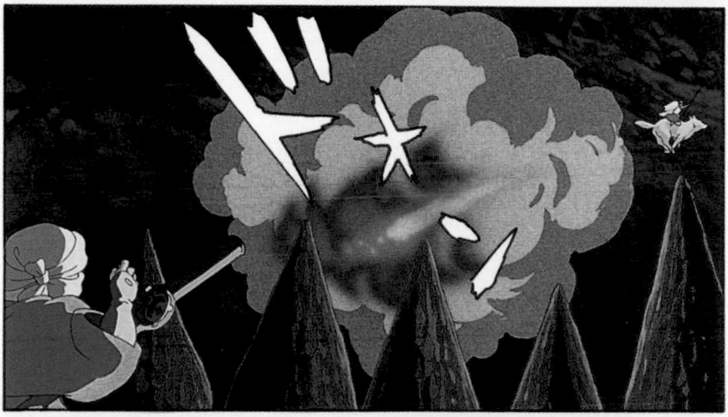
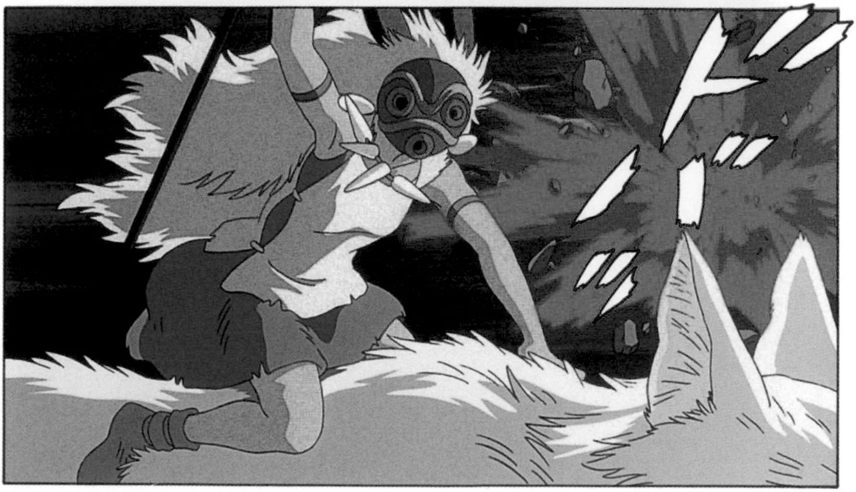

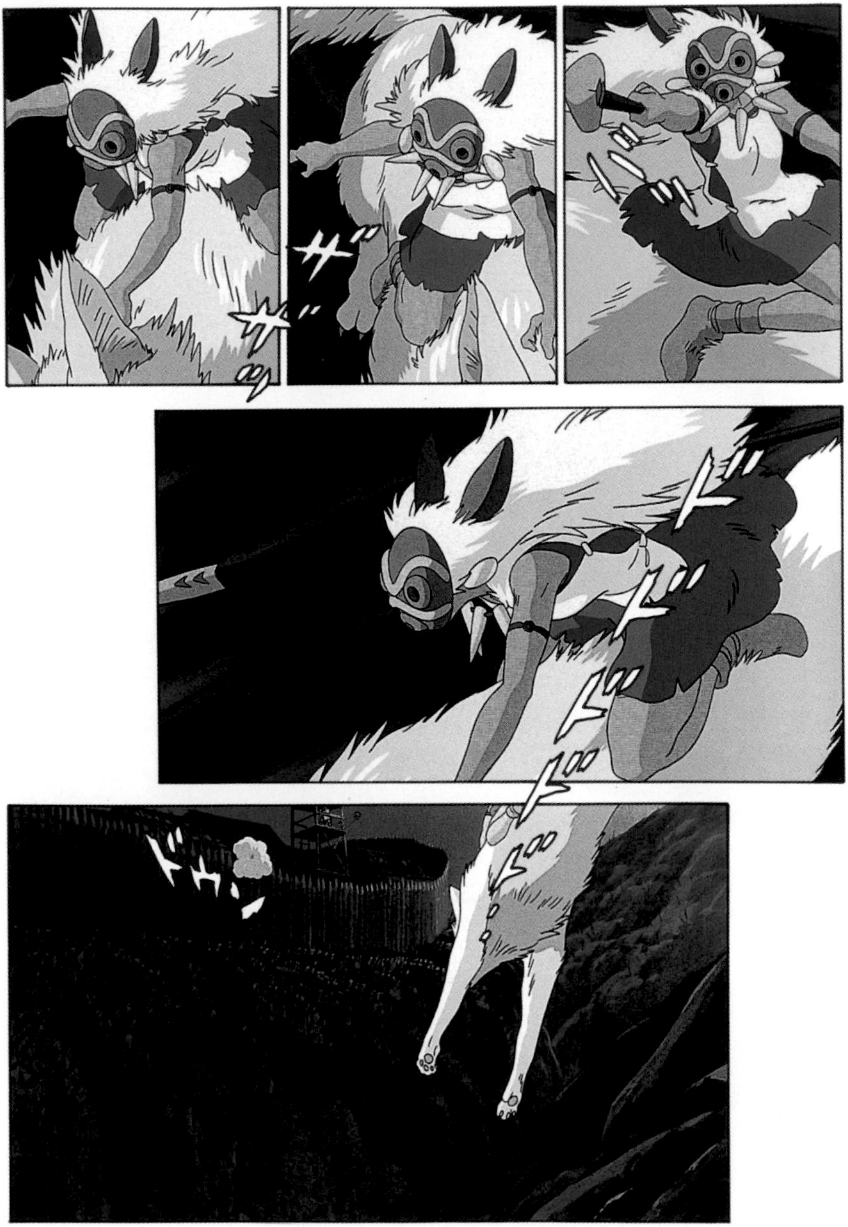
ザ
ザッ
ドッ
ドドドド
ドカッ

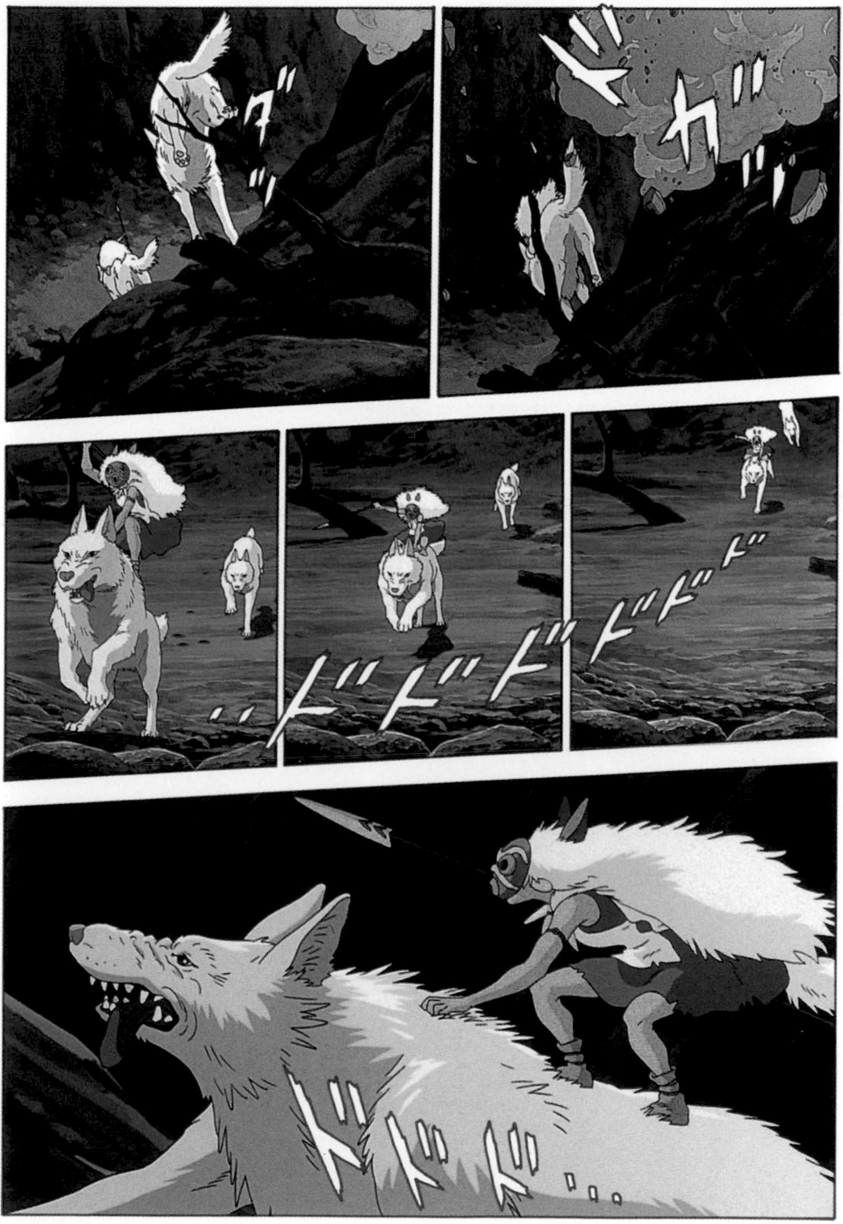
ズガガ
ドドド…

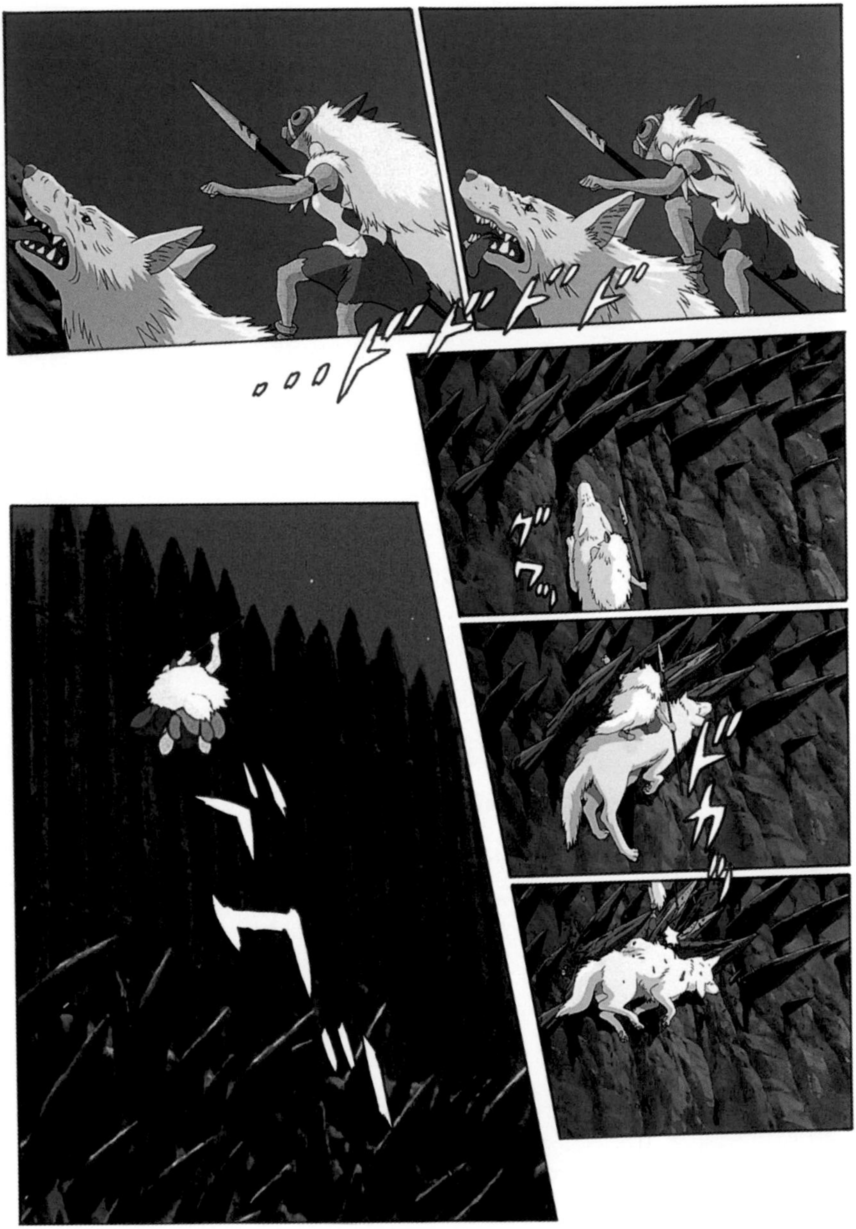
ドドドドド
グワッ
ドガッ

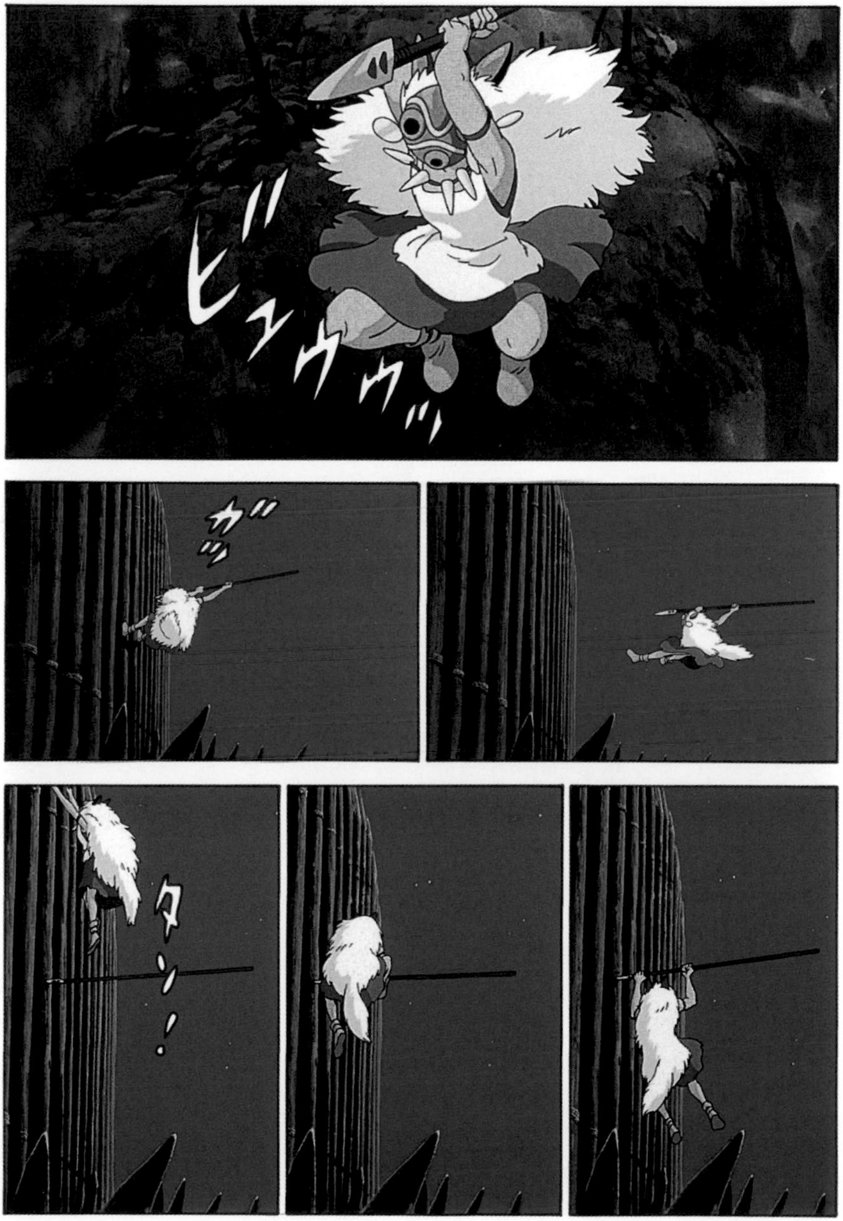
ビュウゥゥッ
ガッ
タンッ!

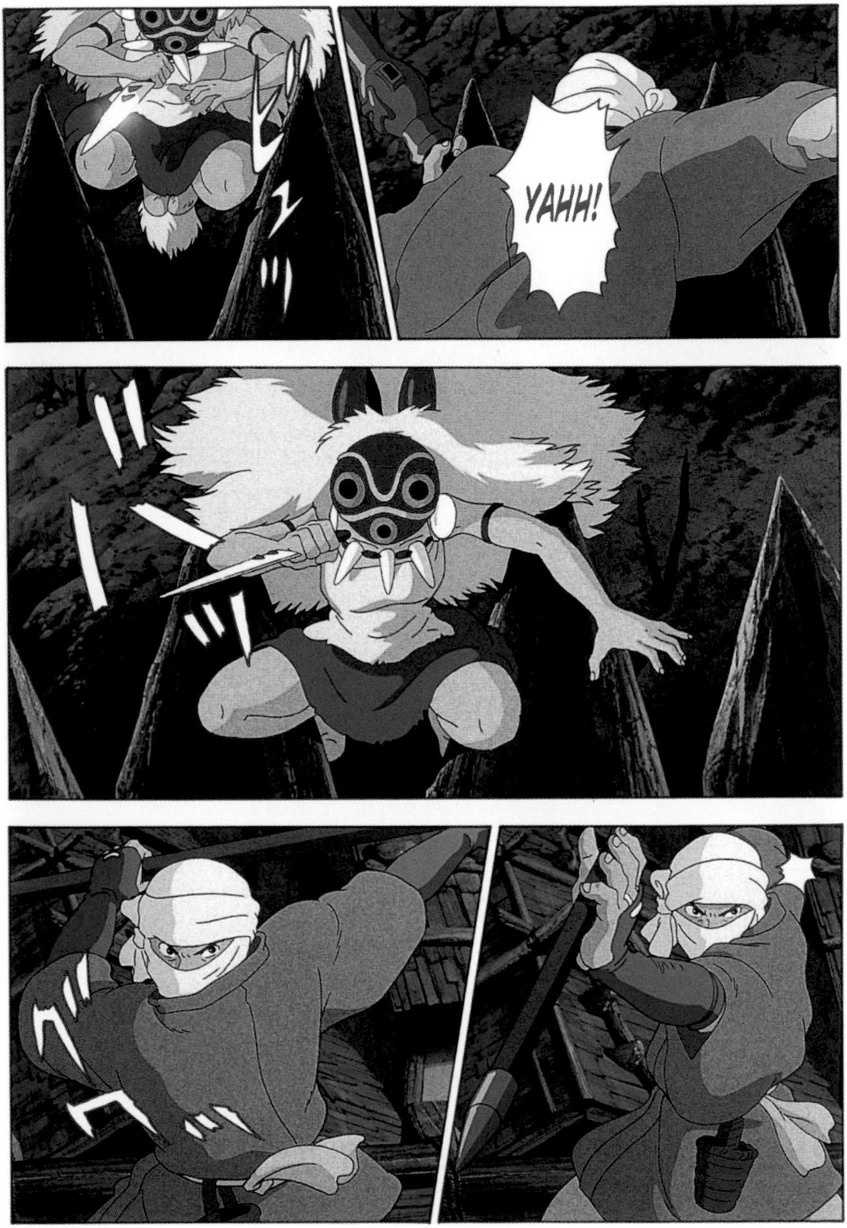
YAHH!

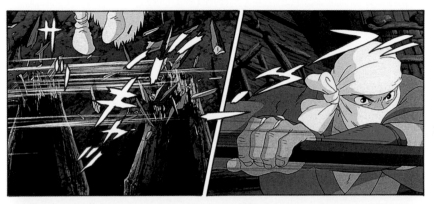

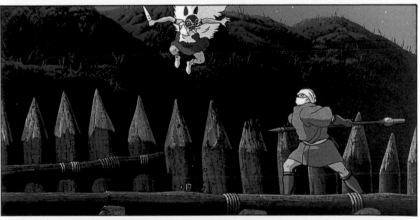

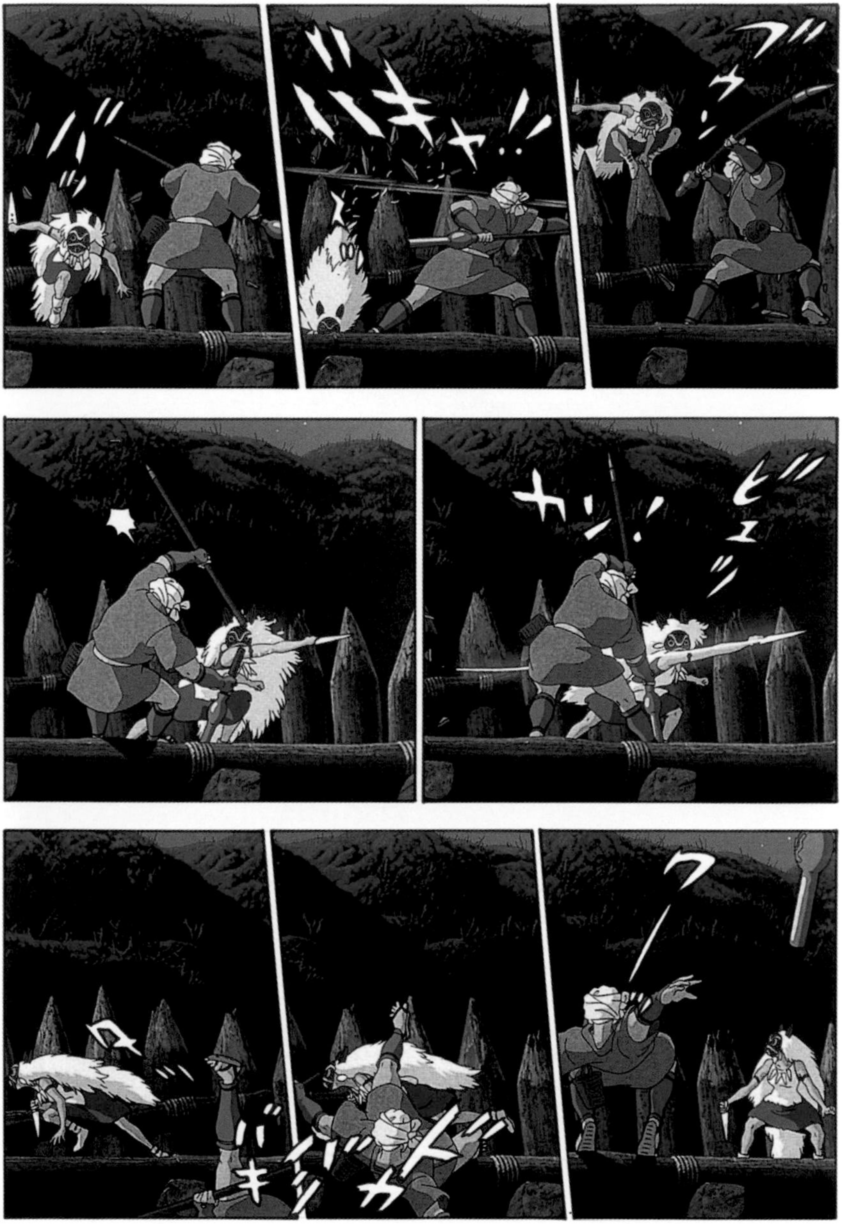
ビュッ
カン!!

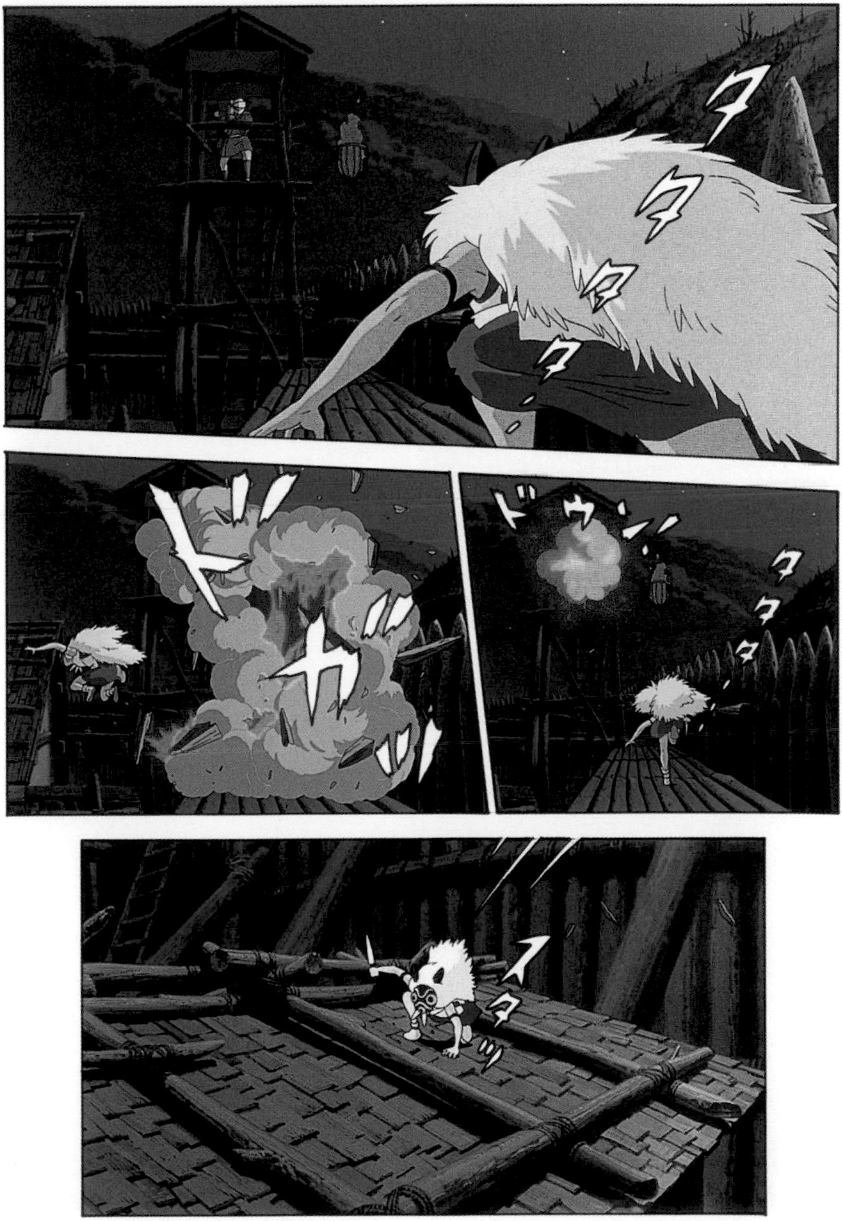
タタタタ
ドウッ!!
タタタ
ドッカッ!!
スタッ

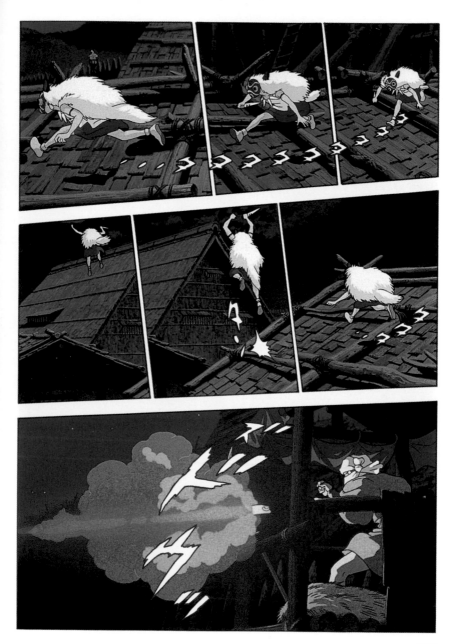

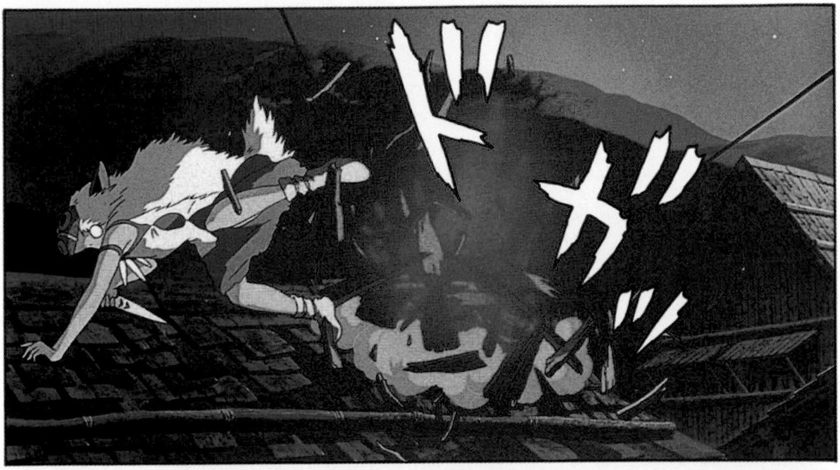

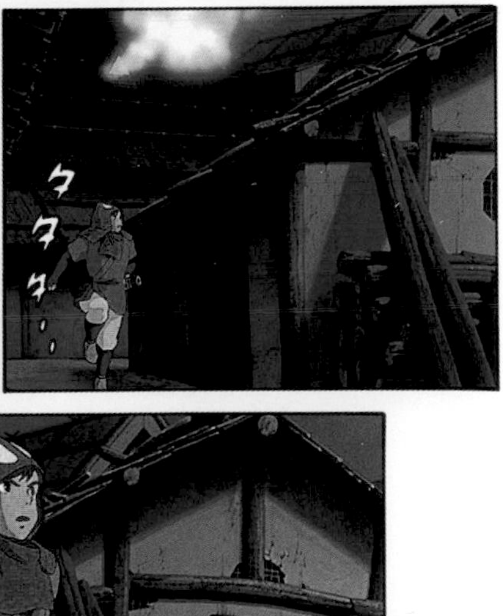

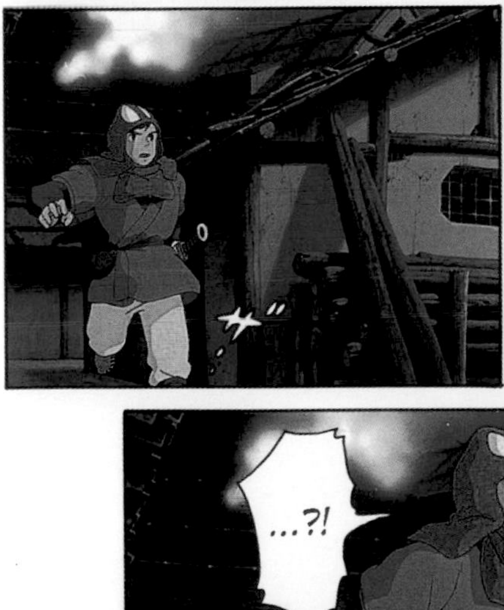

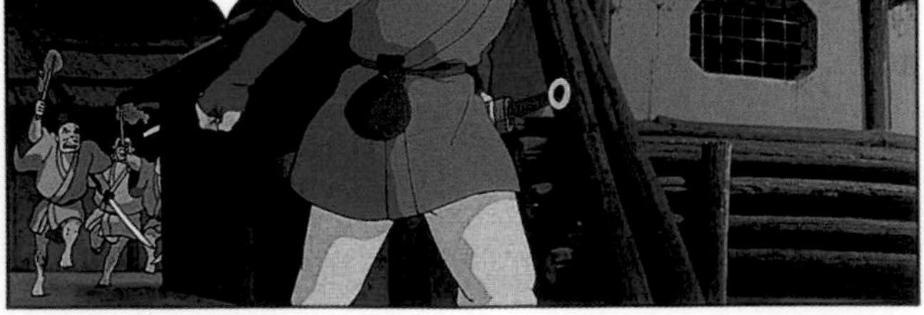
...?!

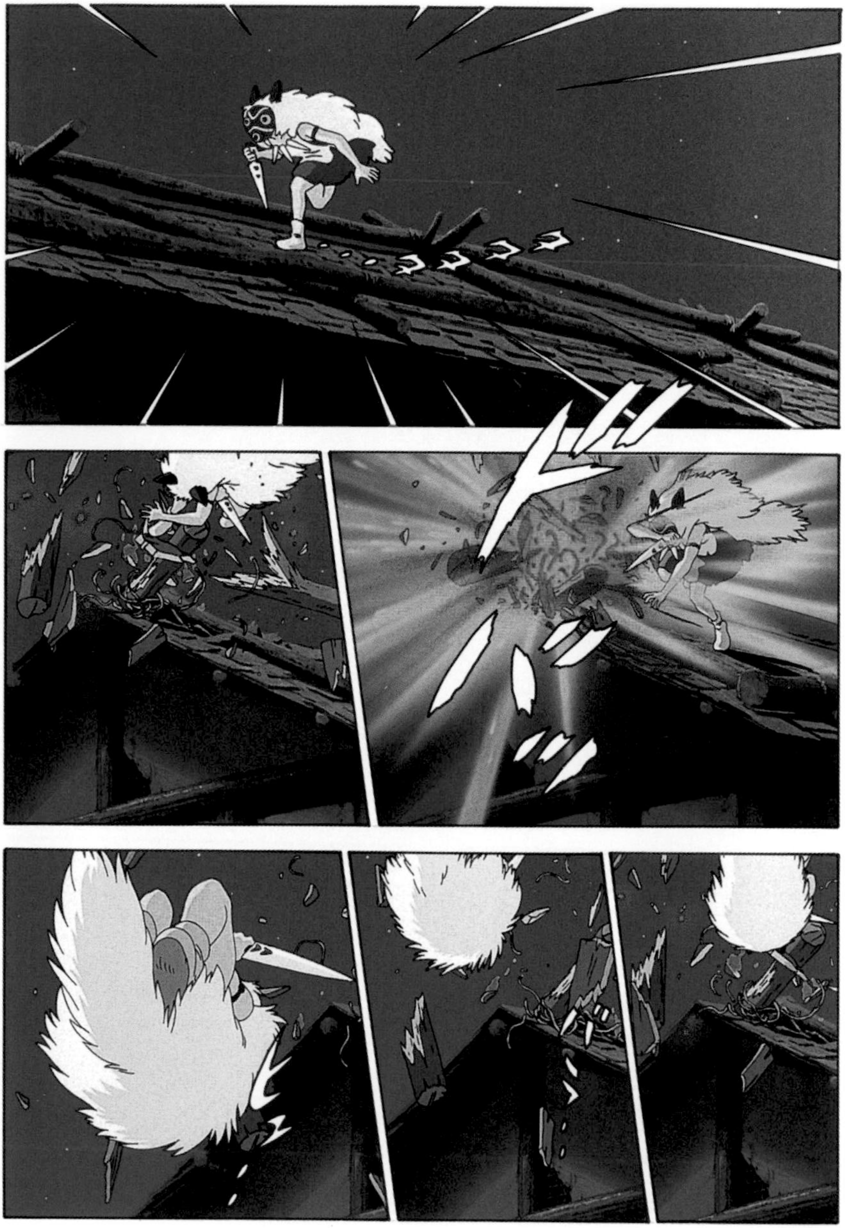

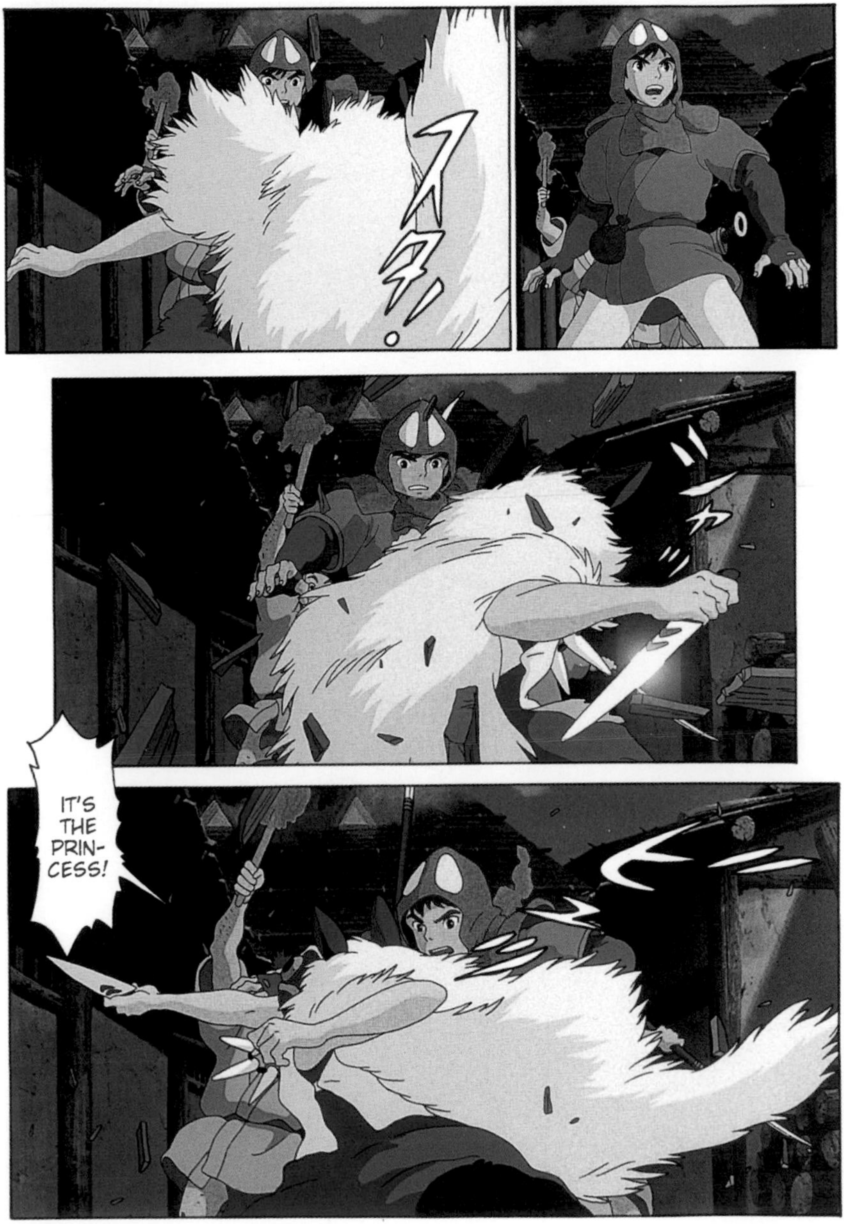
IT'S THE PRIN- CESS!

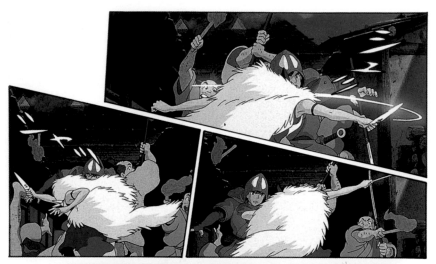

WAIT!

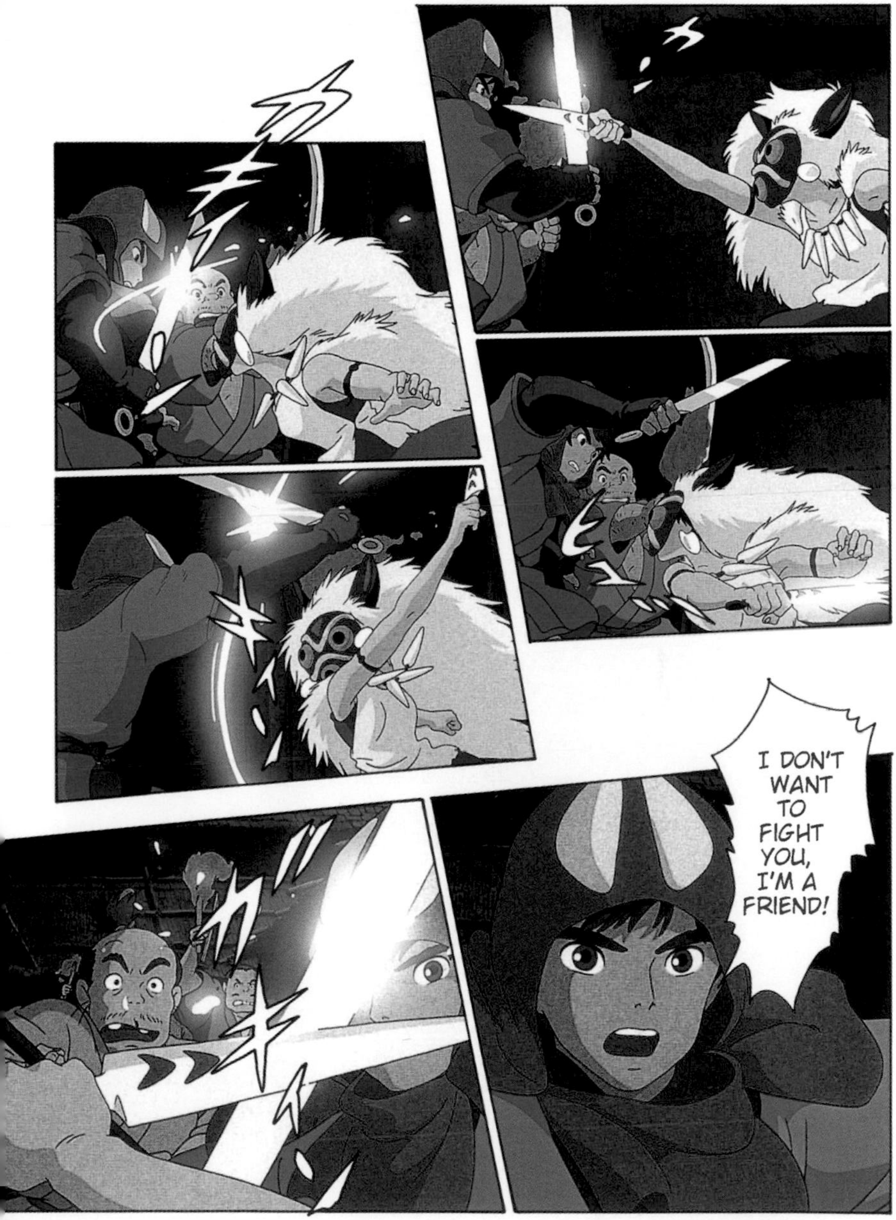
I DON'T WANT TO FIGHT YOU, I'M A FRIEND!

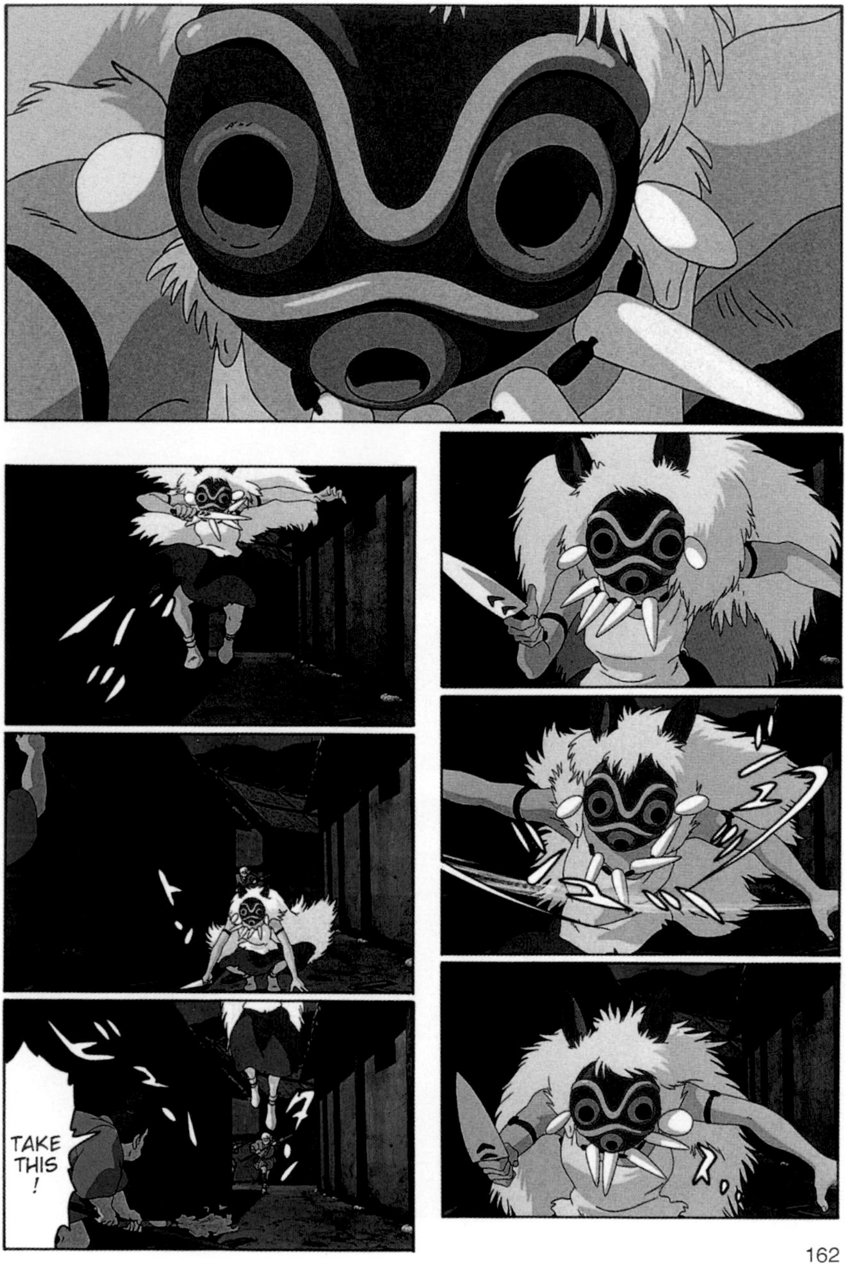
TAKE THIS!

ABOVE !!
SHE'S JUMPED.
SHE'S ON THE ROOF!
SHE'S HEADED FOR THE FORGE!
SHE'S THE ONLY ONE.

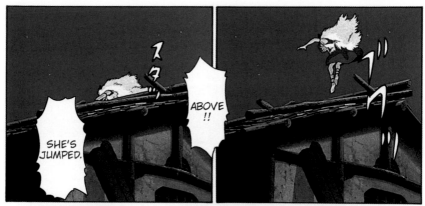

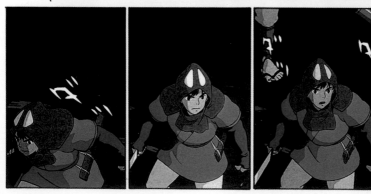

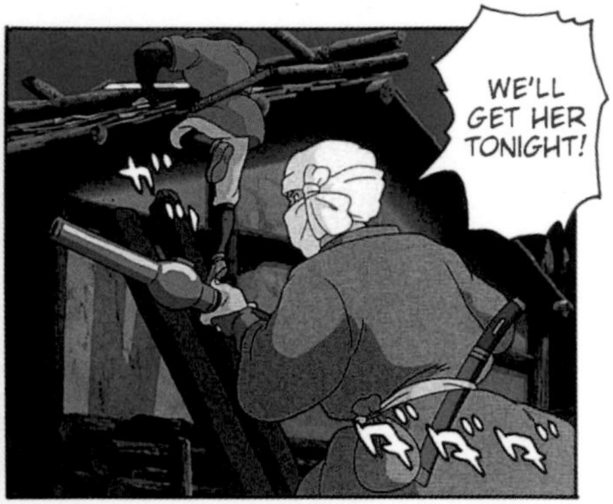
WE'LL GET HER TONIGHT!

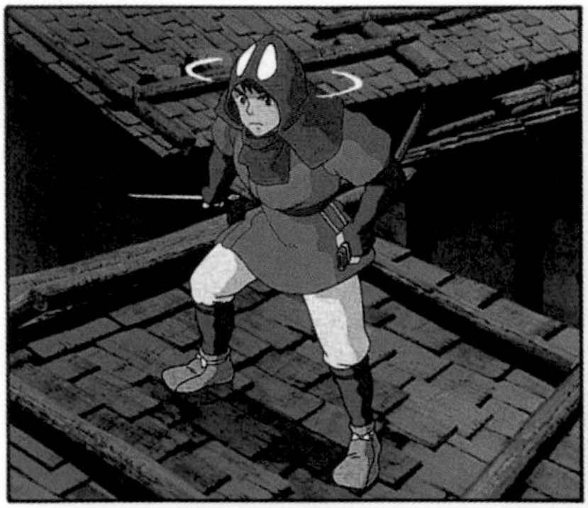

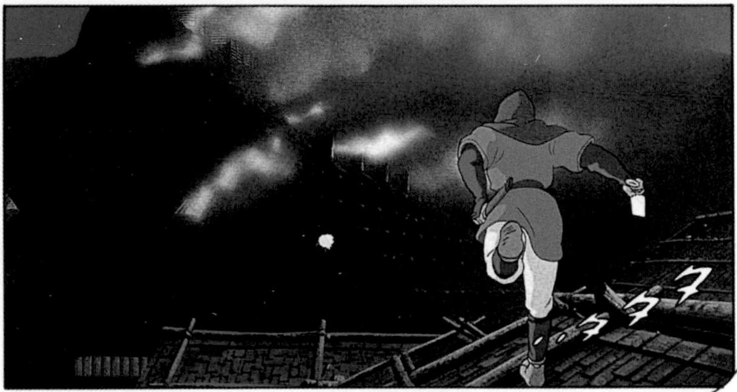

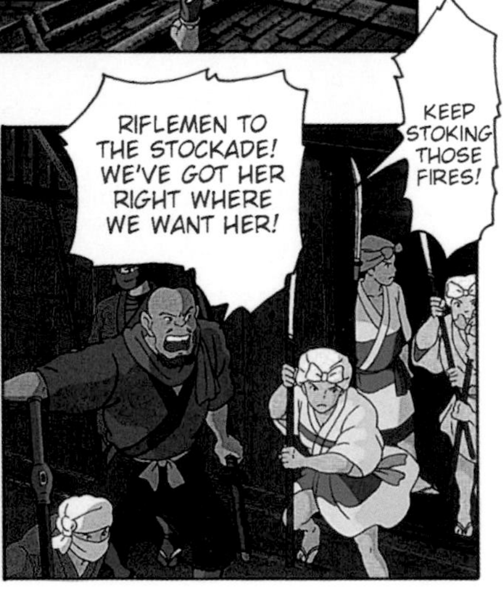
KEEP STOKING THOSE FIRES!
RIFLEMEN TO THE STOCKADE! WE'VE GOT HER RIGHT WHERE WE WANT HER!

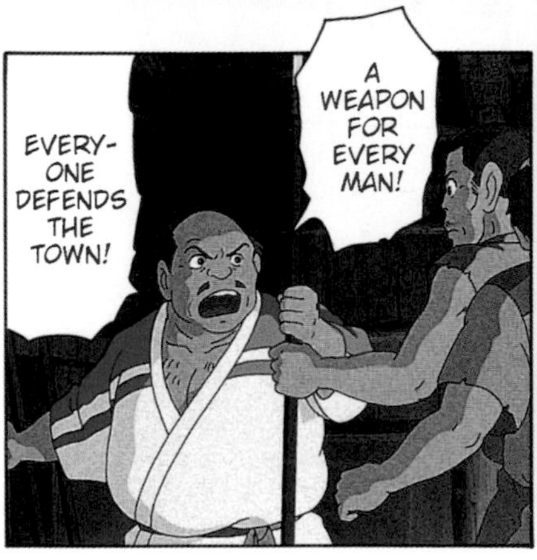
A WEAPON FOR EVERY MAN!
EVERY-ONE DEFENDS THE TOWN!

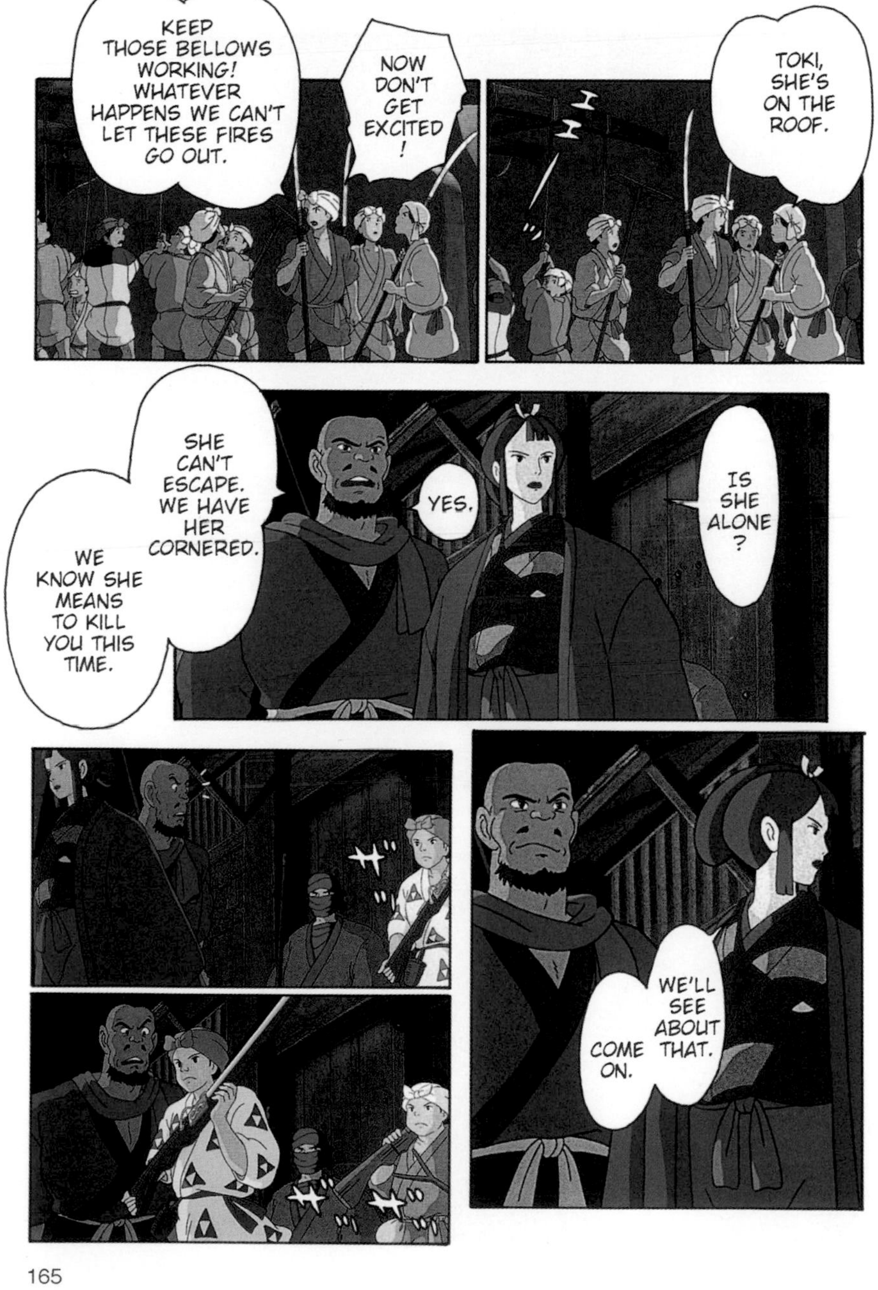
TOKI, SHE'S ON THE ROOF.
NOW DON'T GET EXCITED!
KEEP THOSE BELLOWS WORKING! WHATEVER HAPPENS WE CAN'T LET THESE FIRES GO OUT.
IS SHE ALONE?
YES.
SHE CAN'T ESCAPE. WE HAVE HER CORNERED.
WE KNOW SHE MEANS TO KILL YOU THIS TIME.
WE'LL SEE ABOUT THAT.
COME ON.

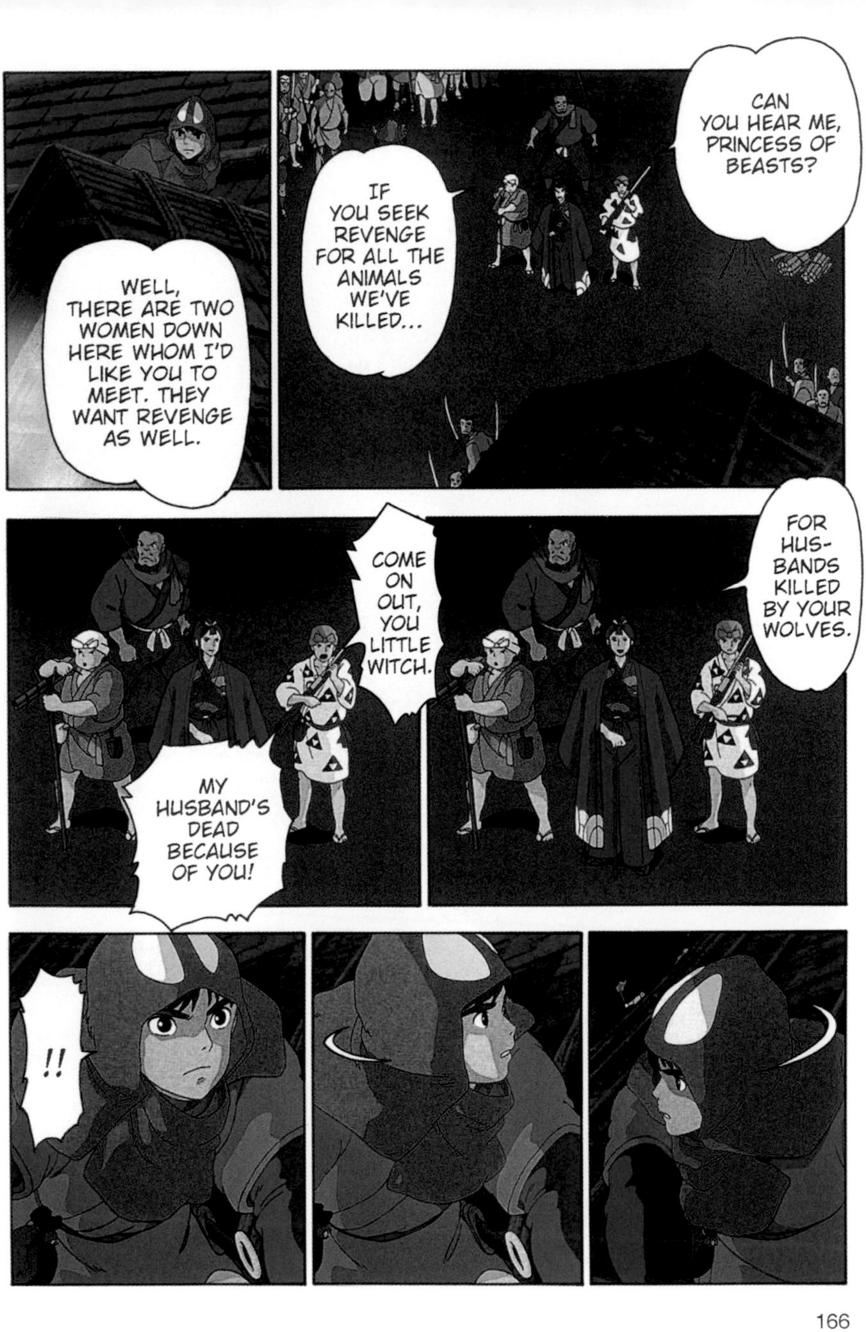
CAN YOU HEAR ME, PRINCESS OF BEASTS?
IF YOU SEEK REVENGE FOR ALL THE ANIMALS WE'VE KILLED...
WELL, THERE ARE TWO WOMEN DOWN HERE WHOM I'D LIKE YOU TO MEET. THEY WANT REVENGE AS WELL.
FOR HUS-BANDS KILLED BY YOUR WOLVES.
COME ON OUT, YOU LITTLE WITCH.
MY HUSBAND'S DEAD BECAUSE OF YOU!
!!

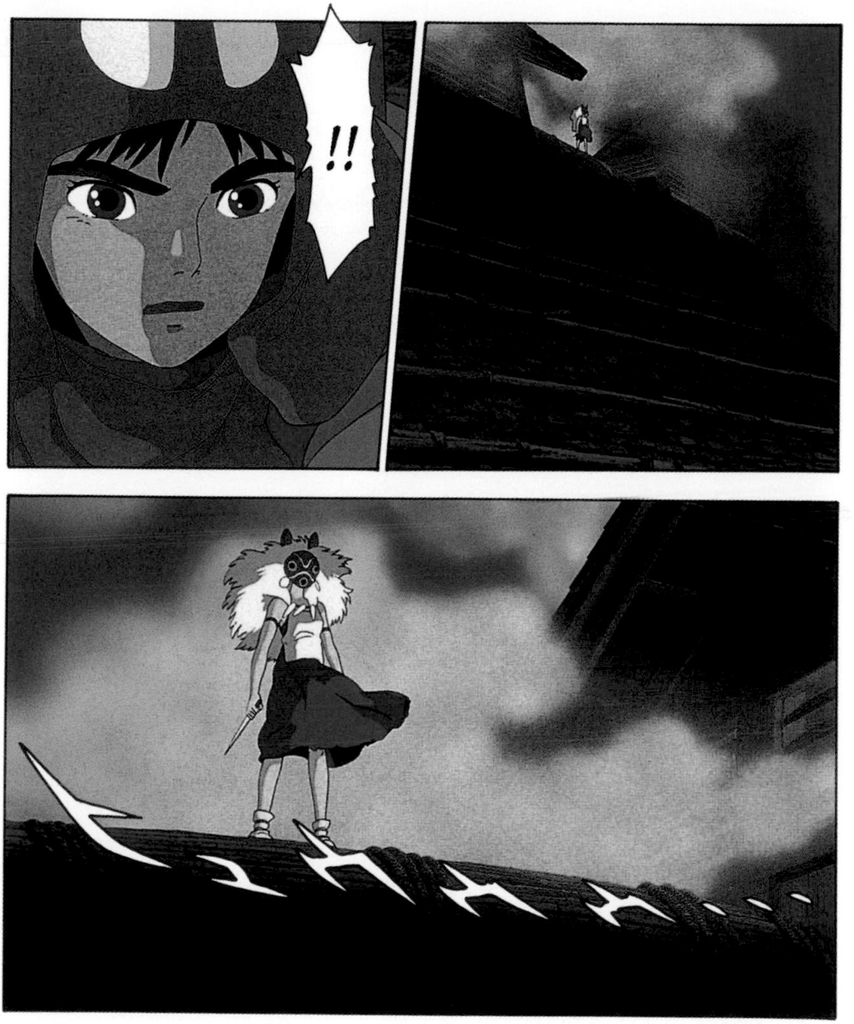
!!

TO BE CONTINUED...

Your Guide to *Princess Mononoke* Sound Effects!

To increase your enjoyment of the distinctive Japanese visual style of *Princess Mononoke* we've included a listing of and guide to the sound effects used in this comic adaptation of the movie. In the comic, these sound effects are written in the Japanese phonetic characters called katakana.

In the sound effects glossary for *Princess Mononoke*, sound effects are listed by page and panel number. For example, 9.1 means page 9, panel 1. And if there is more than one sound effect in a panel, the sound effects are listed in order (so, 106.1.1 means page 106, panel 1, first sound effect). Remember that all numbers are given in the original Japanese reading order: right-to-left.

After the page and panel numbers, you'll see the literally translated sound spelled out by the katakana, followed by how the sound effect might have been spelled out, or what it stands for, in English—it is interesting to see the different ways Japanese people describe the sounds of things!

You'll sometimes see a long dash at the end of a sound effects listing. This is just a way of showing that the sound is the kind that lasts for a while; similarly, a hyphen and number indicate the panels affected.

Now you are ready to use the *Princess Mononoke* Sound Effects Guide!

27.5.1	FX: KATA KATA KATA... [klak klak klak...]	15.4	FX: UUUU [urrrr]	4.1	FX: JIII [sizzz]
27.5.2	FX: SUKKU [foop]			4.2	FX: DOHN [blamm]
		16.4	FX: SUKKU [foop]	4.3	FX: GUWA [arrr]
28.2	FX: KATA KATA KATA [klak klak klak]	17.1	FX: PUUU [hakkk]	5.3-5	FX: HYUUU [fweeee]
28.3	FX: KATA KATA KATA [klak klak klak]	17.5	FX: NU [shoop]	5.5	FX: BAKI [krak]
28.4	FX: SUUU [fsshh]	18.2	FX: SUUU [fipp]	8.2	FX: GASA [fich]
				8.4-5	FX: GOHHH [rrrrrr]
29.1.1	FX: KATA KATA KATA [klak klak klak]	20.7	FX: BA [fsh]	9.1	FX: GOHHH [rrrrrr]
29.1.2	FX: KATA KATA KATA KATA [klak klak klak klak]	21.2	FX: SA [fsh]	9.3	FX: SUTA [fip]
				9.4	FX: TA [tmp]
		22.5	FX: BA [fwoosh]		
31.2	FX: TE TE TE TE [tp tp tp tp]	23.2	FX: TA TA [tmp tmp]	10.2	FX: ZU [fsh]
31.4	FX: TE TE TE TE [tp tp tp tp]			10.3	FX: ZU ZU ZU [fsh fsh fsh]
31.6	FX: TE TE TE [tp tp tp]	24.4	FX: KATA KATA [klak klak]	10.5	FX: TA TA [tmp tmp]
		24.5	FX: KATA KATA KATA [klak klak klak]	11.1	FX: GOHH [rrrrr]
32.3	FX: HAA HAA [huff huff]			11.4	FX: SUUU [fshhh]
32.5	FX: FU FU [ha ha]	25.4-6	FX: SUUU [fssshh]		
				12.1	FX: PIKU [urk]
34.1	FX: GU [tugg]	26.4	FX: KATA KATA KATA [klak klak klak]	12.4	FX: SAA [fshh]
34.4.1	FX: KATA KATA KATA [klak klak klak]			12.5	FX: SUUU [fshh]
34.4.2	FX: KATA KATA KATA [klak klak klak klak]	27.3	FX: SUUU [fsshh]	14.4	FX: MUKU [thup]
		27.4	FX: KATA KATA KATA [klak klak klak]	15.2	FX: GURURURU [grrrrr]
				15.3	FX: PU [hak]

90.2   FX: BAKI [krak]
90.3   FX: DODO [tump tump]
90.4   FX: DODODODODO
        [tump tump tump tump]

91.1   FX: DO HA HA HA [ha ha ha ha ha]
91.2   FX: WA HA HA HA [ha ha ha ha]
91.3   FX: GE HA HA HA [ha ha ha ha]

92.3   FX: DOU [boom]
92.4   FX: DOUN DOUN [blamm blamm]

93.2   FX: DOUN [blamm]
93.3   FX: DOUN DOUN [blamm blamm]
93.4   FX: GOOHHH [rrrrrr]

94.1-2 FX: GOOHHHH [rrrrrrr]
94.3.1 FX: HA HA HA HA [ha ha ha ha]
94.3.2 FX: HA HA HA HA [ha ha ha ha]

95.2   FX: SUU [fshh]
95.4.1 FX: GU [tugg]
95.4.2 FX: WANA WANA [krupp krupp]

97.1   FX: KAN KAN [klak klak]
97.2.1 FX: KAN KAN [klak klak]
97.2.2 FX: KAN KAN [klak klak]

98.1   FX: GOTON [tunk]
98.2   FX: GACHA [chak]

100.2   FX: SUU [fshh]
100.3.1 FX: BA [fwoosh]
100.3.2 FX: GYO [urk]

101.3   FX: SUU [fshh]

104.3   FX: HA HA HA HA [ha ha ha ha]

105.1   FX: AHA HA HA HA [ha ha ha ha]
105.2   FX: SUKKU [foop]
105.4   FX: SUU [fshh]

106.1.1 FX: KON KON KON [tok tok tok]
106.1.2 FX: KOHN KOHN [klaak klaak]
106.2   FX: KAAN KAAN [klang klang]
106.4.1 FX: GOOOH [rrrrr]

65.1   FX: ITETE [ouch]
65.6   FX: ZA [fich]

72.3   FX: HA HA HA [ha ha ha]

73.4   FX: PEKO PEKO [bowing]

74.5   FX: CHIRAA [glance]

75.1   FX: HA HA HA [ha ha ha]

76.1   FX: GUU [tugg]

77.1   FX: KAN KAAN KAN
        [klang klaang klang]
77.2   FX: KAN KAAN KAN
        [klang klaang klang]
77.3   FX: GIII GIII [kreeek kreeek]

78.1   FX: KU KU KU KU [fwooop]
78.3   FX: DOON [fooom]

79.1   FX: HA HA HA [ha ha ha]
79.3   FX: KU KU KU [hee hee hee]

82.3.1 FX: KYA HA HA HA [hee hee hee]
82.3.2 FX: AHA HA HA HA
        [ha ha ha ha ha]

83.1   FX: AHA HA HA [ha ha ha]
83.2   FX: AHA HA HA [ha ha ha]
83.3   FX: HA HA HA [ha ha ha]

84.2   FX: GUBI [slurrp]

88.1   FX: WAAH [yaah]
88.2   FX: DOGA [boomsh]
88.3   FX: DOBAA [fwooom]
88.5   FX: BYU BYU [fwip fwip]

89.1   FX: HYUN HYUN HYUN
        [fwee fwee fwee]
89.2   FX: BUUN [fwoom]
89.3   FX: BA [fsh]

90.1.1 FX: WAAH [aieee]
90.1.2 FX: DODODO [tump tump tump]

39.1   FX: SUUU [fshh]

40.2   FX: SUUU [fshhh]

41.1   FX: CHAPUU [plipp]

46.4   FX: BIKU BIKU BIKU
        [krup krup krup]

47.1   FX: BAA [fwoosh]
47.2   FX: GUU [tugg]

48.2   FX: BASHAN [plissh]

50.1   FX: HAA HAA HAA [huff huff huff]
50.3   FX: CHAPUU [plipp]

52.1   FX: ZA ZA [fich fich]
52.4   FX: BAA [fwoosh]
52.5   FX: ITETETE [ouuch]

54.2.1 FX: KAAN KAAN [klang klang]
54.2.2 FX: GAAN GAAN [kong kong]
54.2.3 FX: KAN KAN KAN
        [klakk klakk klakk]
54.3   FX: UMOOH MOOH [moo moo]

55.2   FX: DOOHH DOOHH [rrrrrr rrrrrr]
55.3   FX: GIIKO GIIKO [krrrr krrrr]

57.1   FX: GUI [tugg]

59.3   FX: ZAWA ZAWA [yadda yadda]

60.1   FX: DOTA DOTA [twump twump]
60.2   FX: TA TA TA [tmp tmp tmp]
60.3   FX: GAYA GAYA [yadda yadda]

61.1.1 FX: ZAWA ZAWA [yadda yadda]
61.1.2 FX: GAYA GAYA [yadda yadda]
61.3   FX: ZABAA [plissh]

62.1   FX: BURU BURU BURU
        [fwip fwip fwip]

63.2   FX: GUI [tugg]

139.3   FX: GOTON GATAN [ftunk ftunk]

141.2   FX: SAA [fshh]

142.3   FX: UUUU [urrrr]

143.1   FX: KI [hmm]
143.3   FX: GUI [fip]
143.4   FX: BASA [fssh]

144.3   FX: DO DO DO [tump tump tump]

145.5   FX: DA [tmp]

146.1   FX: DO DO DO DO
         [tump tump tump tump]
146.2   FX: KAAN KAAN KAAN
         [klang klang klang]

147.2   FX: JIII [sizzz]
147.3   FX: DOHN [blamm]
147.4   FX: DOBA [boomsh]

148.1   FX: BAA [fwoosh]
148.2   FX: ZAZA [fich fich]
148.4-5 FX: DO DO DO DO
         [tump tump tump tump]
148.5   FX: DOUN [boomsh]

149.1   FX: DOGA [boomsh]
149.2   FX: DA [tmp]
149.3-5 FX: DO DO DO DO
         [tump tump tump tump]
149.6   FX: DO DO DO [tump tump tump]

150.1-2 FX: DO DO DO [tump tump tump]
150.3   FX: GUWA [arrr]
150.4   FX: DOKA [thud]
150.6   FX: BUWA [fwoom]

151.1   FX: BYUUU [fweee]
151.3   FX: GA [tunk]
151.6   FX: TAN! [tump!]

152.2   FX: BYU [fwee]
152.3   FX: BA [fwoosh]
152.5   FX: GUWA [fwoosh]

126.1   FX: DOU [blamm]
126.2-4 FX: HYUUU [fweee]
126.5   FX: DOGA [boomsh]

127.1.1 FX: KASAA [fichh]
127.1.2 FX: KASA KASA [fich fich]
127.2.1 FX: KASA KASA [fich fich]
127.2.2 FX: KASA KASA [fich fich]

132.2   FX: SUU [fshh]

133.1   FX: TSUKA TSUKA [tok tok]

134.1.1 FX: GOTON GATAN [ftunk ftunk]
134.1.2 FX: GOTON GATAN [ftunk ftunk]
134.2   FX: SAA [fshh]
134.4   FX: BAA [fwoosh]

135.1   FX: GOTON GATAN [ftunk ftunk]
135.2   FX: GOTON [ftunk]
135.3   FX: GATAN [ftunk]
135.4   FX: GOTON [ftunk]
135.5.1 FX: SUU [fsh]
135.5.2 FX: GOTON [ftunk]
135.6.1 FX: GU [tugg]
135.6.2 FX: GATAN GOTON [ftunk ftunk]

136.1   FX: GOTON GATAN [ftunk ftunk]
136.2.1 FX: KYAH [aiee]
136.2.2 FX: GUWA [fwom]
136.2.3 FX: HA HA HA HA [ha ha ha ha ha]
136.3   FX: AHA HA HA HA [ha ha ha ha]
136.4   FX: HA HA HA HA [ha ha ha ha]
136.5.1 FX: HA HA HA HA [ha ha ha ha]
136.5.2 FX: GOTON [ftunk]

137.1   FX: GOTON GATAN [ftunk ftunk]
137.2.1 FX: HA HA HA HA [ha ha ha ha]
137.2.2 FX: GOTON [ftunk]
137.3   FX: GATAN [ftunk]
137.4   FX: GOTON [ftunk]

138.2   FX: GOTON [ftunk]
138.3   FX: GATAN [ftunk]

139.1   FX: GOTON [ftunk]
139.2   FX: GATAN [ftunk]

106.4.2 FX: KAAN KAAN [klang klang]

107.3   FX: GOOOOH [rrrrrr]

108.1.1 FX: GOTON GATAN [ftunk ftunk]
108.1.2 FX: GOTON GATAN [ftunk ftunk]
108.2   FX: GOTON [ftunk]
108.3   FX: GATAN [ftunk]
108.4   FX: GOTON GATAN [ftunk ftunk]

109.1   FX: GOTON GATAN [ftunk ftunk]
109.2   FX: GOTON GATAN [ftunk ftunk]
109.4   FX: SUU [fshh]

110.2   FX: SUU [fshh]

112.2.1 FX: KON KON KON [tok tok tok]
112.2.2 FX: GII GII [kreech kreech]

113.1   FX: HO HO HO [huff huff huff]

114.3   FX: SUU [fshh]

118.4   FX: GU GU GU [tuggg]

119.2   FX: GU GU GU [tuggg]
119.3   FX: GUU [tugg]
119.4-5 FX: GUWA [fwosh]
119.6   FX: GASHI [fwinch]

120.1   FX: BAA [fshh]
120.2   FX: JARII [fichh]
120.3   FX: GU GU [tuggg]
120.4   FX: GU [tugg]

121.1   FX: GU GU [tugg tugg]
121.2   FX: GU [tugg]
121.3   FX: GU GU GU [tugg tugg tugg]

124.2   FX: GOHO GOHO [koff koff]
124.3   FX: GOHO GOHO [koff koff]

125.1   FX: OOOHN [arrrr]
125.3   FX: GASHA [ksh]
125.5.1 FX: DON! [tunk!]
125.5.2 FX: GACHI [chak]

153.1 FX: BUUN [swissh]
153.2.1 FX: BAKYA [krakk]
153.2.2 FX: SAA [fshh]
153.4 FX: BUUN [swissh]
153.5.1 FX: BAKI [krakk]
153.5.2 FX: TA [tmp]

154.1 FX: BUUN [swissh]
154.2 FX: BAKYA!! [krakk!!]
154.3 FX: BA [fwoosh]
154.4.1 FX: BYU [fwee]
154.4.2 FX: KAN! [klang!]
154.6 FX: WAAH [aah]
154.7.1 FX: DOKA [thud]
154.7.2 FX: BARI [krak]
154.8.1 FX: BAKI [krak]
154.8.2 FX: TA [tmp]

155.1 FX: TA TA TA TA [tmp tmp tmp tmp]
155.2.1 FX: TA TA TA [tmp tmp tmp]
155.2.2 FX: DOUN! [blamm!]
155.3 FX: DOGA [boomsh]
155.4 FX: SUTA [tup]

156.1-3 FX: TA TA TA TA TA [tmp tmp tmp tmp tmp]
156.4 FX: TA TA TA [tmp tmp tmp]
156.5 FX: TAN [tump]
156.7 FX: ZUDOU [blamm]

157.1 FX: DOGA [boomsh]
157.2 FX: TA TA TA [tmp tmp tmp]
157.3 FX: ZAA [fichh]

158.1 FX: TA TA TA TA [tmp tmp tmp tmp]
158.2 FX: DOBA [foomsh]
158.5 FX: BARA [klak]
158.6 FX: HYU [fwish]

159.2 FX: SUTA! [tump!]
159.3 FX: SHA [fwip]
159.4 FX: BYU [swissh]

160.1 FX: SHU [fwish]
160.3 FX: SHA [fwipp]
160.5 FX: BYU [swissh]
160.6 FX: KAKKEEN [klang]

161.1 FX: KAN [klang]
161.2 FX: HYU [swish]
161.3 FX: KAKEEN [klang]
161.4 FX: KEEN [klang]
161.6 FX: GAKEEN [klang]

162.3 FX: SHU SHU [fwish fwish]
162.4 FX: SUU [fshh]
162.5 FX: BAA [fshh]
162.6 FX: TON [tump]
162.7.1 FX: TAN [tump]
162.7.2 FX: BYUN [fwish]

163.1 FX: BUWA [fwoosh]
163.2 FX: SUTA [tump]
163.3.1 FX: DA DA [tmp tmp]
163.3.2 FX: DA [tmp]
163.5 FX: DA [tmp]

164.1.1 FX: DA DA DA [tmp tmp tmp]
164.1.2 FX: GA [tunk]
164.3 FX: TA TA TA [tmp tmp tmp]

165.1 FX: EEEH [huhh]
165.5 FX: ZA [fich]
165.6 FX: ZA ZA [fich fich]

167.3 FX: HYUUU [fweee]

This book should be read in its original Japanese right-to-left format.
Please turn it around to begin!

PRINCESS MONONOKE

Volume 2 of 5

Original story and screenplay written and directed by
Hayao Miyazaki

Film Comic Adaptation/Yuji Oniki
Lettering/Rina Mapa
Design/Hidemi Sahara
Editor/Eric Searleman

Managing Editor/Masumi Washington
Editor in Chief/Alvin Lu
Sr. Director of Acquisitions/Rika Inouye
Sr. VP of Marketing/Liza Coppola
Exec. VP of Sales & Marketing/John Easum
Publisher/Hyoe Narita

Printed in China

Published by
VIZ Media, LLC
295 Bay St.
San Francisco, CA 94133

First printing, October 2007

PARENTAL ADVISORY
PRINCESS MONONOKE is rated T and is
recommended for ages 13 and up. This
volume contains fantasy violence.

HOWL'S MOVING CASTLE
FROM THE NOVEL BY DIANA WYNNE JONES
SCREENPLAY WRITTEN AND DIRECTED BY
HAYAO MIYAZAKI
STUDIO GHIBLI LIBRARY

THE ART OF
My Neighbor
TOTORO

A hardcover book generously packed with concept sketches, character and background drawings, paintings, and cell images!

$29.99

My Neighbor
TOTORO
Picture Book

An attractive hardcover with scene-by-scene film footage and character dialog!

$14.99